THE NUMISMATIST'S FIRESIDE COMPANION

THE NUMISMATIST'S FIRESIDE COMPANION

VOLUME TWO

EDITED BY Q. DAVID BOWERS

PUBLISHED BY BOWERS AND MERENA GALLERIES, INC.

ISBN 0-943161-10-X

Published by:
Bowers and Merena Galleries, Inc.
Box 1224, Wolfeboro, NH 03894

The cover illustration is an original work by Elli Ford of North Jungle Graphics, Center Sandwich, New Hampshire. Elli Ford's sketches have graced a number of our other books, including the cover of *The Numismatist's Bedside Companion*, the predecessor volume to the present text. Note that a *woman* numismatist is pictured, and why not? At various times during 1986 through 1988, when the present book was being planned, women occupied many important positions in the numismatic field. In the area of government, Donna Pope was director of the Mint; in the American Numismatic Association, Florence Schook served as president for the 1985-1987 term, while Ruthann Brettell served as executive director; at *Coin World*, Beth Deisher served as editor, while Ann Marie Aldrich was named as publisher. While men still outnumber women when it comes to being collectors, women do form a very vital part of our hobby—and our cover illustration is a recognition of this.

Much of the work on the present volume was done by the Graphics Department of Bowers and Merena Galleries, Inc. Design and production were by J.E. McCabe.

Table of Contents

Introduction . . . . page 9

Enjoying Coins
by Q. David Bowers, from Rare Coin Review *No. 28, Spring 1977* 11

F.W. Blake
by Douglas McDonald, from Rare Coin Review *No. 64, Spring 1987* 21

A Remembrance of 1883
by Q. David Bowers, from Rare Coin Review *No. 47, April 1983* 27

The Bushnell Sale
by John J. Ford, Jr., from Rare Coin Review *No. 31, 1978* 35

An Adventure in Collecting
by Q. David Bowers, from Rare Coin Review *No. 29, Summer 1977* 45

A Salute to Abner Kreisberg
by Don Alpert, from Rare Coin Review *No. 53, October-December 1984* 63

Reflections on a Connecticut Pond
by Q. David Bowers, from Rare Coin Review *No. 54, January-March 1985* 67

Frossard and Woodward: The Great Feud
by Cal Wilson, from Rare Coin Review *No. 57, Autumn 1985* 75

A Journey to 1958
by Q. David Bowers, from Rare Coin Review *No. 51, April-May 1984* 87

Nearly Extinct: The Pristine American Eagle
by Bruce Lorich, from Rare Coin Review *No. 29, Summer 1977* 93

Legendary 1913 Liberty Head Nickel
by Q. David Bowers, from Rare Coin Review *No. 22, Spring 1975* 97

The Coinage of Vermont 1785-1788
by Codman Hislop, from Rare Coin Review *No. 51, April-May 1984* 111

1785-1985: A Numismatic Bicentennial
by Q. David Bowers, from Rare Coin Review *No. 54, January-March 1985* 119

Q. David Bowers: 30 Years in Numismatics
by Paul M. Green, from Rare Coin Review *No. 50, January-March 1984* 131

Some Aspects of Coin Investment
by Q. David Bowers, from Rare Coin Review *No. 15, August-September 1972* 141

Our Poet Laureate
by Harvey Roehl, from Rare Coin Review *No. 48, June-July 1983* 149

The Pleasures of Forming a Type Set
by Q. David Bowers, from Rare Coin Review *No. 28, Spring 1977* 151

Tom Becker Discusses Coin Collecting
by Tom Becker, from Rare Coin Review *No. 52, June-September 1984* 161

More Than Just a Coin
by Q. David Bowers, from Rare Coin Review *No. 39, July 1981* 165

Louis Eliasberg's Collecting Experiences
by Louis Eliasberg, from Rare Coin Review *No. 30, November 1975* 167

Observations Concerning Coin Collecting
by Q. David Bowers, from Rare Coin Review *No. 51, April-May 1984* 175

Hans Schulman Remembers Virgil Brand
by Hans Schulman, from Rare Coin Review *No. 52, June-September 1984* 191

Garrett Collection Breaks Records
by Q. David Bowers, from Rare Coin Review *No. 34, Winter-Spring 1980* 195

The Austin Collection
by Q. David Bowers, from Rare Coin Review *No. 21, 1974* 201

The Lessons of History
by Q. David Bowers, from Rare Coin Review *No. 39, July 1981* 209

The King of American Coins
by Q. David Bowers, from Rare Coin Review *No. 21, 1974* 213

Index 219

Introduction

Originally I had intended the present book to be Volume Two of *The Numismatist's Bedside Companion,* but upon contemplating the situation, I thought it interesting not to repeat the "bedside" illustration of the first book, but, rather, to come up with a related word. So, now we have "fireside" in the title: *The Numismatist's Fireside Companion.* As before, the cover illustration is by Elli Ford.

Throughout the history of book publishing there are numerous "volume one" books for which no "volume two" was ever issued. When *The Numismatist's Bedside Companion* was published, I did not know whether it would be well received. I had no illusions that it would be a best-seller, for it did not list current coin prices, nor did it tell the reader how to earn a million dollars in one's spare time without work or effort!

Not to worry, it turned out. *The Numismatist's Bedside Companion* has become a surprise best-seller, a situation helped in no small way be enthusiastic reviews. Those who have seen it have liked it. *The Numismatist,* issue of May 1988, ran a review spanning the best part of three pages, by Robert Obojski, titled "Dave Bowers' Lastest Book Entertains and Engrosses." To make a long story short, early in 1988, as *The Numismatist's Bedside Companion* was read by reviewers and countless buyers, it "caught on," and within a month or two of its launching the book was a smash success. It seems that collectors and those involved with coins do indeed like "stories" about them!

The present Volume Two is thus a reality.

Following in the footsteps of its predecessor, *The Numismatist's Fireside Companion* reprints selected articles from past issues of the *Rare Coin Review,* produced by Bowers and Ruddy Galleries through 1982, and by our successor firm, Bowers and Merena Galleries, from 1983 onward. As editor of the *Rare Coin Review,* most of the articles are from my hand, but numerous contributions have been made by others and are so credited.

The topics covered are indeed diverse and range from anecdotes and coin experiences to studies and comments concerning specific issues.

So, take *The Numismatist's Fireside Companion* to your favorite armchair, adjust the light, and settle back for an evening of what I hope will be enjoyable reading.

Q. David Bowers
July 1, 1988

Enjoying Coins

By Q. David Bowers *1977*

How does one *enjoy* a coin or a piece of paper money? Well, there are several ways. . . First of all, there is the coin itself—the touch or feel of it, the sensation of "holding history in your hand," so to speak.

Or, perhaps the design might be especially interesting to you. For example, often when I see a Liberty Standing quarter of the 1916 to 1930 era I think of the Roaring '20s and all of the nostalgia associated with them—flappers, nickelodeon pianos, Laurel and Hardy movies, fancy Duesenberg cars and omnipresent "Tin Lizzies," the great Florida land boom, all the excitement about the stock market, and maybe even F. Scott Fitzgerald's *The Great Gatsby.*

When I see a coin which was minted at San Francisco in the 1850s, I think of the Gold Rush—and the romantic towns, still intact in many instances, in the Mother Lode country—Mokelumne Hill (with its quaint Hotel Leger), Jackson, Sutter Creek, Angels Camp, and so on. Undoubtedly you can conjure similar images in your own mind of events, times, and places of special meaning to you.

Secondly, there is the aspect of what the coin can do for you. Mainly this is an area concerned with investment performance. Just as the buyer of a share of IBM stock back in the 1950s can experience a certain fondness for it now, having seen it go up in value sharply over the years, one can also do this with coins. As numerous studies have shown, including my own *High Profits from Rare Coin Investment* and *Collecting Rare Coins for Profit* books, the investment performance of choice rare coins is second to no other investment medium, at least not to any investment area I know.

With investment, some patience is needed, however. Buy coins today and sell them tomorrow and you are making profits only for the dealer. However, historically, if you have carefully purchased coins and have held them for five to 10 years or more you have done very well. Spectacular performances are the *rule*, not the exception! In my nearly one-quarter of a century in the rare coin business I have helped build fortunes for many collectors and investors. Few experiences are as rewarding as those helping to make someone else rich, and I've done this time and time again.

I consider investment to be an important part, even a *vital* part, behind the motivation of most buyers. This is only natural. After all, if you part with, say, $1,000 for a coin rarity you will do so much more readily if you have a reasonable expectation that five to 10 years from now the same coin might sell for $2,000, $3,000, or even more. On the other hand, if the same $1,000 coin was expected to be worth only $500 five years from now, no matter how beautiful it might be to look at, you would hesitate about buying it—or, probably, not buy it at all. After all, it would be quite a bit cheaper to go see one in a museum!

Apropos of collecting versus investment, one of my favorite quotations appeared in a United States Coin Co. advertisement in 1912:

> Coins as an Investment. Many harsh words are said about collectors who interest themselves in a natural speculation as to whether the coins they are buying today will have appreciated in value 10 years from now.
>
> Numismatists of the old school tell us the true collector is not interested in any such appreciation in the value of his collection but derives his entire profit and pleasure from the coins while in his hands.
>
> We feel, however, the average American collector, while he greatly enjoys his coins also feels very pleased if on disposing of his collection he realizes a profit. . . .

So, in my opinion, the numismatic (romantic, historical, physical, and artistic) aspects of a coin and its investment aspects are intertwined.

In an article written in 1970 and quoted in *Rare Coin Review* No. 27, I said: "To paraphrase Ben Franklin, 'Mind your collection carefully and the investment will take care of itself.' By collecting carefully today, you will build a financial treasure for the future. And, in the meantime you will have lots of enjoyment in the search for the elusive pieces you need."

While I sincerely hope you enjoy the investment appeal of coins and the coming years will be kind to your numismatic holdings, the investment angle is hard to enjoy on a day-to-day basis. Prices don't change that quickly. And, perhaps this is best. I imagine some collectors would become a bit paranoid if they fell into the habit of checking a daily quote sheet to see if a particular coin was worth $87.21 one day, $87.12 the next, and so on! In coins, month-to-month fluctuations are common, and these provide enough concern. The experienced collector/investor realizes that only after several years can the investment performance and the price appreciation pattern of a certain coin begin to take shape.

An example of this is the 1895 Proof Morgan dollar. In that long-ago year, 1895, some 12,000 business strike (intended for use in circulation) dollars were made, plus 880 Proofs for collectors. Somewhere along the line the 12,000 business strikes disappeared. To my knowledge, all authentic 1895 Philadelphia Mint dollars known today are either Proofs or impaired Proofs; I have never seen or reliably heard of an Uncirculated coin or of one possessing mint lustre. It is presumed that when 270,232,722 silver dollars were melted under the terms of the Pittman Act of 1918, the 12,000 1895 Philadelphia dollars were included.

The result is anyone desiring an 1895 Morgan dollar from the Philadelphia Mint must buy either a Proof or an impaired Proof. Thus, the 880 Proofs, or, more accurately, the 500 or so which survive today, are in great demand. In 1977 a nice Proof piece sells in the $9,000 range.

In my *High Profits from Rare Coin Investment* (page 200 of that reference) I charted the prices of this coin in the past. In 1948 a specimen sold for $80, in 1953 $200, in 1958 $650, in 1963 $2,500, in 1968 $4,750, and in 1973 $6,000. As noted, today, in 1977, one is worth about $9,000. The 1948 to 1973 increase was a stunning 7,400%! Today, in 1977, the return on the 1948 investment would be closer to 10,000%!

Over the years I have had quite a few 1895 dollars. I remember well when they were worth $650 in 1958. If in March 1958 a client paid $650 for one as an investment and then tried to sell it in August 1958, he would have taken a 10% to 20% loss, representing my markup. "A crummy investment, for sure," he would have said, or at least have thought! The trouble wasn't with the 1895 silver dollar, nor with my recommending he buy it for $650. The trouble was with his patience, or lack of it! I have seen this happen time and time again. Every week or so Don Suter, who manages our highly successful Collection Investment Program, will receive a letter something like this: "I have been buying coins for a year now, and I would like to sell. Let me know what kind of profit I can make." Such a buyer is usually disappointed. The dealer's margin of profit, often in the 20% range, usually will more than eat up the modest increase in value, if indeed there was one, in that short time. On the other hand, taken over a span of five to 10 years, the nominal dealer's profit fades into insignificance. For example, I am sure that in my earlier illustration of an 1895 Proof dollar selling in 1958 for $650, the buyer would not mind at all paying a commission were I to sell it for him today for $9,000 to $10,000!

So, the *enjoyment* aspect of coin investment is one that hopefully for you will be a feeling of *comfort* and *security* rather than razzle-dazzle day-to-day excitement. Your collection has a reasonable expectation of being a treasure for the future, a valuable equity, a solid financial base for you and your family.

Coins can be enjoyed for their *relaxation value* as well. While I read, or at least skim through, *Coin World* and *Numismatic News* here at the office for "fun" reading, I often take things home. I've spent many nights curled up on the overstuffed brown sofa in the library of my home, with a copy of an interesting numismatic book or publication in my hands. It's amazing how many fascinating tales can be found in back issues of *CoinAge* and *Coins Magazine,* for example. An album full of coins and a shelf full of coin books can combine to take you far, far away from the cares and concerns of your office, factory, or store. It's a well-known fact youngsters with strong interests in hobbies such as coin collecting stay out of trouble much more than their nonhobbyist counterparts. The other day in *Antiquarian Bookman,* the weekly journal of the out-of-print book trade, I saw mention of a study saying dedicated book collectors and dealers apparently have a sharply lower suicide rate than the general public. I suspect the same is true of dedicated coin collectors. The relaxation value of a coin collection can be very therapeutic.

In the area of numismatics, I collect obsolete broken bank notes circa 1790 through 1865 from the six New England states. Often during a busy day at Bowers and Ruddy Galleries I'll spend the noon hour poring over my collection, contemplating the ragged old pieces of paper. Gone are the morning's worries as to how orders are coming in from our latest *Coin World* advertisement, whether we'll be getting that important collection we've been working on in Philadelphia for six weeks, and whether we'll get our next catalogue out on time. My collection represents a different world. A faded and torn $1 bill from the Metacomet Bank in Fall River, Massachusetts, a whole bunch of colorful red and green notes from the Sanford Bank in Maine, a really ratty looking but infinitely interesting $5 note from the Hall & Augusta Bank in Hallowell, Massachusetts, dated April 2, 1806. . .these and others cross my mind and my vision.

When 1:00 rolls around I am refreshed, relaxed, and ready to enjoy the rest of the afternoon.

I want you to enjoy your coins, paper money, tokens, and numismatic items as much as I enjoy mine. How do you do this? The best way I know is to become *aware* of your coins. I've tried to do this with my paper money collection, and it has always led to one delight after another. For example, when I saw my first Hall & Augusta Bank bill I noticed it said "Massachusetts" on it. Being a New England-ophile, I wondered exactly where Hallowell, Massachusetts was. Could it be near Boston? Or perhaps it was in the western end of the state near Pittsfield. I took out a copy of Rand McNally's *Road Atlas* and searched. But I couldn't find it! Well, perhaps it became a ghost town since my $5 bill was issued in 1806. Or maybe it changed its name.

I did know of another Hallowell, this one in the state of Maine. I remembered a visit there about 10 years ago. The main street was lined with old antique shops. I've never seen so many in one place! Well, to make a long story short, after digging out a history book or two I found that Hallowell, Massachusetts and Hallowell, Maine were one and the same! In 1806 Hallowell was indeed in Massachusetts, as was much of the rest of the present-day state of Maine. In 1820 things changed, and Maine became an entity in its own right, and Hallowell, although it hadn't moved an inch, was now located in another state! Interesting? To me, yes. To you? Well that depends. Perhaps you could care less about broken bank notes but, rather, you like Lincoln cents a lot.

What is interesting about a Lincoln cent, you might say. If you buy a scarce Lincoln cent from us or another dealer, make a note of it in your record book or file the sales slip, and tuck the coin away for safekeeping, you will be hard pressed to *enjoy* it. And yet a set or collection of Lincoln cents—and I pick this example because you might consider Lincoln cents to be common and unromantic—can provide many moments of pleasureful contemplation.

When I think of a set of Lincoln cents many stories go through my mind. There's the 1909 V.D.B. cent with Victor David Brenner's initials on the reverse. Brenner, a famous sculptor, was justifiably proud of his work and signed the die accordingly. Soon after the first Lincoln cents made their appearance on August 2, 1909, there was a great uproar about the V.D.B. initials. Within a matter of days the dies were revised, and the V.D.B. initials were no more. The editor of *The Numismatist* pointed out how silly and inconsistent this was, for many other United States coins in use at the time had designers' initials—the B initial for Charles

Barber on the dime, quarter, and half dollar, the M for Morgan on the silver dollar, the ASG monogram for Augustus Saint-Gaudens on the $20 gold piece, and so on!

The 1909-S V.D.B. cent is interesting because of its rarity. It is, of course, the San Francisco Mint's version of the V.D.B. issue. Only 484,000, a low number for a cent, were minted before the controversial initials were removed. Even though a few pieces exceed it in value, the 1909-S V.D.B. has always been the "standard rarity" of the Lincoln cent series. It is certainly one of the most desired of all 20th-century American coins.

The 1914-D is remarkable for its scarcity, especially in higher grades. A couple of years ago a few rolls of Uncirculated 1914-D cents turned up in New Zealand (so I was told). It was interesting to have the opportunity to look through about 100 Mint State (mostly with some light toning) pieces and to pick out a dozen or two for stock! When I first started coin dealing one rule was to watch for phony "1914-D" cents. These, crude in nature, were most commonly made by shaving away part of the digit on a 1944-D cent. In my first year of collecting I looked with interest at every 1914-D I saw, wondering how many of them were altered from 1944-D pieces. Then I finally saw one—and was relieved to learn that the fake was very easy to spot, and that the ones I had seen during the preceding years were all genuine.

The 1922 "Plain" cent is another story. During the minting of 1922-D cents at the Denver Mint a die became worn and clogged, with the result that the D mintmark became weak or altogether missing. A sharply struck 1922-D cent catalogues $60 in Uncirculated grade in the current *Guide Book of United States Coins.* At the same time a 1922-D struck so weakly that the D is missing, in other words, a 1922 "Plain," catalogues for $1,700 Uncirculated! Why? It certainly doesn't stand up to logic. But, then if everything in the coin field were strictly logical, would it be as much fun?

And then there is the 1955 Double Die cent. I've always enjoyed this particular variety, perhaps because Jim Ruddy and I were so involved with these pieces when they first became popular.

One day in 1955 at the Philadelphia Mint a coinage die was being prepared for a Lincoln cent. In the course of impressing the working die with the hub die several times, a slight misalignment occurred. The result was a 1955 cent die with the letters and numbers on the front of the coin all doubled. Instead of reading IN GOD WE TRUST, the famous 1955 Double Die (or Doubled Die as the *Guide Book* now calls it) reads IINN GGOODD WWEE TTRRUUSSTT.

On that particular day several presses were coining cents, each dumping the coins into a box where they were then collected and mixed with the cents from other coining presses. Late in the afternoon a Mint inspector noticed the bizarre doubled cents and removed the offending die. By that time somewhat over 40,000 cents had been produced, about 24,000 of which had been mixed with normal cents from other presses.

The decision was made to destroy the cents still in the box and to release into circulaton the 24,000 or so pieces which were mixed with other cents. This momentous decision was to have an untold effect on numismatics. The coins which were nonchalantly released into circulation subsequently increased in value to hundreds of dollars each!

These 1955 Doubled Die cents were first noticed by collectors later in the same year when they began showing up in upstate New York and in Massachusetts, particularly in the Boston area.

Jim Ruddy, who was operating the Triple Cities Coin Exchange in Johnson City, New York, at the time (in the days before our partnership began in 1958) recalls being offered these freaks for 25c each. Fearful at first of accumulating too large a quantity, he stopped buying them when he had a dozen or so on hand. It seems that in the Johnson City area cigarettes in vending machines could be purchased for 25c per pack at the time. As the real price was 23c, each pack contained two Lincoln cents under the cellophane wrapper as a refund. Apparently, a cigarette distributor was dipping from a Mint bag containing 1955 Doubled Die cents, for cigarette packs are where most of the Uncirculated ones came from! In subsequent years we never heard of Uncirculated pieces being found in original rolls (indeed, no roll would have been purely 1955 Doubled Die cents anyway, as the output from the various cent presses was mixed). Most Uncirculated pieces known today were picked out of change during the days following their first appearance.

While the 25-cent valuation might seem ridiculous today, it wasn't then. There was virtually no interest in collecting mint errors (we recall selling off center Liberty nickels, etc. at a *discount* for they were "defective" and few wanted them; now, of course, mint errors are collected in their own right and bring high premiums), and die preparation errors were interesting but hardly in great demand.

News articles in the various coin collecting publications, spearheaded, if memory serves, by *Numismatic News*, which called the coin the "Shift Cent," began to whet collectors' interest. The price climbed to $1 per coin, and then to $2, and it seemed everyone wanted one! When Jim Ruddy and I formed our business partnership by combining our previous companies in 1958, the price had climbed to over $5 apiece. An early advertisement of ours implored collectors to buy Uncirculated coins for $7.50 each! Dozens of orders poured in; far more orders than we had coins on hand. So, we ran advertisements in New York and Massachusetts newspapers seeking to buy the coins. Soon we were paying $20, then $40 for slightly worn pieces! At one point we had 800 specimens on hand—certainly the largest holding ever!

One man in Greene, New York, not far from our office, really was a treasure hunter and by looking through cents in circulation found 17 pieces to sell us! A nun in a convent near Boston sold us one coin at the time we were paying $20. She was a bit hesitant at first—What's the gimmick? Why would anyone pay $20 for a penny only several years old? But after our check arrived she no longer was skeptical and, in fact, sent us another coin a week or so later.

The demand was on. We sold our holdings and kept buying more. In the meantime the price climbed to $95, then $150, then past $200, then to $300, and in 1977, past the $500 mark for a truly select Uncirculated example!

This "once in a lifetime" error was repeated, believe it or not, in 1972. In that year the so-called 1972 Doubled Die made its appearance. While the doubled lettering was not nearly so sharp as on the 1955 variety, it was doubled nevertheless. Again excitement reigned, and within a few months of the discovery of the 1972 Doubled Die the price zoomed to the best part of a $100 bill (where, by the way, it has more or less remained since).

John Hamrick of World-Wide Coin Co. related to me that in his car trunk he had several bags of 1972 Philadelphia Mint cents which he ordered just to have on hand. When news of the 1972 Double Die reached his ears he thought of the forgotten bags, but did nothing about it. Finally, one day he peeked at a few coins in one bag and was delighted to find several 1972 Double Dies! John says he and his business associate Warren Tucker stayed up the rest of the night looking through the remaining bags and, in the process, found hundreds of the little treasure coins!

1960 Small Date cents have an equally fascinating story. As time and space are short here, I'll refer you to page 180 of my *Coins and Collectors* to read about that. Anyway, the point is an "ordinary" series such as Lincoln cents can provide many fascinating and romantic stories—and I've touched on just a few of them here.

In conclusion, once you pay for your coins, take the time to *enjoy* them.

Coins offer the possibility of being an interesting collection, a profitable investment, and a relaxing pastime. Could anything be more ideal?

F.W. Blake

By Douglas McDonald *1987*

Western Assayer, Banker, and Expressman

The development of the American West in the 19th century encompassed so many events over such a broad area that even today many details still remain to be studied. One such story began with the chance appearance of a small silver ingot in Bowers and Merena's Abe Kosoff Estate auction late in 1985. Accidentally misattributed to a California firm, this piece had actually been issued by an assayer in the Nevada boomtown of Unionville. Slowly the search for data about this ingot-maker led to the unraveling of the life of a little-known pioneer banker, assayer and expressman—Francis Wheeler Blake.

Born in Boston on July 24, 1828, Blake's early years in the East are unknown until he set sail for California in 1852. Choosing the faster sea route over an arduous overland journey, Blake took a ship to Panama, crossed the Isthmus on foot or mule-back, then sailed to San Francisco on board the steamer *Constitution.*

Shortly after his arrival on May 22, 1852, Blake headed for the northern California goldfields of Trinity County. There he found employment as an agent of Rhodes & Lusk Express in Weaverville, but soon realized that he could do much better for himself by opening his own business. Thus F.W. Blake & Co. Express was founded later in 1852 to operate stages between Weaverville and Shasta.

From the very beginning, and for the rest of his life, Blake was closely affiliated with Wells Fargo & Co. At first his line simply connected with their stages at Shasta. Then when he built his Weaverville office in 1854, which was one of the first brick buildings in town and cost the staggering sum of $5,000, he shared space with Wells Fargo, becoming their Weaverville agent. In addition to operating his daily express to Shasta and back, Blake also conducted a banking business which handled gold dust for the miners in the vicinity.

Blake sold his brick office building in August 1857, although he remained in business in Weaverville for two more years. Competition was heavy in both the express and banking businesses, which may have prompted Blake to abandon his ventures in 1859. Wells Fargo transferred their Weaverville agency to Greenhood & Newbauer's Northern Express, and Blake left Weaverville.

By 1861 he had relocated in Carson City, capital of the newly created Nevada Territory. There he operated a storage and commission business in partnership with J.O. Pope, and was a respected member of the business community. In April 1862, Blake was one of the 12 founders of the Odd Fellows' Carson City Lodge No. 4, but within two years he joined the rush to the booming mining camp of Unionville, Nevada.

In March 1864, Blake purchased Block & Co.'s assay office in Upper Unionville, moved the equipment to a more auspicious location in Thomas Ewing's new brick building on Main Street, and reopened in April as "Blake & Co., Assayers." The firm's first ad stated, "Gold and Silver Bullion, and ores of every description melted and assayed; and returns of bullion made in bars or coin, at the option of depositors."

The *Humboldt Register* newspaper reported on July 2 that "Blake's assay office. . .has been glutted, in the past two weeks, with crude bullion from the mail. Things begin to look like 'biz.' " Just how much "biz" was evident a month later when the same paper stated "Blake & Co. received Wednesday, for melting, 16,000 ounces crude bullion." Throughout the next two years similar notices appeared nearly every week stating the various amounts of bullion which he had received or the size of refined ingot shipped the preceding week. Besides his profitable assay business, Blake also served as secretary of the local chapter of the I.O.O.F., as well as secretary of both the Humboldt Salt Mining Co. and the Twilight Tunneling Co.

However, as with most mining booms, Unionville's heady days were short lived. By early 1866 the *Register* was complaining: "The times are dull, and many seek to improve their fortunes by going 'to other scenes and pastures new.' " Thomas Ewing, who operated an extensive retail merchandise store in the same building as Blake's assay office, shipped in April "a monster stock of groceries, liquors, clothing, hardware, mining tools, provisions, and the like" to the bustling new mining camp of

Silver City, Idaho Territory.

Blake must have already decided to move north to Silver City, for his last advertisement appeared in the *Register* on April 28, and he quickly sold his assay business to H.M. Judge, previously an assayer for the Ophir Mining Company in Virginia City. When Ewing left Unionville on April 30 to follow his goods north, Blake was one of those accompanying him. Also in the party was Edward B. Blake, believed to be Francis' brother, but about whom little else is known.

By July the new firm of Blake & Co., Assayers, had begun operations in a building on Washington Street, with E.B. Blake opening a small sign painting business next door, but there was still one item of unfinished business in Nevada. On November 8, 1866, Blake, who was then 38 years of age, married 22-year-old Sarah E. Meador in the tiny Nevada community of Limerick.

The Silver City assay office continued to prosper. In July 1867, Blake & Co. advertised in the *Owyhee Avalanche:* "We guarantee our Assays to conform accurately to the standard of the U.S. Branch Mint. Bars discounted at current rates. Particular attention paid to assays of Ore of every description." A later history of Owyhee County stated that he "was engaged as assayer for all the principal mines and mills in this locality."

When the couple's only child, Edward Meador Blake, was born on August 7, 1867, it is thought that he was named for the Edward Blake who accompanied Francis to Idaho the previous year.

In 1868 Blake became the local agent for the Manhattan Life Insurance Company of New York, and is also reported to have built an imposing stone building known as the Granite Block. The following year he expanded further by purchasing Charles P. Robbins' jewelry and watchmaking store located in the Granite Block, and by early 1870 he had also moved the assay office into this building.

Blake's various business enterprises remained unchanged until October 1873, when the assay office apparently closed. The November 15 issue of the *Avalanche* reported, "Mr. and Mrs. F.W. Blake and Master Eddie took their departure for Boston last Thursday evening. Mr. Blake goes to visit his old mother, whom he has not seen for 23 years, and will return about the middle of next month." The newspaper was in error, though, as Blake did not return to Silver City, and his jewelry store was closed the following April.

The Blake family remained in the East, possibly residing in New York as well as Boston, until they moved to Prescott, Arizona Territory. On October 29, 1875 the *Arizona Weekly Miner* stated that Frank W. Blake had been appointed agent for the new Arizona and New Mexico Express Company which would connect Prescott with the railroad at Caliente.

Returning to the express business was not enough, though, and by August he had opened an assay office in Prescott. The editor of the *Miner* was moved to comment, "We have known Mr. Blake, as an Assayer, for nearly a quarter of a century, in California, Nevada, and Idaho, and have yet to hear the correctness of a single assay of his questioned."

This assay office, like those previously established elsewhere, immediately proved to be a success, enabling Blake to take on the positions of secretary and bookkeeper of the Peck Mining Company. In his spare time he was also involved in locating the Grecian Bend mine in the Tiger mining district, the Atlas mine in the Hassayampa district, and the Apache mine in the Weaver mining district.

Early in June 1877, Wells Fargo & Co. opened their Prescott office, and naturally chose F.W. Blake as their agent. Soon he was also appointed agent and general superintendent for the Peck Mining Company, was elected mayor of Prescott, and once again began selling insurance on the side.

Blake remained Wells Fargo & Co.'s agent in Prescott until 1884, when he allowed the position to be filled by his brother-in-law, John Frank Meador. Mrs. Blake's father had settled in Arizona's Salt River Valley and the Blakes became fairly close to the Meador family.

For the next four years Blake turned his attentions to other projects such as the Walnut Grove Water Storage Co., the Piedmont Cattle Co., the local Masonic chapter, the First National Bank in Prescott, and for a time he even served as cashier of the Bank of Prescott. At one point, a local newspaperman rightfully called Blake "the hardest desk worker in Prescott."

In 1888 Blake again assumed the position of Wells Fargo agent, which he held until ill health forced his resignation in 1895. Edward M. Blake then succeeded his father as agent and held this office until 1899.

On August 1, 1895 Francis Blake died in Prescott of Bright's disease. He was buried in the local Masonic cemetery, where his wife was also laid to rest when she died in 1923.

For 42 years Blake had been an expressman, banker, and assayer, serving countless thousands of people in four states and territories. "He was a man of more than ordinary ability," one obituary stated. "His death will cause a widespread sadness." Blake's integrity and character were without reproach, and perhaps his greatest achievement was the creation of some stability in raw mining camps scattered in the remote regions of the West.

A Remembrance of 1883

By Q. David Bowers *1983*

As we enter the early months of 1983, it is interesting to reflect upon the American numismatic, social, and business scene of a century ago. 1882 had just ended, and the events of the preceding 52 weeks were now memories.

Jesse James, who had been running from the law since the robbery of a Northfield, Minnesota bank several years earlier, had assumed the name Thomas Howard and was living in Missouri. A friend and fellow outlaw, Robert Ford, was tempted by a large reward and killed the fugitive on April 3rd. Soon, a ballad would be written commemorating Jesse's exploits and he would become part of American folklore.

At New York City's Madison Square Garden audiences were delighted with Jumbo, a huge elephant imported from Britain by entrepreneur P.T. Barnum. Standing 12 feet high and weighing nearly seven tons, according to Barnum, Jumbo earlier had been a featured attraction at a London zoo but was sold because he was difficult to care for. A furor arose when Barnum's purchase was announced, and the incident echoed on both sides of the Atlantic, all to the delight of the new owner who was counting the ever-mounting gate receipts! Jumbo, who died in 1885, achieved immortality when his name became a part of the English language to indicate large size.

Although the soft drink Moxie had not yet become a fixture on the American scene, patent medicines were arousing increased concern. A congressional committee was appointed to investigate. It was found that many popular substances consisted of little more than strong alcohol with flavoring added, but that others contained poisonous substances. Interestingly, in later years it was revealed that Drake's Plantation Bitters, a popular drink, was composed in part of the poison strychnine!

Luchow's, a restaurant still very much in business in 1983, opened in New York City. Perhaps among other things it served Canadian Club whiskey, a new product introduced in 1882. Not far from Luchow's the gigantic Brooklyn Bridge, to open on May 24, 1883, was nearing completion.

Although America later became proud of its "melting pot" heritage, in 1880 there was alarm concerning the vast number of foreigners reaching our shores. In that year immigration from Germany reached an all-time high, with many of the newly arrived settling in German-American communities such as Cincinnati and Milwaukee. Congress passed the Chinese Exclusion Act a couple years earlier. Taking effect in 1882, it prevented Chinese laborers from entering the United States for the following decade. Earlier, the Chinese had played an important part in the building of railroads and other enterprises in the West.

Thomas Edison inaugurated commercial electric lighting in 1882 with the opening of the Edison Illuminating Company power plant in Manhattan. Soon, the world would change, the "Great White Way" would transfer Broadway into a melee of nighttime activity, and no longer would activities be mainly confined from sunrise to sunset.

John D. Rockefeller and certain of his acquaintances incorporated the Standard Oil Trust, effectively controlling 95% of the petroleum industry in America. And, to think, OPEC hadn't even been dreamed of back then! Somewhat in a like vein, when William H. Vanderbilt, one of America's wealthiest men, was asked by a *Chicago Daily News* reporter if he ran his railroad for the public benefit, the reply was the now immortal, "The public be damned."

Mark Twain was busy with pen and paper. *The Prince and the Pauper,* published in 1882, achieved success, as would his *Life on the Mississippi* published the following year.

Igor Stravinsky, the Russian composer, was born in 1882, the same year that Tchaikovsky's *1812 Overture* made its debut.

Everyday life in America during the presidency of Chester Alan Arthur usually was serene. In New England, factory workers, including children, tended to their knitting six days a week, looking forward to a Sunday picnic at the company-owned park. In the Midwest the typical farmer rose at daybreak to milk the cows and tend the livestock, to put in a long day and to retire at sunset, perhaps following activities with an hour or two of reading by candle or kerosene lamp. Although the electric light and the telephone had been invented, widespread use was still in the future. Radio, television, and, yes, income taxes, were far in the future and would have been considered the wildest fiction in 1882.

Meanwhile, at the Mint the director reported on October 12, 1882 that "the gold coinage of the mints during both the fiscal and calendar year was greater than that of any previous year in their history." It was observed that at the San Francisco Mint coinage was particularly heavy for larger denominations "because of the great demand for large coins on the Pacific coast, where the large exchanges and settlements are generally effected by the actual use of gold, and less paper is employed for the purpose in other portions of the country."

In the several years previous there had been little call for striking additional nickel five-cent pieces as the Treasury Department had a large supply on hand from earlier times. In November 1881 it was directed that nickel five-cent piece coinage be resumed in quantity and that a supply of large cents and copper-nickel Indian cents in storage be melted to provide the needed metal (the nickel five-cent piece alloy being composed of 75 parts copper and 25 parts nickel).

The big news in the field of nickels for 1882 was not as much the regular coinage as the production of patterns. Dissatisfaction had long been expressed with the shield design. Beginning in 1881, Charles E. Barber produced a new motif that was appealing to many, the head of Liberty wearing a coronet, modeled after the goddess Diana, it was said. By the end of 1882 the design had been refined to incorporate surrounding stars on the obverse and a wreath enclosing the Roman numeral V on the reverse. Curiously, the word CENTS was nowhere to be seen.

In 1883, when Liberty Head nickels of this type were released, it was soon found that they could be gold plated and passed as $5 gold pieces, for no mark of value was on them. Realizing its mistake, later in 1883 the Mint modified the design and added the missing word.

George T. Morgan, who designed the silver dollar of 1878, bore the brunt of much public criticism leveled against the motif. His discomfiture was eased, however, by the knowledge that the 1878 silver dollar had been rushed into production without adequate testing, a situation necessitated by the immediate need to produce millions of silver dollars from bullion purchased by the Treasury in response to political pressure. In 1882, under more leisurely circumstances, Morgan produced another idea for a silver dollar, a piece which became known as the Shield Earring design. Later, collectors would view this as one of the most attractive portraits ever to be produced within the Mint confines. Unfortunately, as often happens with such things, the beautiful design never went beyond pattern form.

As it had done for some years, the Philadelphia Mint struck Proof coins for collectors and offered them as minor sets (containing the cent, nickel three-cent piece, and nickel), as silver sets with the silver denominations, and individually as gold coins. As might be expected, by year's end the minor sets had sold the best, and approximately 3,100 of them had found new owners. The next year, 1883, was to see the fantastically large Proof coinage of 5,219 examples of the new Liberty Head nickel Without CENTS and an even larger number, 6,783, of the modified variety with the word added. This was caused not by a nationwide jump in coin collecting interest, but, rather, by interest on the part of speculators who felt that the issues would become rare.

It turned out that certain 1882 Proof coins would prove to be doubly desirable. Only 1,100 Proof examples were made of the silver denominations. The quarter, half dollar, and trade dollar were to become valued at over $1,000 each before a century passed, simply because business strikes of these same issues were made in small quantities, thus placing additional demand on the Proofs.

The Philadelphia Mint was so busy churning out Morgan silver dollars (eventually 11,100,000 business strikes were coined that year!) that there simply was not enough time to work on quarters and half dollars.

Proof gold coins were issued in modest numbers, with a distribution of 125 recorded for the 1882 gold dollar, 67 for the quarter eagle, 76 for the $3 piece, 48 for the half eagle, 40 for the eagle, and 59 for the double eagle. The double eagle in particular was to become a great rarity, for when the figures were totaled it was realized that only 571 business strikes were made that year, plus 59 Proofs. As exciting as such figures may be to collectors today, a century later in 1983, early in 1883 when the 1882 mintage report became known, few people cared. After all, the face value alone of a double eagle represented nearly a month's pay for many workers.

If someone could have looked into the future to discover that a century later, on the evening of October 29, 1982, a single example of an 1882 Proof double eagle would fetch $34,100 at auction, no one would have believed it!

At the branch mints in Carson City, New Orleans, and San Francisco additional coinage was taking place, with each piece produced being characterized by a distinguishing mintmark. Numismatists could have cared less. The publication of Augustus G. Heaton's treatise on why collecting by mintmarks was desirable was a decade in the future, and mintmarks were almost universally ignored.

Coin collectors were busy with other things, however. Auction sales were being held at a fast and furious pace, perhaps even rivalling the scene of a century later. For example. W. Elliot Woodward alone conducted 11 sales in 1882, with seven more scheduled for 1883!

The Woodward sales weren't furnishing juicy gossip, however. That distinction was reserved for two brash young brothers from Philadelphia, Samuel Hudson Chapman and Henry. A century later numismatic bibliophile John W. Adams was to write:

> The Chapmans had been in business barely a year when they conducted their first auction [October 9, 1879]. Sale one, which consisted of selections from stock, was noted for the quality of its content as well as the innovative introduction of phototype plates. Competitors should have taken this auspicious beginning to heart but, given the extreme youth of the principals [20 and 22 years], they did not. Thus, several years later, in 1882 when the entire dealer profession was maneuvering for the legendary Bushnell Collection, the Chapmans' capture of the prize was greeted with shock and disbelief. These reactions were to escalate into scorn and anger as the young "antiquaries" issued a voluminous, quarto-size catalogue which described the lots in considerably more detail than hitherto had been the custom; it was only adding fuel to the fire to have a plated edition of the Bushnell catalogue which sold for the brazen price of $5.
>
> Critics pointed to a long list of mistakes in the Bushnell text. . . However, the Chapmans had made their mark. The next 24 years saw Samuel and Henry go from one triumph to the next. . . .

Among the critics was Edouard Frossard, a leading dealer who had a strong streak of jealousy. Taking the role of a "spoiler," as a melodrama author might have put it, Frossard felt compelled in the pages of his publication, *Numisma,* to let other collectors know precisely the "truth" about the situation.

Shortly thereafter, in another *Numisma* issue, Frossard discussed the deleterious effects of dipping silver coins in cyanide or potassium, recommending instead that "an excellent means to clean coins not badly corroded is to dip for five minutes in spirits of ammonia, wash with soft castile soap in lukewarm water, dip for a moment in hot rain water, and dry by evaporation." However, he went on to say that an even better way for preserving Proof coins "in perfect condition" was to use six parts of caustic soda dissolved in water until the hydrometer marks 20 degrees. To this solution add four parts of oxide of zinc, and boil down until it is dissolved; add sufficient water to bring the solution down to 10 degrees. Paper or cloth soaked in this solution will prevent the most highly polished or the brightest surface from the tarnishing action of the sulphurated hydrogen, so noticeable in the air of our large cities especially. Coins wrapped in this cloth have been placed in a water closet near the opening for two days and were not changed in the least."

Lyman H. Low, who invited numismatists to contact him at Box 108, New York City, made the offer that "any obscure copper coin [would be] accurately described free of charge." Hard Times tokens of the 1833-1844 years developed into a specialty for him, and by the turn of the century Low had published a book on the subject.

Down in Baltimore, Maryland, T. Harrison Garrett, in his palatial mansion, Evergreen House, spent evenings closeted with his superb collection of American and other coins, a holding rivaled, it was said, only by Lorin G. Parmelee (who, at the time, was busy engaging in his trade as a bean baker in Boston).

In January 1883, the *American Journal of Numismatics* published a two-page article by Patterson DuBois, who was associated with the Philadelphia Mint. The dissertation sought to heighten the appeal of patterns with collectors and noted, in part:

> Open for me your cabinet of patterns, and I open for you a record, which but for these half-forgotten witnesses, would have disappeared under the finger of Time. Read to me their catalogue, and I read to you, in part, at least, the story of an escape from the impractical schemes of visionaries and hobbyists—a tale of national deliverance from minted evil. These are to be enjoyed as bygones, though there lingers a fear for the spark that still smoulders under the ashes. Laws have been framed for them, words have been warred over them. Now, only these live to tell the tale of what "might have been," only to remind us of what has been weighed, measured and set aside among the things that are not appropriate, not convenient, not artistic, in short, that are not wanted.
>
> But the lesson of these negations is positive and pertinent; these denials are emphasized affirmations, if but we see them so. They are the records of failure that suggest success. They are a dead language bristling with living thoughts. One cannot but reflect how nearly some of them have grazed the edge of success and missed being the types and forerunners of millions. . . I am not sure but that the minting and numismatic sciences of the future will look with singular interest upon a case of our patterns. They will profit

> nearly as much from the knowledge of what we do not want, as of what we do want. . . The pattern is to be viewed in the light of an honest experiment, of bona fide purpose, with some pretentions as a coin; in short, a true pattern. All experiments prove something, even if it be no more than their own failure. It is quite as important sometimes to be warned from the wrong road as directed to the right one. . . .

DuBois continued his flowery prose, culminating with the observation that "the pattern goes forth on a mission, weeding from the ravelling threads of what might have been, the prophetic picture of what ought to be."

It was exceedingly important that numismatists desire patterns, for one of the main "businesses" of the Philadelphia Mint was the unofficial production of such pieces for sale by government officials to collectors. Indeed, numismatic historian Don Taxay was later to characterize the Philadelphia Mint as "a workshop for their own gain." Early in 1883, however, it might not have been realized that the year marked the end of the trade dollar. It is probable that the exceedingly rare 1884 trade dollar (10 minted) and the even rarer 1885 (five struck) were not yet even a gleam in the eye of the coiner.

January 1883 reports of recent coin club meetings held in Boston, New York, and Philadelphia showed that a variety of items which would be considered esoteric today, 1983, attracted wide interest on the part of those who saw them. William S. Appleton showed the so-called Washington half cent of 1793, a famous forgery, and an 18th-century medal of the Social Club of Charles Town, South Carolina. Among the items shown by Sylvester S. Crosby was a medal of Lincoln by Franky-Magniadas. "Mr. Woodward exhibited several interesting pieces, among which were the silver 10-franc coin of Geneva. White's Halifax farthing, and some gold," while it was reported that Frossard brought with him "two mortuary medals of George Whitefield, the cofounder with John Wesley of Methodism in America."

Prof. Charles Anthon, one of the most respected and knowledgeable numismatists of the time (whose collection was also being sold in several installments during this era), showed "the so-called North Carolina or Raleigh medal," with the legend, "As soon as wee to bee begune, wee did beginne to be vndone," a coin which a century later, 1983, remains mysterious and unresearched. Another interesting item back then must have been the "Florida half dollar" exhibited by Mr. Betts.

The era was not without its humor, even in numismatics, so it is perhaps fitting to close the present article with a joke printed in the *American Journal of Numismatics* a hundred years ago:

"Sooner than have a light dollar leave the Mint, the authorities give it a weigh."

The Bushnell Sale

By John J. Ford, Jr. *1978*

An 1882 Sensation

Each decade during the past century has included a numismatic event of such singular importance that it continues to reverberate, influencing our aims and interests, even to this day. A particularly appropriate example of such an occurrence is the sale of the Charles I. Bushnell Collection, over 100 years ago, which heralded the beginning of a new era in American numismatics.

C.I. Bushnell died, at the age of 70, in his New York home on September 17, 1880. He was well known as the author of two numismatic works, published in 1858 and 1859, concerning tradesman (merchant) and political tokens and the first three business tokens of New York. It was a popular opinion that Mr. Bushnell possessed an unsurpassed knowledge of colonial and early American coins. His collection, one of the most famous ever assembled, was unusually strong in Americana, particularly colonial coins, medals, tokens, cards, and similar items.

Within a few days of Mr. Bushnell's demise almost all of the well-known dealers attempted to contact his family with ill concealed interest relative to the purchase of his estate. The collection was initially offered by the son and Mrs. Bushnell, the executrix, at the round figure of $10,000 without finding a purchaser. The opportunity to carefully examine the collection was difficult to obtain, but, eventually, several people obtained a fair view of the coins, and as much as $7,500 was offered by a New York party. W.E. Woodward, H.P. Smith, H.G. Sampson, and other dealers, including the indefatigable Ed. Frossard, all attempted to obtain the collection, and at one time or another, all seemed to have an equal chance of success.

The aforementioned gentlemen did not, however, stop to consider the young and extremely precocious Chapman brothers of Philadelphia. The Chapmans, Samuel Hudson and Henry Jr., were but 23 and 21 years of age at the time of Mr. Bushnell's passing. Both had served an apprenticeship with dealer John W. Haseltine and both were extremely capable young men, well versed in the mysteries of their chosen profession. As in similar situations, the bright-eyed and ambitious, however earnest and sincere, were constantly waylaid and badgered by their contemporaries. On the other hand, the Chapmans were fully aware of their knowledge and other sterling attributes, and were not, at that time, susceptible to anything resembling modesty.

Ed. Frossard, a former professor of languages and a partially disabled veteran of the Civil War, cleverly described the success of Messrs. Chapman in regard to the acquisition of the Bushnell estate. "While the fray at the front gate of the citadel was waxing hot, the Chapman brothers, by a brilliant strategic movement, having secured an ally within, entered through the postern gate in the rear, and captured the stronghold, much to the dismay of the craft in general, for few, excepting well-informed observers, had more than 'an ally within' to aid them in obtaining the Bushnell material for sale."

"The ally without," in this situation, was a Boston bean baker by the name of Lorin G. Parmelee. Parmelee began collecting in earnest about 1865 and after obtaining the Seavey, Adams, and Brevoort cabinets, rapidly became the foremost collector in the country, his interest becoming stronger as Bushnell's diminished. By 1880, he owned the finest existing collection of colonial coins and regular U.S. Mint issues and had, for several years, been negotiating with C.I. Bushnell for the purchase of his collection. After Mr. Bushnell's death, Parmelee would naturally be a most interested party, as the acquisition of a few pieces from the Bushnell estate would make his collection one of the most complete ever formed. Finally, Lorin G. Parmelee bought the Bushnell Collection, at a figure still unknown, but probably over $7,500 and a little under $8,500. By this shrewd purchase, he secured at apparently high, but really nominal prices, the few rarities needed to complete his superb holdings.

While the owner of the Bushnell Collection and privileged to withdraw the most interesting items, Parmelee placed the entire estate into the hands of the Chapmans and requested that they catalogue it for sale. Thereby, he could remain in the background and legitimately buy, against open competition, the coins necessary to round out his collection. Why the Chapmans were selected to sell the Bushnell estate is not clear, unless of course, it is understood that they were said to be nephews, by marriage, of the late Charles I. Bushnell.

In course, as it always must, the word went around and the Chapmans made a statement, through Frossard, which appeared in a supplement to the March 1882 issue of *Numisma*. "The rumors which have been circulated, by those envious of their success, to the effect that a certain number of rarities are withdrawn by previous arrangement with a certain Boston numismatist, who was said to be their backer in the negotiations with Bushnell's son, are unfounded and untrue. Every coin, medal, die and duplicate, of which there are many, will go in the sale, and everything is to be sold, without reserve, to the highest bidder."

Within a very short time, the Chapmans prepared an announcement for the forthcoming sale, consisting of a circular, describing a sumptuous catalogue, corresponding in size, and forming a sequel to Crosby's *Early Coins of America*. This was somewhat unusual, as the catalogues of the period were small affairs, offering brief descriptions and limited commentary, often little better than lists of the material to be sold. The announced length of the Bushnell catalogue and subsequent sale was also somewhat startling, as the total number of lots approached 3,000, and the sale itself was to be conducted for six days. The most radical departure however, as announced by the compilers, was an asking price of $5 for a limited edition of the catalogue with 10 Phototype plates. This, coupled with the 50 cents asked for a plain catalogue and the $1 for a priced one, plus the claim that the "magnum opus" would prove a sequel to as well as matching S.S. Crosby's work in size, was too much for several critics, including Ed. Frossard, who later observed—"It must be stated that while 50 cents is only a fair price for this large and handsomely printed catalogue, $5 is too much by half for the illustrated one. There is but one opinion among collectors on this point. The former ridiculous pretentions of the compilers to the effect that the catalogue would form a sequel to Crosby's masterly work *The Early Coins of America*, also fall to the ground. There are in fact very few colonial coins described not found in Crosby, and as no new light is shed on his work, and the borrowed information, conveyed with painful labor, belongs to the descriptive rather than the historical, it can neither supplant nor explain Crosby, but rather needs the explanations of the latter to make itself intelligible."

The actual appearance of the catalogue itself, early in 1882, brought forth extensive comments, including several snickers, the majority of which originated with the gentlemen who had an axe to grind. The Bushnell catalogue contained 136 pages and exactly 3,000 lots. Correcting the announcement, the sale was a five-day one, June 20 through 24, 1882, and as previously mentioned, the $5 edition contained 12 plates rather than the 10 originally contemplated.

Bushnell's collection was always considered somewhat mysterious as he bought secretly and through others and generally under an assumed name. It is said that even his closest friends had little knowledge of the full extent of his cabinet. The appearance of the catalogue was eagerly looked for with interest and curiosity by collectors in general as the final dispersion of the collection seemed of the greatest importance.

The initial criticism concerned itself with the contents of the collection. The progressive element of the period righteously bewailed the lack of U.S. Mint issues in the Bushnell cabinet. Regardless of how complete or how fine a collection Bushnell had made of colonials, American medals, and store cards, the breast-beaters wondered why he had neglected the rarities of the silver series; the 1804, 1851, and 1852 dollars; the 1796 and 1797 halves; the 1823 and 1827 quarters and the rarer dimes and half dimes, as well as the later pattern issues of the U.S. Mint. The fact that Bushnell had collected for a number of years, particularly when rarities were cheap and collectors few, was oft brought to the fore, in several instances in rather derogatory terms. A comparison was made with the Mickley Collection, sold in 1867, and as Frossard acidly remarked, "The Mickley cabinet still remains the best, most complete, as well as the most valuable American collection ever offered for competition in this country." Of course, the fact that Bushnell was a sincere collector and student of Americana, with little regard for the ersatz productions of the Mint, including the 1804, 1851, and 1852 dollars, made little difference to the critics of the day. The Chapmans alone seemed to appreciate Bushnell's lack of love for the regular Mint silver issues.

Professor Frossard's *Numisma* appeared about five years after he took an active interest in numismatics, and today upon its yellowed pages we find extensive comments concerning the Chapmans, especially in connection with their catalogue of the Bushnell sale. In May 1882, No. 3 of Vol. 6, we find the following tirade, obviously penned upon receipt of the catalogue. "As regards the arrangement and composition of the catalogue we remark with pleasure that the carelessness in composition, indifferent grammar and tautology, found in the former combined productions of Messrs. Chapman, have to a certain extent been avoided in this. A good story must be well told, or it loses its charm, and it would have been a pity to see such adjectives as "Uncirculated, bold and sharp impression," or "unique, exceedingly rare, and only specimen known," thrown in unending and tiresome repetitions throughout the catalogue. It looks indeed as if a person of mature judgment, sound learning, and accustomed to utter good English, had drawn the Messrs. Chapman from the inextricable tangles into which they have been wont to fall when endeavoring to make a point. If such be the case his name should have been mentioned as a collaborator, but it is quite as probable that they have simply followed the recognized authorities without referring to their lists or works, and this is the most unpleasing peculiarity of the catalogue, and one that cannot be overlooked. Except where it could not be avoided, the names of every American authority on coins and medals have carefully been excluded. Messrs. Chapman apparently prefer to leave the collectors in the dark rather than to commit themselves so far as to mention a single name."

Later, in another issue of his house organ, that of July 1882, No. 4 of Vol. 6, immediately following the sale, Frossard became somewhat snide and altered his earlier opinions to an actual attack. "A plain and correct catalogue would have reflected honor on its compilers, but the Chapman brothers apparently exhausted themselves on the plates and mechanical part of the work, unconscious of the fact that a proper use of English terms, an intelligible construction, also general accuracy in statements made, are of greater importance in work of this kind than thick paper, new type, and gilt letters. Careless proofreading, tautology, and exhibition of boastful egotism can be overlooked; hazardous, overdrawn, incorrect statements of history, rarity, and condition, cannot; the latter, rather than the former, are the chief defects of the catalogue, but all combining, help make the Bushnell sale catalogue, as published, unworthy of the collection it is supposed to describe."

The sale itself began promptly at 3:00 p.m., Tuesday, June 20th, 1882, in the salesrooms of Bangs & Co., 739-741 Broadway, New York City. Lot No. 1, a Sierra Leone penny of 1791, was purchased by Frossard and presented to Edward Cogan as a souvenir of the sale. Number 2 was bought by H.G. Sampson and presented to W.H. Strobridge for a like reason. Lorin Parmelee bought the Good Samaritan shilling for $650, as well as the cream of the Massachusetts silver, plus the Lord Baltimore penny at $550, together with a large number of other desirable colonials.

The monotony of the second day of the sale was broken by a gentleman who sat at the rear of the room and loudly criticized the descriptions of the various coins. The Chapmans purchased a large number of rare colonials, and Ed. Frossard obtained the most desirable item offered, the Brasher doubloon, for a paltry $505. Parmelee continued to buy odd pieces to round out his already magnificent collection.

The third day's bidding was enlivened by the presence of a Baltimore collector who obtained the finest of the Washington medals offered. Parmelee purchased many of the first-grade Washington coins while other room bidders actively fought for the balance.

The fourth day's sale was made noteworthy by the spirited interest in early Mint patterns, almost all of which brought record prices. Parmelee again led the bidders, although the majority of the items offered were snapped up about the room. The last day of the sale, June 25th, was marked by the offering of the regular United States material. Frossard purchased a Fine 1800 silver dollar and on behalf of the bidders, with the exception of "Long John" (Haseltine) and the two brothers, presented it to the auctioneer as a pocket piece.

Observations made at the time of the sale are rich in human interest. The bidding generally was spirited and rapid, the Chapmans starting at a round figure, and when not going up quickly enough, were said to occasionally attempt bidding against each other. Richard Cogan had charge of the coins while on exhibition, and kept a record of the sales. The New York press attended the sale, due no doubt to the extensive publicity it had received. Among others, the *Tribune, World, Sun,* and *Times* were represented. One observer remarked that the man from the *Times* was intelligent and dressed faultlessly.

Lorin G. Parmelee was the largest buyer, adding $3,800 worth of material to his famous collection. The Chapmans were next, having spent some $3,000 for stock. The other heavy buyers were Frossard ($2,500); George W. Cogan ($1,600); H.G. Sampson, and J.W. Haseltine. In all, the collection which probably cost Bushnell about twice the amount, realized $13,901 and was seemingly very profitable to Parmelee.

All in all, it was a lively and successful sale, the average daily attendance being about 25, including buyers and spectators. Among those present were Professor Charles Anthon, Ed Cogan, Sr., Daniel Parish, Jr., W.H. Strobridge, W. Poillon, William S. Appleton, Parmelee, F.W. Doughty, George W. Cogan, Lyman H. Low, Charles Steigerwalt, H.P. Smith, Major Nicolls, J.W. Scott, and David Proskey, all famous names in the glorious history of American numismatics.

It is said that humorous little incidents and remarks between the auctioneer, Mr. Merwin, and the audience, relieved the general monotony and kept everybody in good humor. A reflection upon the times is contained in a comment made earlier by one of the cataloguers for Bangs & Co. "Patent portable spittoons cost only 50 cents apiece, and it costs $5 to have the auction rooms on Broadway scrubbed after each coin sale. Not being interested in the sale of the patent article, we only throw out the suggestion as a friendly hint."

Frossard, while generally caustic on the subject of the Bushnell catalogue and its youthful compilers, made a few references which seem decidedly complimentary—"One feature for which Messrs. Chapman deserve praise is the care they appear to have exercised in pointing out all coins which our numismatic authorities have since the Mickley Sale discovered to be spurious; in all such cases they boldly announce the fact, no matter what the cost may have been to Mr. Bushnell. In questions of authenticity therefore, we grant them the merit of having been painstaking, intelligent, and honest."

However, the professor, in future issues of *Numisma,* continued to tear into the Chapmans and seemed to delight in heaping abuse upon the Bushnell Sale. He was joined by W.E. Woodward, who, in his catalogue of the Montreal Sale, July 1882, made a scathing attack upon the two brothers. After questioning the origin of several lots, Woodward remarked as follows: "There are many other pieces in this celebrated collection around which a veil of mystery has long been thrown, which, if they could be illuminated by the light of truth, would have their lofty pretensions sadly lowered—notwithstanding 'our opinion,' which throughout the catalogue is apparently regarded by the young gentlemen who compiled it, as amply sufficient to settle any mooted question in American numismatics."

Those among us who follow every current sale of this generation with unyielding enthusiasm must wonder at the obvious freedom enjoyed by our forefathers. The publication in a numismatic journal today of similar gross indignities would, in effect, be responsible for a catastrophe of no little magnitude.

In an effort to completely overshadow the earlier criticism of his own and of others, Frossard, in a final attack, listed in detail every lot in the Bushnell Sale that he could find fault with. Actually, many of these comments are quite amusing and should be followed carefully by every owner of the Bushnell catalogue. They indicate obvious dissatisfaction for a work that is currently valued by many leading authorities as a standard reference.

A Little Dry Reading for the Antiquaries

By Ed. Frossard

Nos. 14, 16, and 17; counterfeits.

145. Bogus and modern; why did not Bushnell say whence he obtained the piece? If from England someone must have sold it to him; but the piece is known to be a fraud from the fact that the man who bought Hub No. 2844, said "that he bought the hub because he had the piece."

176. Crosby right; bogus.

186, 187. Nothing to do with Florida and 188 a Spanish medal.

241. Counterfeit.

247. More than one dozen known; probably a restrike.

266. Counterfeit casting.

289 and 1544. "Knawing" is good.

291. "It is our opinion." *For shure.*

337. W.E. Woodward has had a dozen.

349. "Two or three known." —*Bosh.*

362. "Cast copper silver plated." —*Original.*

537. Was there ever a Colburn Sale?

608. "We do not think so." Oh! Fountain of wisdom! Deep well of knowledge!

620. Cast, not stamped.

653. "One of the most," etc.—*Bosh.*

712 and 715. *More bosh.*

740. "Very rare and the rarest variety." Good English.

775. Counterfeit of the period.

778. "Celebrated;" who celebrates it?

878, 887, 896. "Five known," "Five known," "Three known," how known and whence did the antiquaries derive this bit of gossip?

920. Too much bosh! Crosby's original statement correct.

1005. Edge engrailed (with a chisel).

1017, '26, '38, '52, '64, '69, '81, '90, 1107, '14, '16, '21; none silver.

1212. "Imploring of him;" good Irish. Poor English.

1217 and '35. What is "A band of clouds?"

1244. A marvelous discovery and statement. This piece was later bought by Scott and Co. at $7.50. *Query.* How did it get in the Bushnell Sale?

1265 and 1303. "Rays diverting," the description is diverting, the rays diverge.

1289. "Licking the calf," and "Minding the baby;" quite classical.

1335 and 1343. Electrotypes.

1375. Marvin 705; a mute.
1400. "Sund disk" is good.
1553, '75, '78, and '79. Electrotypes.
1605. "This is one," etc.—Bosh.
1616. "Medal awarded Congress;" when?
1660. W.E.W. has the dies.
1748, '49, '51. "Arctic" "Artic;" bound to have the spelling correct.
1764. U.S. Mint at Philadelphia, which has been cleaned in acid; when?
1848. Electrotype.
1843, 1929, '67. What Express? Adams?
1976 and '82. And is it Alex. Hamilton?
2183. "Similar but very different;" Clear as mud.
2205 and '06. "Beath' and "Uncirbulated" are good.
2230. Not silver.
2279, and '82. "Sewn" and "Sewen" of course not sewed.
2617. "We believe," "We had," "We sold,' "We have." By the way, quite a number of the cents were polished with stove blacking; all the '94s, 1814, '27, etc; none of the 1794 cents were struck as Proofs, and they rated from Very Good to Uncirculated; all the Fine silver medals had been cleaned.
2635, etc. "Variety to last;" to, good. Many of the half dollars did not belong to Bushnell's collection. "Bless my heart," innocently exclaimed Major Nicolls, suddenly looking up from his catalogue, "Why, I never knew I had so many uniques in my collection!"
Auct. "Three cents, going at three cents to Proskey."
Pr. "No sir, I did not bid on these."
Auct. "Beg pardon, I thought it was yours from the size of the bid."
Auct. (To H.G.S.) "No sir, you can't have that Silly Head cent, that belongs in Philadelphia."
Sampson. "How about the Booby Head?"
Auct. "That goes there too, *it makes up the pair.*"
Smith (Loud) "That's bogus."
Chapman. (Sotte voce) "Shut up Smith."

Originally written by John J. Ford, Jr. for the Coin Collectors' Journal *(published by Wayte Raymond).*

An Adventure in Collecting

By Q. David Bowers *1977*

This article is adapted from the "Joys of Collecting" series written by Q. David Bowers, which is currently appearing in Coin World. *Subsequently, much of the following appeared in the book,* Adventures With Rare Coins, *published in 1978.*

Numismatic Fascination

In today's era of high numismatic values in many areas, it is refreshing to know that often a modest budget will build a superb specialized collection. In the last issue of our *Rare Coin Review* I told of the pleasures of building a set of United States coins by design types and how a collection quite impressive in scope and appearance could be formed in one way for $3,446. Or, by spending $11,656 one could come up with a very comprehensive collection in this field—or, for $30,572, one could build a type set a museum would be proud to exhibit.

"What do you collect?" is a question often asked of me. While I think it would be delightful to form a type set of United States coins, to do so would compete with my customers' needs. And, besides, I work with United States coins every day, have been doing so for nearly 25 years, and collecting them would not be as "fresh" to me as a new field.

It has been my experience that most numismatists tend to form many different collections over a period of time. My good friend, the late Oscar G. Schilke, who lived in Connecticut, was a numismatist's numismatist—and appreciated coins for the many *pleasures* they offered. As I have related in my *High Profits from Rare Coin Investment* book, Oscar combined collecting with investment and, as a result, built a financial treasure over the years.

At the same time, Oscar was always seeking the byways, the little-traveled roads, of numismatics. To be sure he had a type set of United States coins, a superb one. And he had a collection of 1793-1857 large cents by dates and varieties. And then there was a superb display of quarter eagles from 1796 to 1929, including many Proofs. But there were other things too; pieces which were not as valuable but which were equally fascinating from a numismatic viewpoint. Oscar had a collection of rolled-out coins issued by penny arcades and as souvenirs in expositions. You are probably familiar with the type of rolled-out Lincoln cent with the Lord's Prayer on one side. Well, Oscar had dozens of different types—including pieces dating back to the 19th century. . .rolled-out coins from the 1893 Columbian Exposition, for example. Seeking to make an "original" contribution to his collection of rolled-out coins, Oscar visited the 1939 World's Fair in New York with two 20-cent pieces from the 1870s in his pocket. He picked two pieces in Extremely Fine grade with fairly heavy toning. His theory was that an Uncirculated coin would be too "bright" and when rolled out would lose its design detail. He went up to a concessionaire and watched as each of his 20-cent pieces was rolled out. Presto! He had what probably remain to this day the only rolled-out 20-cent pieces from this 1939 event! Silly? Perhaps. But to Oscar and to a collector of rolled-out coins, such a story is fascinating.

Here at my firm we sell lots of numismatic items in just about every field imaginable. It's also rather commonplace for us to sell major rarities—coins in the $10,000 to $100,000 range or more. The other day, for example, we had an order for the magnificent Proof 1875 $3 gold piece listed at $110,000 on page 55 of our last *Rare Coin Review* issue. The new owner of the coin, a wealthy investor, really appreciates the coin and its history. I know that it has a fine new home.

While selling an 1875 $3 gold piece for $110,000 makes interesting reading and, of course, is pleasurable from both a business and a numismatic viewpoint, the fact remains that my average client simply does not write out $110,000 checks. And yet each collector wants to have a sense of importance and fulfillment. While great rarities are fine for those who can afford them—just as in another context Rembrandt paintings are fine for art connoisseurs who have champagne budgets—the fact remains that there are vast areas of numismatics in which small sums will go a long, long way. Some of these other areas have a very high degree of numismatic and historical interest.

If you are interested in coins, whether as a collector or as an investor or, as what I consider to be ideal, a combination of both, you will double your enjoyment if you take the time to delve into the history and background of the coins or paper money you buy. Numismatics can be *fascinating.* Now in 1977, after having handled just about every major rarity in the book, scarcely a day goes by without my learning something new and interesting! The following experience, representing my current collecting interest, is shared not to entice *Rare Coin Review* readers to collect my specialty (heaven knowns, I don't need more competition!) but to show how fascinating collecting can be—and to show that a sense of collecting importance and fulfillment can be obtained for a relatively modest cost.

A Visit to Clark's Trading Post

In 1976, following the American Numismatic Association convention at the Americana Hotel in New York City, I joined my two sons, Wynn and Lee, and two friends from Boulder, Colorado, Beverly and John Rives, and drove in a Hertz rental car to North Woodstock, New Hampshire.

North Woodstock, at the entrance to Franconia Notch (known for the "Old Man of the Mountains" or "Great Stone Face" rock outcropping), has as its best-known attraction Clark's Trading Post. Managed by Murray Clark and his family, Clark's Trading Post does a land-office business with vacationing tourists visiting the White Mountains. On view to be seen and enjoyed are such diverse items as a standard-gauge steam locomotive and passenger cars (which depart from the ornate 1880-style railroad station once located in New York City's now-defunct Freedomland Park and since relocated piece-by-piece at Clark's), an arena and show featuring trained black bears, a very nice exhibit of coin-operated nickelodeons and orchestrions (a favorite interest of mine), an old fire station with some really ingenious equipment (including a wonderfully complex-looking old Amoskeag horse-drawn pumper), the Americana Museum (a large structure with a wide array of exhibits, including old radio and telegraphic equipment, probably the world's largest collection of memorabilia relating to Moxie soft drinks from the turn of the century, children's toys, old steam engines, and many other things), some old cars and trucks, a roll-operated circus calliope, the "Yankee Wisecracker" (a clever coin-operated "talking" scale which, when stepped on, delivers such messages as "I'm a scale, not a freight elevator!"), a well-stocked gift shop (advertised as "the largest in New Hampshire"), and, on the more serene side of things, two nicely marked nature walks through the New Hampshire hills.

During our late August and early September stay there, my sons and

I and John and Beverly Rives enjoyed the different facilities of Clark's Trading Post and visited surrounding areas as well—including a nice afternoon spent going up the Mt. Washington Cog Railway, managed by Murray Clark's brother Ed, and which actually features original authentic equipment first put in use in the 1860s and 1870s!

One evening Murray Clark and I were discussing numismatics. Murray has been a numismatist for many years. In his gift shop he features a small numismatic-souvenir section which enjoys a brisk trade during the summer months selling $2 notes, tokens of various kinds, modern Proof sets, silver dollars, and other pieces—mainly priced from a few dollars up to $10 or so. On the personal side of things, however, Murray goes into it a bit deeper—and is forming a nice collection of obsolete and United States currency, with emphasis on the issues of New Hampshire.

Murray showed me many obsolete pieces of scrip issued by New Hampshire merchants during the Civil War era when coins disappeared from circulation and notes were privately issued as an emergency measure. Then came an array of notes from New Hampshire banks of the 1830s, 1840s, and 1850s. Then Murray took from a portfolio some beautiful stock certificates and bonds issued years ago by New England railroads. What impressed me was not the value of the pieces, for most cost Murray all of $5 or $10 or so, and some just cost a dollar or two, but their beauty and historical significance. Within an hour I became absolutely fascinated with the collection!

A Collecting Interest Begins

My interest concentrated on his obsolete currency issues. Being a director and owner of one of America's largest numismatic firms, a company in business for nearly a quarter century by 1977 (we celebrated our silver anniversary the very next year!), I have handled lots of obsolete currency—sheets, bulk lots, and so on. However, these have all come and gone through the firm—with scarcely any time taken by me to *appreciate* them in depth, apart from the time needed for proper cataloguing. So, here at Clark's Trading Post I was in effect seeing obsolete currency and its true significance for the very first time in my life!

Murray had one referenc ebook on the subject, *North American Currency,* by Grover C. Criswell. We spent 15 minutes leafing through it, with Murray guiding the "tour." He pointed out that obsolete currency, or *broken bank notes* as they are often called, was issued in many really unusual denominations. The People's Bank of Paterson, New Jersey, for example, produced such esoteric denominations as $7, $8, and $9! Other banks issued such values as $1.25, $1.75, and $6.25!

I was not a complete stranger to this, for in 1975 I purchased two collections of $3 bills. One of these was subsequently given by me as a gift to the American Numismatic Association Museum in Colorado Springs. The second was put into a bank vault where it remained ever since the day of purchase—for it was something I thought might be interesting if I ever had the chance someday to look into it. In the meantime it had been all but forgotten. The thought of it did cross my mind a few months before my visit to Clark's—and I asked the person from whom I had bought it if he would like to buy it back! His answer was negative; his collecting interests had turned elsewhere. So, you see my interest in the $3 notes was just about as low as it could be!

As Murray kept talking about obsolete currency I resolved that one of the first things I would do upon my return to the Bowers and Ruddy Galleries office in California would be dig out the collection of $3 notes and look through it carefully for the first time!

"How do I begin a collection of obsolete currency? Where are some places to buy? How much should I expect to pay?" I asked questions like this of Murray, just as I have heard similar questions in other areas asked of me for many years.

Murray related that he made purchases from a number of different sources, but that Roland Hill, a Massachusetts dealer in currency, was perhaps his most steady supplier and sent him frequent shipments. He gave me Mr. Hill's address and I said I would write to him as soon as I returned.

All too soon the visit ended, and my sons and I were aboard a United Airlines 747 en route from Boston back to Los Angeles.

The first chance I had on my return I took the collection of $3 notes from the bank vault and spent a number of hours studying it carefully. I decided that my main area of interest was New England, so I separated the collection into two parts—$3 notes of New England (of which there were nearly 200) and $3 notes of other states (of which there were about 500). The notes from other states went back to the bank vault with the idea in mind of selling them as a lot or trading them someday. The New England $3 notes were carefully sorted and put into individual holders.

So, I had an "instant collection" of New England obsolete currency—all of the $3 denomination. Now I wanted to add to the group. Looking through the classified and display section of *Coin World,* through the periodical publication of the Society of Paper Money Collectors, and through the monthly publication, the *Bank Note Reporter,* I came up with about 25 names of dealers who specialized in broken bank notes. To that list I added Murray's friend, Roland Hill, and a few others I knew from previous business transactions.

Out to many different areas of the United States went a letter stating that I was beginning a collection of New England obsolete currency and welcomed price quotations, approvals, and correspondence pertaining to the subject. Within a matter of a week or two shipments from Richard Hoober (accompanied by some very interesting historical commentary), Rarcoa, Don Embury, the Brandywine Company, Roland Hill, Bob Medlar, Byron Cook, Commercial Coin Co., Currency Times Past, and Julian Leidman were on my desk. I sorted through these with care and picked out a couple hundred additional notes. Most were priced in the range of about $5 to $10, although some were higher and a few were lower. In the weeks that followed additional sellers responded. Some sent me several shipments.

Julian Leidman, the well-known coin dealer from Silver Spring, Maryland, who often deals in obsolete currency, told me I should get in touch with John Ferreri of Connecticut. John, Julian said, was really enthusiastic about New England currency and had specialized in it for quite some time. Subsequent correspondence revealed that John, whom I had recently met in person, is a really likeable person—full of interest, enthusiasm, and spirit concerning his specialty. Over a period of years he has assembled approximately 1,500 different notes from the six New England states—Connecticut, Maine, Massachusetts, Vermont, New Hampshire, and Rhode Island. His advanced interest paralleled my beginning interest, so I have learned quite a bit via correspondence from him.

I have always been oriented towards study and research, and an early goal was to read as much as possible on the subject. I quickly found that most of the area of obsolete New England bank notes is uncharted. Grover C. Criswell's *North American Currency* gives an overview of the subject, but does not go into comprehensive detail. For example, among obsolete currency of New Hampshire only 91 different notes are listed. This is not a deficiency in the book, for the author did not envision it to be the final word on the subject. In fact, the foreword states: "This work is by no means complete, nor is it intended to be . . . I set about compiling a book which would list the more common varieties . . ."

From Quarterman Publications in Massachusetts I obtained a copy of *The Obsolete Bank Notes of New England,* by David C. Wismer. This publication, which sells for $25, is a condensation of a series of articles originally published serially in *The Numismatist,* journal of the American Numismatic Association, from 1922 through 1935. To Mr. Wismer's writings of years ago has been added an interesting modern introduction by George W. Wait. This reads in part:

> In our daily activities we spend paper money and seldom look at it, except to notice the denomination . . . The Treasury Department emphasizes that all of our $1 bills carry the portrait of Washington, all of our $5, Lincoln, all of our $10, Hamilton, and so on. Such was not the case in 1860. A buyer might pay for his purchase with any one of many kinds of bank notes or a combination of them. These bank notes were issued by state-chartered institutions with varying degrees of solvency. A famous token dated 1857 bore the words *Never Keep a Paper Dollar Till Tomorrow.* Not only were there many banks of questionable integrity, but a large proportion of the floating supply of paper money was counterfeit . . .
>
> Obsolete bank notes provide a most interesting field for collection, not only for the bank note collector but for the historian, art lover, and student of engraving . . . Those interested in the process of engraving may trace a simple early design from black and white to the very elaborate color notes of the 1850s and 1860s. Bank presidents tried to outdo each other in picking the best of thousands of designs, including depictions of lavish scenes and beautiful women. And, of course, the fancier the note, the more difficult it was to counterfeit. Because a great many banks went broke, the term *broken bank notes* has been commonly applied to all early bank notes, whether or not they were good. This is really a misnomer, since more genuine bills were redeemed and, in a very few instances, will still be redeemed by banks still in business or by their successors. The collecting of these obsolete notes is probably one of the most interesting, educational, and rewarding of all branches of numismatics, although it was not recognized as such until quite recently . . . .

A Beginner Learns More

The Wismer book vastly expanded my horizons. Whereas the Criswell reference lists 91 different notes from New Hampshire, the Wismer book lists 528! By making a rough tally of the Wismer listings I noted that the volume listed 683 notes of Connecticut, 754 of Maine, 2,419 of Massachusetts, 528 of New Hampshire, 1,215 of Rhode Island, and 579 of

Vermont. This meant a grand total of 6,178 different types of New England currency listed.

I quickly found that perhaps 50% of the notes I was receiving in the mail were not listed in the Wismer reference. By simple mathematics this would mean that about 12,000 different varieties had been issued totally. But, considering that I have only received shipments of currency for about a year now, I am sure that this proportion will grow as time goes on. Perhaps the number of notes originally issued was far greater—15,000 to 20,000 or more! And, New England broken bank notes are considered to be scarcer than those of certain other areas such as New York and Georgia—so what the total population of broken bank notes issued from all different places in the United States was, is anyone's guess!

From Julian Leidman as a surprise gift one day came another reference on the subject, a red clothbound book published by the Society of Paper Money Collectors in 1972, entitled *Vermont Obsolete Notes and Scrip,* by Mayre B. Coulter. This book, a fairly comprehensive dissertation on the subject of paper money from the Green Mountain State, gives rarity ratings and approximate values for many different issues. Even so, I learned there are numerous varieties which weren't listed and, best of all, my beginning collection had some of them!

I soon realized that there was no definitive volume on the subject and that I had to "fly by the seat of my pants." Collecting obsolete currency is like sailing in uncharted waters. Complicating this is the situation of price. Within a couple of days I received in the mail from two different sellers the same variety of $4 note from a bank in Portland, Maine. One note was priced at $18, the other at $90. Was the $90 note vastly overpriced? Probably not, for there are few price guidelines to go by. I have found that seller A can price a note at $20 and seller B can price the same note at $10. In the next shipment, another variety of note will be priced by seller A at $10 and seller B at $20! So, there really aren't any rules. I have to pay what I think a note is worth to me. If I pay $15 for a given note today and then next week the same note is quoted to me for $8, all I can do is shed a secret tear. On the other hand, if the same note is later quoted to me for $25, a smile crosses my face!

I soon found that rather than being a problem, this uncertainty was part of the fun. It is interesting to obtain a note for, say, $15 and find that it is unlisted in any of the standard reference books and, for all I know might be the only such note in existence! Or, perhaps it is quite common and I just don't know it. To me this contributes to the "thrill of the hunt" and is more interesting than following a standard price list and simply ticking pieces off the list mechanically as I acquire them.

Two months after I started collecting I sent John Ferreri in Connecticut, who by that time was a good mail order "friend," a listing of some of my duplicate notes—and was delighted to learn that he, an advanced collector with many years of experience, was able to find seven different pieces which he didn't already have!

A number of intereting facts soon became evident. The Wismer book, which lists over 6,000 varieties of New England notes which were once printed, is in no way representative of notes which exist today. The reason for this is that Wismer used old banking guides, counterfeit detection manuals, and other references from the 1830-1860 period to compile his list. Many of the notes therein were issued only in limited quantities and have all been redeemed since or in some instances may never have been issued at all but were merely contemplated. As his references mainly date from 1830 onward, nearly completely absent are the thousands of issues from the 1790-1830 period, even very common notes. Also absent are the scrip or private fractional currency issues from the 1860s.

I have learned that particularly rare are high denomination New England broken bank notes. While Wismer lists *numerous* $500 and $1,000 notes, the only one I have in my collection is a Proof $500 note—and I have never been offered any others. John Ferreri reports having found only one $1,000 note in his many years of collecting, and, recently, another friend-by-mail, Leonard Finn, reports that he owns but one each of the $500 and $1,000 denominations, both notes being from the Franklin Bank of Boston. I would find it immensely interesting to own a $500 or $1,000 note which actually circulated. What an immense sum of money this would have represented originally—in an era in which a year's salary for a working man would be on the order of $200 to $400 in many instances!

$3 Notes and Counterfeits

While $3 notes are unheard of today and, in fact, the expression "queer as a $3 bill" denotes something which isn't logical or desirable (witness Maria Muldaur's song of the early 1970s, *You're Just a Three-Dollar Bill)*, at one time $3 notes were very common in America. In fact, $3 notes from the early 19th century are no more unusual than are, for example, $2 notes, $10 notes, or $20 notes. In fact, $10 and $20 notes are scarcer!

When the United States government commenced issuing its own currency in 1861 it was decided to issue $3 notes as part of the series. Preparations were made for doing this. When currency was actually issued, the lower denominations were made only in the values of $1, $2, and $5—with the $3 forgotten. Somewhat related to $3 bills are such coins as $3 gold pieces (minted 1854-1889) and three-cent pieces (made in silver 1851-1873 and in nickel 1865-1889).

I learned that counterfeit notes are avidly collected, and in many instances sell for as much as or even more than the originalsr! I have in my collection a $3 note which purports to have been issued from "The Hamilton Bank" of Boston in 1857. Across the note is an old counterstamp which reads COUNTERFEIT. Examination of the piece reveals that the word "HAMILTON" is fuzzy-appearing and is a slightly different shade than the rest of the features.

The other day when looking through my collection of notes I found another $3 bill, a genuine issue from the Lafayette Bank of Boston. I noticed that it was quite similar in appearance to the note I had from "The Hamilton Bank." Putting the notes side-by-side I noticed that the "Hamilton" note had the same inked signatures of bank officials as did the Lafayette note! So, the "Hamilton" note had been produced years ago by rubbing out or otherwise obliterating the word "LAFAYETTE" and carefully hand-inking "HAMILTON" in its place!

What probably happened is that the Lafayette Bank failed or its notes became worthless. Someone in the 1860s found himself possessing a Lafayette Bank note which could not be redeemed. In those days $3 was a lot of money and represented the best part of a week's salary. At the same time the Hamilton Bank of Boston was a going concern and its notes were accepted. So, presto-chango, with a few hours' work the worthless Lafayette note became a valuable "Hamilton" note! To me such a situation contributes very much to the joys of collecting the series. The cost involved? The counterfeit note cost me $20 and the genuine set me back $11. It is my guess that if I were to take these two notes and arrange them in a display case at a convention, surround them with a picture of the Lafayette Bank and the Hamilton Bank (if I could find these in a book of old engravings), and tell the interesting story of how they were made I am sure that it would be of great interest to numismatists. And, who knows, perhaps it would even be awarded a prize of some sort. And, yet, here is an exhibit that would cost me just $31—certainly a nominal sum in monetary value—but still possessing untold numismatic and historical significance.

Not all counterfeits were made by altering notes. There are other types.

Sometimes the corner designs of a $10 bill would be pasted on a $1 note to raise its denomination. Other times—quite often—counterfeiters would make up false plates and print the notes they needed. Usually the workmanship is not up to the standards of the New England Bank Note Co., the Graphic Co., and other early issuers, but sometimes the quality is indeed quite good. Occasionally a ludicrous error is made, as in the case of a note in my collection which has the state name spelled as *New Hampshier.* But, not all mistakes are counterfeits. I have two other notes from the same state, scrip notes (denominations less than $1) issued during the Civil War, absolutely genuine, with the state spelled as *New Hamshire.*

I learned in a subsequent conversation with my friend Murray Clark that certain notes which were stamped "COUNTERFEIT" were really genuine notes which had been redeemed, and when they were redeemed they were marked "COUNTERFEIT" so that they would no longer circulate. This is particularly true of notes of many issuers called in by two early-day clearing houses, the Bank of Mutual Redemption and the Suffolk Bank, both of Boston. Of course, in most instances those marked "COUNTERFEIT" really are. The more usual way of marking genuine notes when they were redeemed was to cancel them with one or more small punch holes—or, in the case of the State Bank and the South Royalton Bank, both of Vermont, to cancel them with huge holes.

Some Observations

In the nearly one year's time since I have been collecting obsolete currency of New England some nice surprises have come my way. Ed Leventhal, genial proprietor of Boston's J.J. Teaparty Co., learned of my interest and asked me if I would like to purchase his specialized collection of obsolete Massachusetts currency which he had been forming over a period of years. I asked for more information, acquired same, found the price to be reasonable, and now have added this group to my collection. Grover Criswell sold me a nice collection of Proof notes (notes which were not actually issued but which represent trial impressions on special paper), including pieces once owned by early author D.C. Wismer. Dr. John Muscalus and Jess Peters furnished substantial numbers of interesting pieces. So, note by note, group by group, the collection grows.

The motifs featured on the notes are fascinating. A girl feeding chickens, a sailor in a crow's nest high on a mast, railroad trains of all sizes, shapes, and varieties, pigs in a farmyard, an Indian raid, stately bank buildings resembling Grecian temples, steamboats, whales, figures of Liberty and Justice seated, standing, and even flying, factories, pioneer scenes, trees, George Washington seated, standing, wearing a uniform, wearing a toga, and on horseback, trees, boy and girl lovers . . .these are just a few. A commmon set of notes from the West River Bank of Jamaica, Vermont, features a series of illustrations or *vignettes,* as they are called, of cupids playing with United States silver dollars. As George Wait has expressed, it is almost as if early bank presidents were playing oneupmanship with each other in the area of elaborate designs.

Condition of the notes is sometimes paradoxical with regard to their numismatic value. Often Uncirculated or *New* notes, as they are referred to by collectors, are the least valuable and really wretched-looking ones are the most valuable! Why? The reason for this is rather simple. When a bank failed often it had on hand vast quantities of unissued notes. These notes, in New condition, have found their way into numismatic channels and in many instances are extremely common today. John Jay Ford, Jr., a well-known enthusiast in the field, recently related to me (at a dinner at the Copenhagen Restaurant on West 58th St. in New York in the evening following a coin show) that during the 1950s he once had an eight-inch-high stack of West River Bank (Jamaica, Vermont) notes and was doing a land-office business selling them for 60 cents each! (Which, by the way, is about 1/100th of their value today; broken bank notes, like many other areas of numismatics, have been an excellent investment.) On another occasion he bought from a New Orleans seller 14,000 sheets of obsolete Louisiana bank notes.

In the field of New England issues, New notes from such institutions as the Stonington Bank (Stonington, Connecticut) and the Bank of New England (East Haddam, Connecticut) can be obtained in certain instances today for $3 to $6 each. Indeed, original sheets containing four different notes are often priced from $15 to $25 or so.

On the other hand, notes which actually circulated are apt to show extensive signs of wear, tear, and soiling. In these instances the original notes were entirely dispersed into circulation. In intervening years most were redeemed or lost. Thus the "finest known" might only be in Fair or Poor grade, perhaps with a corner missing!

Strange Doings in Vermont

One of the most interesting of the reference books I have been able to gather on obsolete New England bank notes is a small green-covered pamphlet entitled *Historical Account of Vermont Paper Currency and*

Banks, by Terrence G. Harper, undated, reprinted from *The Numismatic Scrapbook Magazine.* The following account of strange doings in Vermont is largely quoted from that source.

But first, what if I were to tell you that some of the most historical of all American paper money—notes with an absolutely fascinating and romantic and adventurous history—could be obtained for $10 to $20 each? Would you be skeptical? Well, after having read this article this far you probably wouldn't be—but if I had mentioned it to you in any other context you probably would have pooh-poohed the idea. Anyway, I spent a nice evening at home reading Terrence G. Harper's 48-page monograph. I was fascinated with a three-page account of the history of the Franklin Bank of St. Albans, Vermont. After reading the article I was eager to return to the office to get from the bank my Vermont notes. Lo and behold, I found I had several different varieties from the Franklin County Bank! The cost? In the $10 to $20 range, closer to about $10 per item. Now I'll tell you of Mr. Harper's account and you can judge for yourself whether or not these relatively inexpensive items are among the most fascinating pieces of numismatic Americana one could own:

> The Franklin County Bank at St. Albans was chartered in 1849 with a capital of $100,000. Bills were issued of the denominations of $1, $2, $5, $10, and $20. From 1849 to 1865 the president was O.A. Burton. Cashiers were Edward W. Parker from 1849 through 1858 and M.W. Beardsley from 1858 through 1865.
>
> Immediately after the *St. Albans Raid* the Franklin County Bank was liquidated. It paid all of its debtors but refused to redeem its bills unless a satisfactory account of proper possession could be proved. The story of the Raid is fascinating. This bank, along with the St. Albans Bank (notes of which are also common and inexpensive, by the way), was involved in one of the most daring robberies in Vermont history, the so-called "St. Albans Raid."
>
> This daring adventure of October 19, 1864, aroused not only local but national excitement. Thousands of words have been written about this affair, some true and some romanticized. No history of Vermont is complete without its mention, and it fits in nicely with the present discussion.
>
> A band of armed and desperate ruffians, representing the interests of the Confederate States of America, 22 men in number, succeeded by a secret and well-planned movement in robbing these banks in open daylight and escaping with their plunder to their base of operations across the border in Canada.

That a robbery so daring could be accomplished by a force so small in a village of the population of St. Albans might seem very improbable. To carry it out it was necessary to make it a complete surprise.

The citizens of St. Albans, like those of New England villages generally, were occupied during that October 1864 day with their private affairs at offices, shops, and stores—with no suspicion of danger and with scarcely a weapon of defense. After all, the Civil War conflict had never extended even close to Vermont, and the northernmost holdings of the Confederate States of America lay hundreds of miles to the south!

The rebel plan was indeed a bold one and, as it developed, was very skillfully carried out. Bennett H. Young, who apparently was the leader, accompanied by two others, came into town from the city of St. John's in Canada on October 10th and stayed at the Tremont House. Two others on the same day stopped at the American Hotel. On the next day three others arrived. These men spent the next week in and around the village of St. Albans and learned the habits of the people, the location of the banks and their safes, and the places where horses could be obtained when they were ready to leave. The desperados attracted no more attention than did other strangers who arrived on nearly every train into this village and who customarily stayed at the same hotels.

On October 18th, the day before the Raid, two more came to breakfast at the Tremont House and were joined later by four more at dinner. On the 19th, the day of the Raid, five came to dinner at the American Hotel and six at the St. Albans House. It was later proved that two of these late arrivals came in a carriage from Burlington, Vermont, and that the others arrived on the Montreal train at noon.

The raiders learned that Tuesday, being market day, would be an unfavorable one for their purpose, but that the day following would be the dullest of the week when there probably would be only a few people in the streets. It so happened that on this particular Wednesday nearly 40 of the leading citizens and most active men of the town were in Montpelier, Vermont, attending the Legislature, then in session, and in Burlington awaiting the progress of important cases before the Supreme Court.

The names of the raiders, as far as can be ascertained, were Bennett H. Young, Squire Turner Treavis, Alamanda Pope Bruce, Samuel

Eugene Lackey, Marcus Spurr, Charles Moore Swager, George Scott, Caleb McDowell Wallace, James Alexander Doty, Joseph McGroty, Samuel Simpson Gret, Dudley Moore, Thomas Bronson Collins, and William H. Hutchinson. They were mostly young men from 20 to 36 years, except McGroty who was 38.

The afternoon of Wednesday, October 19th, was cloudy, threatening rain, and the streets were particularly quiet. By prearrangement, immediately after the town clock had struck the hour of three, the banks were entered simultaneously by men with revolvers which had been concealed on their persons.

Hutchinson and four others were deputized to rifle the coffers of the Franklin County Bank. Marcus W. Beardsley, cashier, sat by the stove conversing with James Saxe. Jackson Clark, a woodsawer, was also in the room. Hutchinson came in shortly after three, and Mr. Beardsley arose and went behind the counter to see what was wanted. Hutchinson wished to know what the price of gold was. Beardsley replied that the bank did not deal in it. J.R. Armington then came in with money to deposit, and Hutchinson was referred to him. While Beardsley was counting the money left by Armington, Hutchinson sold the latter two gold pieces for greenbacks. Saxe and Armington then went out, leaving Hutchinson standing at the counter, keeping up a conversation with Beardsley.

Immediately after this, four others came in and stood in the corner of the room a few moments. Then one of them advanced a few steps, put his hand deep into his side pocket, drew out a heavy navy revolver—which he then pointed directly at Beardsley, looking him straight in the eye, but without saying a word.

Beardsley thought he must be some insane man and at first was inclined to run—but he did not, and stood returning his gaze. Two others stepped forward, drew their revolvers, and pointed them like the first, without a word from either. Hutchinson, who had kept his place at the counter, then said in a low but very decided tone, "We are Confederate soldiers. There are a hundred of us. We have come to rob your banks and burn your town."

Clark, a bank employee, made a dash for the door but was ordered back with the threat of instant death if he moved. Hutchinson said, "We want all of your greenbacks, bills, and property of every description." They came behind the counter and into the vault, taking everything they found of value.

When they had secured their booty and were ready to leave,

Hutchinson told Beardsley that he must go into the vault, where Clark had already been placed. Beardsley remonstrated against an act so inhuman, told him the vault was airtight and that no man could live long in it, and that if they were left outside of the vault they would raise no alarm.

This did not impress Hutchinson at all. He grasped his prisoner by the arm, led him into the vault, and fastened the door. Beardsley supposed that they would carry into execution their threat to burn the town, and had before his imagination the horrid prospect of being burned alive.

Hearing voices in the room, he rattled the door of his prison, and soon heard his name being called by Armington. He told him how the door could be opened, and he was soon released—his confinement having lasted about 20 minutes. As he emerged from the bank he saw the robbers galloping off to the north.

The robbers succeeded in getting across the line into Canada, but 13 were arrested there and held for trial. The money found on them amounted to $80,000. The prisoners were brought before Justice Coursel, and after a long and tedious examination at great expense to the government of the United States and the Franklin County Bank, the judge concluded that he possessed no jurisdiction in the matter, ordered the men to be discharged, and the stolen money to be returned to them. Having regained their ill-gotten funds, the raiders left immediately!

Four or five were later re-arrested, and another attempt was made to extradite them to the United States. They were brought before Justice Smith at Montreal, and after much more additional expense the judge ruled that the transactions of the robbers in St. Albans were acts of war and were not liable to international extradition. The Canadian government, however, did not sympathize with the magistrates and their decisions. Parliament appropriated $50,000 in gold to be paid to the Franklin County Bank and others as partial compensation for the money successfully taken by the raiders. At the time $50,000 in gold was equal to $88,000 in currency.

The entire amount taken by the robbers was $208,000. The currency loss was therefore a net of $120,000. To this might be added a sum of not less than $20,000 which was expended in the arrest of the robbers and the attempt to secure their extradition.

The Vermont bank commissioner later reported that: "I have visited the Franklin County Bank two days after the St. Albans Raid and have found by examination of their books that they suffered a loss of $72,443. I found by an examination of July 27, 1865, that they had recovered $31,857 of the stolen funds, making $40,586 their actual loss; surplus on the day of the Raid and unpaid interest then due reduces the deficit to $33,890.93. The act of Legislature relieving this bank from its liability to redeem its bills after June 1, 1865, leaves $54,031 not redeemed, of which $40,586 is in stolen funds, leaving $13,445 in honest circulation, which the directors are willing to redeem."

So, it is apparent that most of the currency of the Franklin County Bank still in existence—including hundreds of notes in collectors' hands—has a good chance of being among the treasure carried off on October 19, 1864 by the raiders!

Conclusions

I have been collecting New England notes for less than a year. I enjoy it immensely, as you probably can tell! I have the satisfaction of knowing that there are many other stories, presently unknown to me, which will come to light concerning different issues. I know that many of the notes I will acquire in the future, mostly for sums in the $10 to $20 range, and some for even less, will be one-of-a-kind and not even the most advanced collector or museum will have a duplicate copy! I know that hundreds of hours of fascination await me. Also in the offing are some nice friendships. I look forward to the possibility of meeting more of my friends who are known to me now only by mail. For example, Richard Hoober, the currency dealer who lives in Pennsylvania, always has a personal paragraph or two on his invoices. The other day, by fantastic coincidence, while looking through a reference book about American picture postcards I came across a reference to a special 1909 card announcing the marriage of a Mr. Hoober, who lived in Pennsylvania. I mailed a copy of that book page to Richard Hoober and was delighted to learn that it was one of his close relatives! It's a small world!

Perhaps collecting New England notes isn't your cup of tea. Actually it's fine if it isn't—for, heaven knows, I don't need any more competition! Why not try the more generally available and cheaper notes of New York, New Jersey, Pennsylvania, and Georgia—just to mention a few other states. Or, if budget isn't a consideration you might try broken bank notes of Colorado and other western areas. Did you know, for example, that Clark, Gruber & Co., issuers of territorial gold pieces, some of which featured Pikes Peak as their motif, also issued broken bank notes in the

1860s? John Jay Ford, Jr. said he offered some of these a few years ago for about $600 each. Perhaps their value is even higher today. Hardly inexpensive!

Or, did you know that the Mormons, who prior to their move to Nauvoo, Illinois and, later, to what is now Salt Lake City, Utah, stayed for awhile in Kirtland Safety Society, which issued bank notes, many of which were signed by Brigham Young? Did you know that some obsolete currency was once printed on the back side of wallpaper? There are hundreds of stories and anecdotes, and to relate even a small fraction of them would take up hundreds of pages—but you get the idea.

In today's world of numismatics there are many fields and areas of specialty which provide the collector a vast opportunity for fascination and numismatic satisfaction. It is well and good to be interested in the financial investment area of numismatics for the investment return in many areas has been spectacular over the years. But, at the same time take time "to smell the roses," to enjoy the romantic, historical, artistic, and other considerations. You'll increase your enjoyment of numismatics, you'll increase the satisfaction and enrichment of your life, and the knowledge gained will enable you to make wiser and better buys—which will lead to, if you please, your holdings being a better financial investment.

What is your area of interest? For me at the moment it is New England obsolete currency circa 1790-1865, for another it might be trade dollars 1873-1883, for another it might be New Jersey cents minted during the 1786-1788 years, for many it is the formation of a United States coin collection by design types, for a recent correspondent of mine it is Michigan emergency currency issued when banks in that state were closed in 1933.

Consider the possibilities. Do some investigating. Buy some books for your library (always a good idea!). Discover what area is just right or you. A new world of fascination will be yours!

A Salute to Abner Kreisberg

By Don Alpert 1984

It has been our pleasure to have known Abner Kreisberg for many years. So, it was with a particular degree of interest we read an article which appeared in the Los Angeles Times, *May 24, 1984—a feature by Don Alpert—which spotlighted one of our very favorite professional numismatists. The article is reproduced herewith:*

At 80, still in circulation. Just because a coin is 80 years old is no guarantee that it is particularly rare or valuable. But an 80-year-old coin dealer—now that's something special.

Well, on Monday, Abner Kreisberg, will celebrate his 80th birthday, and Kreisberg, to the uninitiated, is one of the deans of American numismatics, a 50-year veteran who has handled some of the great rarities and sales of modern times. But Kreisberg does not live in the past. He continues to operate out of Rare Coin Galleries, 344 North Beverly Drive, Beverly Hills, recently puchased by Joel Rettew, another veteran dealer.

"I owe my time to the people who trusted me through the years," Kreisberg said, "and as long as I'm around, I'll service them. I enjoy it. Most of my good friends are numismatic acquaintances. Some of them started as young boys. You give them as much attention as adults. If they specialize, who knows, they can become experts.

"That's how Dave Bowers got started when he was a kid. (Q. David Bowers is a noted numismatist, coin dealer, and president of the American Numismatic Association.) His father used to bring him in, and they bought coins from us in New York. There were Abe Kosoff, Hans Schulman, and myself, and we were partners. We started the first coin department at Gimbel's department store in New York. (Actually, the trio is virtually legendary in coin circles.)

"Most of our customers were not real wealthy people. Some of them were change makers on the subway in New York. That's where they found a lot of their coins. They later retired on their profits. There are lots of stories. Lots. Some day, if I stay alive. . .I just don't remember all of them any more."

Kreisberg got into numismatics through the back door.

"I was in the refining business in New York," he said. "Well, actually I was an old-gold peddler, really. Two of my friends were about to be drafted—I was too old—and they both wanted me to take over their business until they got out. One was Abe Kosoff. The other was Sidney Balaban. We tossed a coin and the coin business won out. As it turned out, neither one of them was drafted But Abe and I formed the Numismatic Gallery in New York City at 42 East 50th Street."

Menjou and Farouk

"We later had some of the finest auction sales. We sold the World's Greatest Collection of Gold and Silver coins in 1946. There was the Fred Boyd Collection, also the Adolphe Menjou Collection, the Beck Collection, the Moskowitz Collection, the Gainsborough Collection, the Shipkey Collection.

"We sold coins to King Farouk. There was the Kahn Collection of Chinese coins, which was sold and then sold again to the British Museum. I forget all the names. Our sales were mostly held at the Waldorf in New York and here at the Beverly Wilshire and Century Plaza."

Does that mean that collecting is just for the rich?

"Not at all," Kreisberg said. "Many people bought coins just because they were interested. Then people started to buy because it was a good investment. I liked it better the old way when a numismatist came in, looked at a coin for three hours and spent $9. That was real numismatics. Now, somebody stands guard over you with a gun. We never used to have that. It was all trust then."

The veteran dealer also deplores what has been happening with coin grading and the Mint State scale of one to 70 that has been adopted by most of the professionals in the business. He says it goes back to Dr. William H. Sheldon's book on large cents, which was aimed strictly at copper coins. This grading system was later expanded to include gold and silver. But Kreisberg knows as well as anyone that grading is subjective.

A Very Fine Difference

"It depends," he said, "on which side of the counter you're standing; whether you're buying or selling. I don't think anyone can tell the difference between MS-63 and MS-65. I don't do it. I never did. I grade the old way, AU, VF, XF (Almost Uncirculated, Very Fine, Extra Fine), which was good enough for everyone in those big auction sales that we held."

Among the coins Kreisberg has handled is the gold pattern Indian Head 1907 $20 rarity, which went to King Farouk for $1,500 around 1946. It was bought by Julian Leidman in April 1979, for $500,000 and auctioned in August 1981, for $475,000. "There's only one. It's called the Indian Head double eagle, a design that was adopted on $10 (eagle) gold pieces. But the $20 design is a standing Liberty, called a Saint-Gaudens after its designer."

Kreisberg also was involved with Louis Eliasberg, a storied collector who was determined to own one each—preferably the finest known—of every date and type coin struck by the U.S. Mint. "Eliasberg bought his last two American coins from me to complete his set," Kreisberg said proudly.

Proud of His Sons

Kreisberg keeps up with modern times. He goes to a gym two or three times a week, golfs regularly Wednesdays and Saturdays, collects art and sculpture, and is proud of his sons, one a dentist, the other a veterinarian.

"They didn't care for my business," Kreisberg said. "That's OK. I didn't care for my dad's. He was a dentist, too."

"The main thing to do," Kreisberg said, "is keep your mind active, otherwise you disintegrate."

And while Kreisberg isn't the oldest coin dealer in the country (Norm Shultz of Salt Lake City is a little older), he's one of the most refreshing. Yet he's the one who considers himself lucky.

"I've met a lot of nice people," he says.

Reflections on a Connecticut Pond

By Q. David Bowers *1985*

Among my favorite recollections are those involving Oscar G. Schilke and his wife Olga, who lived on the shore of Dodge Pond in Niantic, Connecticut, not far from New London. During the 1960s I visited there once a year, sometimes twice, usually alone but sometimes with Jim Ruddy, who was my business associate at the time.

Oscar was certainly a "complete" coin collector and would fit in nicely with the ideal numismatist envisioned in my article, "The 'Compleat' Coin Collector," which began on page 35 of our *Rare Coin Review* No. 53. Indeed, in my *High Profits from Rare Coin Investment* book I gave Oscar as an ideal example of a person who truly enjoyed coins for their many aspects and who, at the same time, found them to be a wonderful investment over the years.

Oscar, who died in 1971, had a long and distinguished involvement with coin collecting. When his interest began, I don't know, but he was heavily involved by the mid 1930s. These were the years of the Great Depression, but, somehow, coin collecting was immune from many of the Depression's effects. Indeed, the coin market, after suffering some setbacks in 1930 to 1933, strengthened considerably, and by 1935 and 1936 a boom of sorts was underway, spearheaded by nationwide interest in commemorative coins.

Outside events often influence numismatics, and in my own experience dating from the early 1950s, I have seen numerous instances in which, almost like an astrological prediction, something out of the control of coin collectors has had a deep impact. In 1957 it became popular knowledge that earlier Proof sets ordered from the Philadelphia Mint had proven to be spectacular investments, so the public jumped on the bandwagon. While many noncollectors limited their activities strictly to current Proof sets, others became involved more deeply and went on to be specialist collectors. In 1960 the Small Date Lincoln cent set off a nationwide treasure hunt, setting the tone for the modern coin market as we know it today. *Time* magazine, television shows, and others told of success stories—how a barber found a $50 sack of 1960 Small Date Lincoln cents and sold it for more than $10,000—spurring everyone to scramble to find the precious little copper things. *Coin World* was launched and within a few years climbed to dizzying heights in circulation, achieving subscriber figures not equaled since. The teletype machine, something formerly relegated to hotel reservation desks, newspaper newsrooms, and the like, became a fixture on the numismatic scene, and by the end of 1962 or 1963, well over 100 coin shops could communicate with each other via this medium. At one time the Professional Numismatists Guild even had its own teletype circuit.

Later outside influences having a profound effect on the coin collecting hobby included the Great Treasury release of silver dollars in 1962, the advent of the 1964 Kennedy silver half dollar, the tremendous public interest in gold bullion in 1971 through 1973 with the concurrence of double-digit inflation, the OPEC oil scare, the weakness of the American dollar overseas, and high bullion prices of the 1979 to 1980 years.

In each of these historic instances outside interest in coins has caused prices in the numismatic market to rise sharply. In each instance prices fell all the way back down after the popular passion subsided, but prices never went back to what they were before the cycle started. Indeed, a charting of numismatic market prices over the years will look something like a saw laid on edge, with many peaks and valleys, but the sawblade is angled upward. The long-term trend has been one of price appreciation.

Anyway, Oscar Schilke had his own business problems in the early 1930s. Economic times were tough, and Oscar in later years never quite got over the instance of a Connecticut contractor who owed him $10,000 but who filed for bankruptcy, thus evading the debt. Years later, the same contractor in the same business was to become immensely wealthy, but he made it clear to Oscar that as he did not *legally* owe him anything, Oscar was out of luck. Oscar, who had consummate faith in human nature, felt otherwise.

I first met Oscar Schilke in 1955 at an early Metropolitan New York Coin Convention. These shows, staged on the lower level of the old Park

Sheraton Hotel (which since has changed its name several times), were under the direction of Ray Gallo. Ray took a personal liking to me and in following years I was always favored with a nice position right next to the entrance. Of course, after a few years this position was earned, as by the 1960s there were many dealers setting up at the show who had not been in business back in 1955.

Oscar liked stories connected with coins. In many instances he would offer me an unusual piece and state the price would be cheaper if I could tell him its background, a procedure Wayte Raymond, the well-known dealer of the 1930s and 1940s, had followed with Oscar earlier.

A scholarly numismatic student Oscar was not, but he did have a broad and general appreciation of all sorts of coins from colonial pieces through current Proof sets. One wall of his den in the basement of his home on Dodge Pond was devoted to numismatic reference books and old auction catalogues. Back in the 1960s when I made my visits, there were not nearly as many references in print as there are today, in 1985. Still, Oscar managed to have hundreds and hundreds of different information sources. Later, Oscar's library was purchased by Hank Spangenberger, the Ohio antiquarian.

A typical day at Dodge Pond would be prefaced by arrival the night before. Then would come wake-up time, usually around 8:00 or 9:00. After dressing and straightening up the guest cottage not far from the water, I would make the short hike up the hill to see Oscar and Olga in the main house. On deck would be a sumptuous repast of pancakes, eggs, and other breakfast delights served in a kitchen decorated with a strawberry motif. And, *decorated* is an understatement for *everything* was done in strawberries—the wallpaper, the dishes, the china knick-nacks on the sideboard, and even Olga's apron. When the Strawberry Patch Restaurant opened here in Wolfeboro a few years ago it featured an omnipresent strawberry motif, prompting me to think of the "good old days" on the shores of Dodge Pond.

Oscar and Olga loved to eat, and their substantial figures reflected this. The best preparation for a visit to Dodge Pond would be to go on a diet the week before!

It wasn't proper to start looking at coins for sale at the beginning of my visit, although the ultimate purpose for coming was Oscar's invitation to buy a few coins and sets—he was making an orderly disposal of his collection acquired over a period of years. There were certain social aspects to be followed. And, this was fine with me. Right after breakfast we would retire downstairs to the den, take up a couple of easy chairs, and start talking coins, without a hint of any actual buying or selling. Like other old-timers in numismatics, Oscar liked to reminisce. And, he liked coin people. He was acquainted on a first name basis with anybody who was anybody in numismatics in the northeastern part of the United States. He told of Tom Elder, who had a strong personality (to put it mildly) and who conducted his New York dealership through a metal-cage window, like a bank teller. Elder, who once boasted he could catalogue 1,000 auction lots per day, seemed to always be in a hurry about things, according to Oscar. State your business, conduct it, then leave, seemed to be the modus operandi. And, if some person offended Elder, the use of four-letter words was not spared.

The pace of 1,000 auction lots per day—if indeed this was ever achieved—or whatever fast pace he used—took its toll on accuracy, for of the leading dealers in the New York area, Tom Elder was the loosest when it came to grading, according to Oscar. This furnished endless opportunities for Monday morning evaluations of coin sales by other dealers and his customers. Such-and-such didn't sell well because it was overgraded or, worse, was not genuine. These stories were numerous. Tom Elder had many positive attributes, and one of these was intense promotion of the coin collecting hobby. He gave many talks and discussions before groups, often illustrating them with unusual pieces, particularly in the field of obscure tokens and medals.

At the 1939 World's Fair held in Flushing Meadows, not far from Manhattan, Oscar saw a machine that rolled out various coins fed into it. Of course, it was intended that Lincoln cents be used, but the device was such that it would accept nickels, quarters, and other coins larger than cents. Oscar fed a few Lincoln cents through the machine and quickly noticed that new pieces, when rolled out, lost their design, for the rolled-out piece was simply a strip of bright copper. However, a worn Lincoln cent, particularly one that was slightly dirty, would be rolled out with the date and other features sharply visible. This sparked an idea, and on a subsequent visit Oscar brought two 1875-S 20-cent pieces from his collection. Back then such coins, probably in what we would call Extremely Fine grade today, were apt to be worth less than a dollar each. The idea of having a rolled-out 20-cent piece was immensely appealing, for he had never seen such before and was going to be the first to create one! To be sure the coin would not be confused with the rolled-out quarter and to make certain the legends would be visible, Oscar deliberately darkened each piece. Then each 20-cent piece was fed into the maw of the machine, run through the rollers in its innards, and disgorged as an unusual and "extremely rare" rolled-out 20-cent piece, with the date and mintmark on each sharply visible.

Several times each year, Oscar would make an arrangement with banks in Waterbury, Naugatuck, Bridgeport, and other towns to have a "coin day." Advertisements of each bank, placed beforehand, noted that on a given day a coin expert would be on hand. Oscar was given a corner in the lobby to look over any items brought in. There would be no charge or obligation. Oscar would take up a position in a lobby chair, have a copy of the *Standard Catalogue of United States Coins* at hand, and would be set up to greet all comers. Although the typical bank customer had few coins of value, each day would yield a few gold coins, some scarce Indian cents, and perhaps even a rarity or two. At one time he was brought an 1842 United States Proof set, complete from the half cent through the silver dollar, a set that today (1985) would be worth many tens of thousands of dollars. Included in the set was a Proof example of the 1842 Small Date quarter, a fantastic rarity in its own right. The specific coin from this set later went to the Hollinbeck Coin Company, then to me, then to the collection of H.B. Hinman (The Century Collection), which I subsequently catalogued for auction for the Paramount International Coin Corporation in the mid 1960s. The 1842 Proof set had rested in a dresser drawer in an upstairs dresser in a mansion for many years before Oscar saw it. Whether the set was brought into the bank lobby or whether Oscar was led by the hand to the house and extracted the Proof set from its resting place, I don't recall, but I do know this was one of Oscar's foremost prizes. Another prize was a beautiful framed fractional currency shield which belonged to a former governor of Connecticut, who acquired it in the 1860s at the time of issue. This shield was displayed for years on Oscar's den wall. It was a matter of special pride during one visit to Dodge Pond when Oscar sold it to me. Today it proudly hangs on my office wall.

Oscar once told of visiting a toll house located, I believe, near Boston Harbor. The facility had been active in the early part of the last century in the years prior to the Civil War. Oscar told of visiting the abandoned toll house, going down a flight of stairs to a stone basement, and being shown a safe or storage vault in the floor. After considerable exertion, the lid to the metal vault was wrested off, and revealed was a cache of United States large cents, all dated 1826! The condition varied from well-worn pieces to coins numismatists might call Extremely Fine or About Uncirculated. Obviously, they had been collected over a long period. Why the date 1826? Oscar never found out. Perhaps the year was significant in the life of the toll collector. In any event, hundreds and hundreds of 1826 cents were extracted from their underground tomb. Over the next few years, all dealers in the New York City and New England area were well equipped with examples of this particular issue.

After a morning of "coin talk," the time came for lunch, again in the strawberry kitchen. Typically, Olga had spent the morning preparing a delightful repast, usually a sandwich board with sliced turkey, ham, beef, and other selections. After lunch it was downstairs again and more tales of Wayte Raymond, the Stack brothers, Elder, and other old-timers. Oscar and his collecting friends liked to play one-upmanship with certain of the dealers in the city, who often thought they knew a lot and had seen everything (which perhaps was true). The story was told of a tale fabricated by a young couple who visited Morton Stack and showed him an Uncirculated 1793 large cent. The couple claimed they had found a group of them in an old broken-down grist mill they had recently explored on a farm which they had purchased. Morton, of course, was wide-eyed at the possibility of acquiring such a rarity, especially in multiples! However, the couple didn't want to sell it—not just yet. They went on to tease the dealer, then left with the coveted 1793 cent feigning they hadn't the slightest idea that it was worth much but, in any event, they wanted to keep it and others in the hoard as souvenirs.

Coin clubs played an important part in Oscar's life and he was a regular attendee at the New York Numismatic Club meetings each month. The Fairfield County (Connecticut) Coin Club was another interest, and occasionally the group had a picnic at Oscar's home during the summer. Photographs were taken, and in later years Oscar delighted in sharing these with me. He could review a picture of two dozen Fairfield County Coin Club members and spend 15 minutes telling about each person! These were from the days when Oscar lived closer to New York City—before he retired to his lakeside home in Niantic.

The afternoon of a typical day on the shore of Dodge Pond would come and go with lots of coin discussions, but nary a word about the actual buying and selling to take place. Then would come dinner, my treat at a restaurant to be picked by Oscar and Olga. One of their favorites was the Latchstring which, I believe, was in New London. Perhaps it still is in business today. I remember once we commented that the word "latchstring" was unusual in having six consonants—"tchstr"—in a row, certainly an unusual situation in the English language. Oscar was always noticing trivial details like this, and that is what made the visits so interesting and so memorable. On one visit he gave me a detailed tour of New London, showing me the Electric Boat Company where atomic submarines were made. As it happened, the *Nautilus* was streaming by, with the upper part out of the water, a grand and historic sight to behold. I found it interesting that there were so many private residences right across the river from the submarine facility. It would have been easy, I thought, for a foreign power to set up any number of spies under the guise of being New London citizens. All one would need would be a medium-power telescope to see what was going on.

After dinner it was back to Dodge Pond and some more talk, but not much, for Oscar and Olga usually turned in early. The next morning the scene changed, and it was down to business. From some hidden location Oscar would extract a number of coins—the ones he wanted to sell. Each time he had something specific to offer. Once it was a beautiful collection of large cents, another time it was a comprehensive group of California small denomination or fractional gold pieces, and still another time it was a virtually complete set of Philadelphia Mint quarter eagles from 1796 onward, including all of the 1796 through 1834 early issues (which I later sold intact to Abner Kreisberg and Jerry Cohen) as well as a complete set of Matte Proofs 1908 through 1915. Such things were fantastic rarities, of course, but back in the early 1960s the values were not all that great. In later years a single item such as the 1796 quarter eagle would be worth more on its own than the entire collection was when I bought it!

Oscar would hand me a set of coins—an evenly matched Uncirculated collection of Flying Eagle and Indian cents comes to mind as I write this—and ask me to make an offer. Knowing there would be some dickering ahead, I might offer, say, $2,000. "I was thinking of more than that," Oscar would say, always with a twinkle in his eye. Oscar maintained his charm at all times, and even during intense negotiations, he had a smile on his face and was as cheerful as could be. And yet he was firm. Finally, after at least one-half hour of discussing the quality of the Indian cents, how rare they were, and so on, we would compromise on a price, say $2,500, after which the set would be mine. In the meantime, I was told exactly where the 1877 came from and why it was a special piece, how he found the elusive 1871 and 1872, about the 1909-S and how it came from B. Max Mehl (leading into a number of side stories about the well-known Texas dealer) and so on—great fun! Speaking of Mehl, Oscar mentioned once he bought a coin in one of Mehl's mail auctions but was not pleased with the condition. He dropped a note to Max, of whom he was a close friend, and stated he didn't like the coin at all and would take it up with him in person when he saw him soon at the forthcoming American Numismatic Association convention. Well, early in the convention Max spotted Oscar first, came over, shook his hand, and promptly invited him out for a grand dinner—at which time all thought of bringing up the unwanted coin was promptly dismissed from Oscar's mind!

I never knew the depth of everything Oscar collected, for he liked to maintain an air of mystery and would continually offer me surprises. I did, however, get to see his grand type set of United States coins and paper money and remember the prooflike 1796 quarter, other early silver issues, and other delights. Similarly, his currency collection, by design types, was of the finest quality. Oscar mentioned offering it to me sometime in the future, but his death intervened, and I do not know what ever happened to the collection. After his death I was told all of his coins had been sold earlier.

It was shortly before Thanksgiving, 1971, when Olga telephoned me to say that Oscar had died. She wanted me to be a pallbearer in his funeral, and I accepted. It was a very heart-rending and sorrowful occasion when Oscar was laid to rest. With his passing the life of one of America's finest numismatists ended.

The coins I bought from Oscar over the years have long since disappeared into collections around the land, but the memories will always be with me. Often in an idle moment I reflect upon the good times on the shore of Dodge Pond and recollect another one of Oscar's anecdotes. There must have been hundreds and hundreds of stories, and I only wish I had recorded them in detail.

Frossard and Woodward: The Great Feud

By Cal Wilson 1985

The following article is by Cal Wilson, the California numismatic bibliophile who has written extensively on "the good old days" in the coin collecting scene and who is a leading student of and dealer in old numismatic literature. The more things change, the more they are the same, and the following article points out that controversies are nothing new.

Walter Breen, considered by many collectors to be the leading authority on American numismatics, recently published a masterful work titled *Walter Breen's Encyclopedia of United States Half Cents, 1793-1857.* As is so often the unfortunate circumstance, a few collectors of America's "Little Half Sisters" chose to malign the work by pointing out a number of minor flaws in the reference. Whether the criticisms of the book are valid is of little consequence; but the flap did stir memories for the present writer with respect to the "great feud" which was waged between Edouard Frossard and William Elliot Woodward in the latter portion of the 19th century.

W.E. Woodward is generally regarded to be one of the first three important coin dealers in the United States, having set up shop in 1860 in Roxbury, Massachusetts. Edward Cogan, the "father of professional numismatists," had been a full-time dealer since 1856, and the venerable and respected William Harvey Strobridge entered the trade in 1862. These three gentlemen held a veritable lock on the trade for more than a decade and handled the sale of virtually every major collection during that period.

Woodward, born in Oxford, Maine in 1825, was a pharmacist by trade. He operated his apothecary in Roxbury from 1848 until his death in 1892, and still found the time to catalogue no fewer than 111 auction sales between 1860 and 1890. Included among the many cabinets sold by Woodward are such legendary collections as those of Rev. J.M. Finotti, Henry Holland, William Marvin (definitive Masonic medals), Herman Ely, J.N.T. Levick (of store card fame), and perhaps the finest of them all—the Joseph J. Mickley cabinet. It would be difficult to name more than a handful of dealers who have sold more important collections than Woodward. Indeed, today his catalogues are among the most eagerly sought by numismatic bibliophiles due to the depth of information and quality of descriptions contained within their pages.

Ed. Frossard appeared on the numismatic scene nearly 20 years later, in 1878. He was born in Switzerland in 1837 and arrived in America around 1858. Well educated, he took a position as a teacher at the Brousand Academy in Brooklyn, where he taught languages. At the outset of the Civil War, Frossard enlisted and served with distinction in the Union Army. Often decorated and twice wounded, he rose to the rank of colonel by the end of the conflict. Upon entering the coin trade, Frossard also commenced publishing his own house organ, a tasty little periodical called *Numisma*. This publication, as might be expected from one so learned as Frossard, was written in a very scholarly manner and contained numerous informative commentaries on virtually all facets of the hobby. At the same time, Frossard also utilized the journal to criticize the abilities and practices of his contemporaries in the coin trade. And here is where our story really begins.

In the January 1881 issue of *Numisma,* Frossard penned the following comments directed toward W.E. Woodward:

> It appears almost incredible that a man whose name is cited as an authority on American coinage, and who handles coins from morning 'till night six times a week all the year round, should ignore the difference between genuine half cents in the '40s, and the mint restrikes of the same dates, but such appears to be the case. Mr. W.E. Woodward, the compiler of the Mickley Sale catalogue, avows himself still unable to distinguish the reverses of the restruck half cents from the reverses of the genuine half cents of the same dates. (See his remarks, page 39, sale Dec. 8, 9, 10, 1880). To point out the differences which stamp one class of half cent as genuine emanations of the Mint, made in the years corresponding with the date on the coin, and in the other class as coins produced at a subsequent date, with a reverse that did not exist when the genuine pieces were issued, would be on our part, an exhibi-

tion of "cheap learning" we wish to avoid, at the present time.

It is enough to state that the differences exist, have frequently been pointed out, notably in the *American Journal of Numismatics,* are marked, easily recognizable, and that no one offering coins at public sales to the purchasing/collecting public has the right to ignore these differences. At this rate we shall soon have compilers of catalogues ignoring for instance the difference between the original Confederatio cents, worth 10 times their weight in gold, and Bolen's close copies of the same, or between a genuine 1796 half cent and one of Dr. Edward's copies.

As regards the 1831 and '36 half cents, their genuine reverse has the bar under the words "half cent," while the few restrikes known (one sold in Haseltine's sale, Nov. 23, 1880) have a reverse identical to the reverse of the Mint restrikes of dates 1840-49. The 1831, '36, and '40-49 Mint restrikes were all struck after 1850, and with the reverse which is supposed to have been the reverse of the 1856 half cent—but whether '55, '56, or '57, is a matter of slight importance. They are restrikes and no amount of even the most plausible arguing can make them pass for the genuine article.

At approximately the same time the subject issue of *Numisma* was being distributed, Woodward auctioned the fine cabinet of William Jenks (Jan. 10, 1881). One lot in the sale—No. 468—is described as follows:

468 Pescennius Niger. Head of Pescennius Niger facing right; "Imp Caes Pes Nigerius," etc. rev., figure standing, facing left; "Concordia." Aureus; pierced over the head, in other respects fine; of the greatest rarity.

It is well known that a gold coin of Pescennius Niger was for a long time one of the treasures in the cabinet of the King of France, and that the coin was stolen many years ago, the general opinion being that it went to the crucible. The suggestion is presented of the possibility that such was not the fate of the piece in question, but that, saved from destruction, it here appears again. The owner of the piece is able to trace it in responsible hands for more than 30 years, which period carries us well back toward the time of the robbery alluded to. In brief, the story is this: Mr. Connor was, for many years prior to 1870, an owner and manager of real estate in the city of Boston. About 1850 he had in some of his houses quite a colony of Italians. The rent falling due, one of his Italian tenants was unable to meet it, and placed in Mr. Connor's hands this coin as security, exacting a promise that it should be kept and returned to him, stating that he prized it highly because it was a gift to him from a nobleman whom he knew in Italy, and who had presented it to him a long time before he left his native country. Not being redeemed, the coin was retained by Mr. Connor until his death, which occurred a few years ago, when it was inherited by his son, who, having no appreciation of its value, though perfectly aware of its great rarity, pierced it and wore it for a watch charm 'till last year, when it was sold to me.

Alas, poor Woodward! The coin proved to be a fake. Ever on the ready to take advantage of a competitor's woes, Frossard published the following allegory in the March 1881 issue of *Numisma:*

The False Talisman

Let it be known unto the people that there are men both learned and wise who are the possessors of ancient talismans and tokens of gold, silver, and brass, inscribed with the cabalistic signs and characters of kings, princes, and potentates who ruled of old; and these wise and prudent men have stores of these talismans, and keep them in their secret chambers, and set great store by them, and if by reason of trouble and affliction their hearts fail within them, they betake themselves unto their talismans and gaze upon the same, and interpret the signs thereon, and their hearts are cheered as with good tidings, and they come forth like strong men and go on rejoicing.

Now there dwelt in a distant country, called the Land of the Sun, a youth who inherited a vast estate, and ancient talismans in gold and silver and brass without number, and this youth wasted his inheritance and sold his talismans unto the sons of Israel, yea, he sold them all but one, and this one the sons of Israel would not buy, for being wise and learned they interpreted the signs thereon and explained them unto the youth, and said, "It is not a true talisman of Pescennius, surnamed Niger, whose superscription it bears, but is false, and the work of a sorcerer, one Becker, who dwelt in the forests of Germania." And the youth put the false talisman (which, through his foolishness was all that was left of his inheritance) into his bosom, and saith, "Peradventure I may find elsewhere a purchaser for this talisman." And he departed from his native land, and took ship, and sailed upon a wide and tempestuous sea, and a storm arising, he and his companions were cast upon a bleak and desolate shore.

Now there came forth one of the chief men of the land, and took him, and made him his slave, and set him to dig canals, him and his companions, and gave them a pittance and a hovel for their abode, and exacted from them a monthly tax. And after a time it came to pass, that because of hard toil, disease preyed upon the body of the youth from the Land of the Sun, and he laid upon his couch, sorely afflicted, for many days, and no one comforted him. And the lord of the canal came unto him, and said: "Give me the monthly tax that is due me or I will cast thee in prison." And the youth arose from his couch, and fell at his master's feet and saith: "Behold, my lord, my substance is exhausted, and I have nothing to satisfy the demand, save a talisman of gold worth 1,000 pieces of silver, bequeathed unto me by my father in my native land; and if thou wilt set me free from this bondage and let me return to my native land, I will give it to thee." Then pulled he forth the false talisman, and gave it unto his master, and forthwith found favor in his eyes, and his master released him from his bond, and from his tax, and gave unto him 100 pieces of silver, and the youth took ship, and returned to his native land, and bought a vineyard, and took unto himself a wife, even the daughter of a prince, and grew wise and prosperous.

But the lord of the canal saith, "Behold I have a talisman of great price, and I will sell the same, and enlarge my possessions, and buy mules, and a house, and an estate." Now there dwelt not far from him a mighty man, a soothsayer and apothecary, one versed in the knowledge of the talismans of his own country, who bought and sold the same, and whose name was known throughout the length and breadth of the land. And the lord of the canal took a sharp instrument and bored a hold through the talisman, and hung it with a golden chain around his neck, and mounted his mule, and rode to the apothecary, and showed him the talisman. And the apothecary went into his secret chamber, and took a book of chronicles of the Kings of Gaul, wherein are recorded the names of all the mighty rulers and potentates who coined talismans in days of old, and behold on a certain page in the book was written the name of Pescennius, surnamed Niger, and the apothecary did read, and his understanding was enlightened, for he saw it recorded that the priceless talisman of Pescennius, surnamed Niger, had been stolen from the King's treasury, and that the robbers had fled to a foreign land, and he saith until himself, "In verity this talisman is the same that was stolen from the treasury of the King of

Gaul, behold it is of great price and value." Then he came forth and spoke unto the lord of the canal and saith, "I will give thee for this talisman 500 pieces of silver," and he spread a feast unto him, yea beans and pork, (for the flesh of the swine is not accounted impure in that country) and gave unto him a drink from the fountain of living waters that is in the southwest corner of his shop, and they ate, and drank, and were merry. And when the feast was ended the lord of the canal took the money, even the 500 pieces of silver, and bestrode his mule, and returned unto his native place.

Now the apothecary had many other talismans in gold, silver, and brass, and he forthwith issued a proclamation unto the people of the land, wherein was an enumeration of the talismans and of the names of the Kings, rulers, and potentates who made them in days of old, and he told the people that on a certain day he would sell the talismans unto them. And he went to a large city on the border of the sea, where dwelt the sons of Knicker, and spread his treasures before them, the talismans, and the jewels, and the precious stones, the pearls and opals and rings and amulets, and likewise the books. Now the children of Knicker looked upon all these previous things and said to another, "Yea, they are good to behold and of great virtue, and we will buy thereof and enrich our treasuries, and for the talisman of Pescennius, surnamed Niger, we will give unto the apothecary 1,000, nay perchance 2,000 pieces of fine silver, and it shall be our chief talisman, and we will keep it in our chief chamber, with sentinels to watch over it day and night, lest it be stolen from us as it was from the King of Gaul." But there dwelt among the children of Knicker a stranger from the distant land of the Parisii, a man wise and learned in the interpretations of talismans of ancient Kings and rulers, and when they showed him the talisman of Pescennius, surnamed Niger, he shrugged his shoulders after the manner of the people of his own land.

Now the children of Knicker were wise after their generation, and they interpreted this and said: "It is not a true talisman of Pescennius, surnamed Niger, but is false." And on the day appointed for the sale the apothecary stood before the children of Knicker, and the high steward, who was the custodian of the talismans and other precious things, sat on a throne and called out the number of each talisman, and the children of Knicker sat on the ground before him, and spread out their money, and each talisman was given to the one who offered the highest price. And the children of Knicker, and the people of distant towns, who had gathered together, freely purchased the talismans of the Angli, and of the Galli, and Americani of the high steward, but when he called out the talisman of Pescennius, surnamed Niger, and on a platter of pure alabaster held the same before them, they remained silent, and would not offer their silver for the same.

Then did the apothecary marvel and saith: "Will ye not give me even 1,000 pieces of silver for this rare and precious talisman?" And one of them, a man fearless and strong, their spokesman, arose and spoke unto the apothecary with a loud voice and saith: "It is bogus," which signifieth false. Then did the apothecary perceive his error, and he saw that the talisman was false, and he was angered with himself for his foolishness, by which he had lost much money, even 500 pieces of silver, and he forthwith betook himself unto his own country, and returned to his shop, and put the false talisman in a crucible, and took a bronze pestle in his right hand, and with one mighty blow broke the false talisman of Pescennius, surnamed Niger, into a thousand pieces, and scattered the dust thereof on a field behind his dwelling and put on sackcloth and ashes and fasted and mourned for seven days and nights. And when the days of his fasting were over he stood by the fountain of living waters, that is in the southwest corner of his shop, and took an oath upon the same, and said: "The talismans of Pescennius, surnamed Niger, and other ancient rulers, behold, I am as a babe, and I know nothing, and I will never again buy them, nor sell them, nor harbor them in my house." And he kept his oath, and bought and sold tailsmans and drugs, and precious ointments, and out of his fountain he sold water to the wayfarers and weary, and he bought and sold the tomahawks and pipes of peace, pearls, and precious stones, and patent medicines, and trafficked much, and abode in his shop, but visited he not again the children of Knicker for a season; and behold the field where he cast the dust of the false talisman became bare and sterile, and is so even to this day.

Understandably outraged by Frossard's commentary, Woodward, in his April 1881 catalogue of the Clogston Collection offered Lot 1307, a copy of Andrews' work on late date large cents. Following the description, Woodward saw fit to make the following comments:

This unpretending little book of 54 pages is the work of an original investigator, and is a real and not pretended contribution to numismatic science. It may with truth be said of it, "A work of ab-

> solute necessity to Collectors of American Copper Coins." With the exception of Maris' *Varieties of the Copper Issues of the United States Mint in the Year 1794,* and Crosby's account of the Cents of 1793, published with Levick's plate in the *American Journal of Numismatics,* and Appleton's *Issues of the Mint of the United States,* printed in the same journal, and reprinted in a small edition, it is the only work that has ever appeared on this specialty of any importance whatsoever. *True, a sumptuous and presumptuous volume has been printed on the subject,* but a diligent perusal will convince any person that it is perhaps the only book ever written, from which no new fact could be gleaned. Having carefully read it, I fail to discover in it anything new, except numerous ridiculous blunders of the author, who I judge wrote his book in a hurry, to suit his pictures, and published it under the impression so elegantly expressed by one of his learned coadjutors, that "the Americans are fools and will buy anything."

Of course, Woodward was referring to Frossard's *Monograph of United States Cents and Half Cents,* published two years earlier. Still, not feeling he had extracted enough revenge for the comments appearing in *The False Talisman,* Woodward, in his June 1881 catalogue of the Jenison Collection, took the time to offer a satirization of *The Legend of Sleepy Hollow,* with Frossard taking the place of Ichabod Crane. Unfortuantely for today's collectors, only the very early press run copies of the catalogue contain the narrative which follows:

> Whatever sails up and down the North River, can but be impressed with the picturesque beauties of its shores, the lofty palisades, the hills and valleys, and the distant mountains, so impress their features on the mind of the voyager, that the lovely picture can never be erased.
>
> Every reader of history as related by that delightful and veracious chronicler, Diedrich Knickerbocker, knows by heart the biography of Rip Van Winkle, particularly the account of his protracted slumber; and the traveler who visits the Kaatskills and voyages leisurely down the river and comes abreast of that little hyphenated village on the Eastern shore, if its somnolent influence does not overcome him, he is immediately impressed with the idea that Rip, if he had any notion of taking a long sleep, ought to have crossed the river, dropped down to that little burg and there fallen asleep; for had he done so, his nap might have been uninterrupted for a century at least.

Now it happens that the same historian records the life and adventures of Ichabod Crane. He not only treats us to a charming picture of Ichabod as schoolmaster, as playmate of the boys and girls, but he gives us an insight into his love affairs: he tells us how Ichabod, invited to a quilting frolic, borrowed a nag of Hans Van Ripper, and went wooing the buxom daughter of old Baltus Van Tassel; how he was jilted by the fair Katrina, and chased on horseback on his way home by a fearful spectre, who carried his head in his hand; how, just as the luckless schoolmaster crossed the keystone of the bridge over which, it is generally believed, goblins and witches cannot pass—and we pause to remark that this philosophical view is greatly strengthened by the history of Tam O'Shanter's midnight ride—the goblin rider, with one mighty effort, threw his head at the poor retreating pedagogue, who, though he sought by dodging to avoid the missile, was felled to the earth. The horse of Van Ripper was found in the morning at his master's door; the saddle, which fell off in the race, was found trampled and torn by the heavy hoofs of the goblin horse, but Ichabod never more was seen. True, our historian intimates that the weird, headless horseman was no other than Brom Bones, Ichabod's rival with the blue-eyed Katrina, that the head, which we, as students of the occult sciences, know was fleshless and bloody, was but a harmless pumpkin, and that Ichabod simply ran away; that he afterwards became a lawyer, an editor, and what not, and traded and grew rich, and went to the Legislature. All this, however, is mere surmise, authenticated by no shadow of evidence. Up to this point the history of Ichabod Crane, like that of Rip Van Winkle, is without a break or a flaw, the relation is in each case, as it were, a chain of evidence; each fact supports and strengthens every other fact, but it is quite clear that from the moment the bridge was crossed, history failed and imagination filled its place.

Recent events have, in a measure, cleared up the mystery. There appeared, a few years ago, at Sleepy Hollow, a gentleman, the very counterpart of Ichabod, somewhat rounded out to be sure, from his former angular proportions, but still bearing enough of his peculiarities of character and appearance to make the likeness observable if not unmistakable. On his arrival, which was by way of Castle Garden, this gentleman settled down immediately into Ichabod's profession of pedagogue. We hasten to present the facts and to the development of our theory; further on we shall offer evidence in its support more conclusive by far than that by which the existence of Symme's Hole has been demonstrated.

Little more than 20 years ago it became necessary to repair the bridge over the haunted stream which Ichabod crossed on that fateful night, the stream near Wiley's Swamp, for a full account of which we refer to Diedrich's History. When, on the second day, the workmen renewed their labors in the morning, a plank was removed near the edge of the stream and at the end of the bridge, and under the plank, wonderful to relate, were found impressed in the hard earth the exact form and outline of Ichabod Crane, the small flat head, the huge long ears, the lanky arms and legs, the flat feet, which might have served for shovels, all were there as in a picture, and more wonderful than all, the hole was still warm, and scarcely a doubt existed in the minds of the workmen, to whom the facts of Ichabod's disappearance were well known, that, awakened by the operations of the day before, he had risen in the night and taken himself off. So far it was all clear to the minds of those serving men; but how Ichabod could have been concealed there for all the long years, was not so certain. Just here science and philosophy come in. It is clear that when Ichabod was struck by the ghastly skull, he was stunned; in his pain and terror he crawled under the bridge, where he fell asleep. The influence of the headless horseman—for an account of whom we again make reference to our historian—the nature of the haunted brook, the close proximity of Andre's tree, and the drowsy character of all around him, did the rest; and here, all unknown to the historian, was repeated the phenomenon of the Kaatskills; something the like of which never happened and never will happen except on the lovely sleepy shores of the North River.

It was not for some years after the event so minutely described, that the strange newcomer appeared at Sleepy Hollow, and, as all the friends and pupils of Ichabod had passed away, the appearance of identity was not observed by any of his neighbors, and the great discovery was finally perfected by a man from Boston, a place famed for inventions and great discoveries; principal among the inventions is ranked—no allusion to the pork-baked beans, but amongst the discoveries the one here chronicled "takes the cake."

The stranger that was, though a comparatively long residence makes him a stranger no longer, this sentence seems a little mixed, but the reader is assured there is no pun here, if he expects to find one, has been numerously interviewed, but he wisely keeps his own counsel as to all that concerns his hibernation. He is fond of talking about his residence in "Parree," a place that none of his neighbors know anything about, but which they suppose is over in Jersey, and after dinner he sometimes boasts of being in the army during the late war, which he says he entered as a non com and from which he emerged as a colonel, with shoulder straps, brass buttons, and things. When his back is turned the neighbors pityingly tap their foreheads and say the nom com part is evident enough now, but we "can't see" the colonel. Forgetting his love of the last century, if he be the veritable Ichabod, he has taken a wife, one of the fair daughters of the Empire State; he has become an editor and an author, and his fame now extends from Irvington-on-Hudson all the way to Harlem and back again. Men know him generally as the sage of Sleepy Hollow, but if any title next to colonel—which by a pleasing fiction he still claims to be—pleases him best, it is that of Contributor to American Numismatic History.

That the sage and historian is the *successor* in office of Ichabod Crane, is established beyond peradventure; that he is the *original,* some ignorant, unphilosophical men may doubt, but with due respect to other men's prejudices and superstitions, we avow our own unwavering belief in our own theory that the sage is the original, sleeping, it is true, for a long time, but now redivious. By this theory as an article of faith and practice, we shall abide.

1. For the facts concerning this event we refer to the great Scottish historian, Bobby Burns.

2. *Symmes' Theory of Concentric Spheres,* demonstrating that the earth is hollow, habitable within, and widely open at the poles. 12mo. Cincinnati, 1826.

3. We must not interrupt the narrative; but for a full account of all the interesting events, places, etc. to which we make only the briefest allusion, we refer once more and finally, to the old chronicler Knickerbocker, whose works can be found in the Boston Public Library, the Astor Library, and it may be in other repositories of learning.

4. If it happens that a strange proclivity to lying and fondness for dirt has been observed in our hero, it may perhaps be accounted for by his long continued lying in the dirt. This explanatory suggestion can but commend itself to the metaphysical mind.

5. Non Com, in the vernacular is short for Non Compos Mentis,

in which sense the neighbors use it; just what our hero means by it he has never explained.

The Frossard-Woodward war continued for quite some time subsequent to the above diatribe. In the January 1882 issue of *Numisma,* Frossard printed a letter received from one of his clients:

> In a former catalogue Mr. Woodward mentions that he knows no difference between the original and restrike half cents. You, wishing to impart wisdom to all ye mortals who seek it, kindly call his attention to the fact that there is really such a thing, and he like a wise man accepts the information and imparts it again in his Burton catalogue as though he knew it since childhood. Therefore, let all give thanks to you and *Numisma.*

Frossard then made the following closing comments:

> Thanks for a good opinion. We lay no claim to the discovery of differences in half cents. These have always been known and recognized among well posted coin dealers and collectors. The greater part of the half cents were restruck at the Mint at a time when the governing officers desired to increase the collection of Washington medals at the Mint by exchange, and were coined with that object in view, not as is generally supposed for speculative purposes.

Eventually, Frossard and Woodward ended their feud, and in later years they actually were known to praise one another from time to time. Commenting on the results of Woodward's sale of the J.N.T. Levick Collection in the September 1884 issue of *Numisma,* Frossard noted: "As a work of reference it (the catalogue) is simply indispensible, while as a literary production, if we may use the term in speaking of a compilation of this class, it is one of the best examples of Mr. Woodward's vigorous, terse, and entertaining style."

The feud has ended.

A Journey to 1958

By Q. David Bowers *1984*

Many publications are fond of recalling "the good old days"; times which seem from modern perspectives to be incredibly nostalgic, problem free, even romantic. Thus our local newspaper tells what happened in its columns 10 years ago and 30 years ago, *Forbes* magazine turns back the pages of time and recounts happenings of long ago, and others do the same. So, we follow suit and do it now!

To get the maximum effect we could go back to 1953, when our firm was established. But, at hand as this is being written in 1984 are a bunch of price lists from 1958, so we will pick that date.

Popular music of the time included *The Purple People Eater* (a song which perhaps is best forgotten), *Catch a Falling Star, Volare,* and Alvin and the Chipmunks singing the *Chipmunk Song*. Teenagers, the present writer included, were captivated by *Diana*, by Paul Anka, age 15, who was to go on to a brilliant career. In a more formal vein, Van Cliburn won the Tchaikovsky Piano Competition that year in Moscow.

A visitor to a book store might pick up a copy of *Parkinson's Law* and learn that work expands to fill the time available to do it in and that expenditures expand to equal income. Also on display would be copies of *The Ugly American, Exodus, Breakfast at Tiffany's,* and *Only in America*.

The United States and Russia were engaged in saber-rattling, and in reaction students and others plastered walls with peace symbols. The New York Giants relocated to the other side of the continent in San Francisco and enjoyed their first season at Candlestick Park, despite unfamiliar winds which caused problems, a situation that did not affect the transplanted Brooklyn Dodgers who were playing in Los Angeles. The Yankees, still in New York, won the World Series by besting the Milwaukee Braves in a full program, four games to three. Johnny Unitas of the Baltimore Colts captured the admiration of millions who watched him on TV lead his team to the NFL championship.

In the days before popular transatlantic jet travel (although one could go on a DeHavilland Comet flown by British Overseas Airways Corporation) many hopped aboard the four-motored planes offered by TWA and others, stopped at Gander, Newfoundland for refueling, then touched down at Shannon, Ireland, and then went on to the continent, perhaps to attend the World's Fair held that year in Brussels, Belgium, highlighted by the Atomium, a molecule-shaped building. All the while, tourists had their noses buried in the latest edition of *Fielding's Travel Guide to Europe* to learn where "undiscovered" restaurants were and, heaven forbid, to learn how to "influence" customs agents at the border (a pack of cigarettes was said to be just dandy to make the agent look the other way). "Beatniks," first originating in California, spread their word throughout America, and before long college students and others were "dropping out" to pursue more attractive lifestyles, perhaps as "flower children."

In Kansas City a new food establishment, Pizza Hut, opened. The founders did not dream that years later they would have hundreds of millions of dollars worth of sales and more locations than could ever be visited by a single company executive. McDonald's, with its lighted golden arches, was expanding, and for this purpose a two-engine airplane was acquired to check on prospective locations and for executive travel. IRS questioned the feasibility of such an expenditure for a hamburger business. Holiday Inns, another enterprise, was growing, and the "great signs" were sprouting up along well-traveled highways.

In California the Bank of America introduced BankAmericard, making it possible for customers to buy from subscribing merchants and pay their bills on a monthly statement; an innovation. Not to be outdone, American Express introduced a credit card which it hoped would become popular with restaurant, hotel, and auto-rental customers, perhaps even giving the long-established Diners Club (which started business in 1950) a run for its money. The economy was having problems, as it always seems to have, and unemployment in America reached a postwar high. The next year President Dwight D. Eisenhower said "not to worry," for things were improving, as indeed they were.

On the numismatic scene many things were happening, not the least important of which was the formation on April 1st of Empire Coin Company by Q. David Bowers and James F. Ruddy, who earlier operated their own businesses. After jointly conducting the Penn-New York auction in 1957 they decided their talents could be best combined in a single entity. "The combination of facilities, numismatic knowledge, reference libraries, and customer mailing lists make possible complete numismatic service," a notice published in May 1958 observed.

A new publication, *Empire Topics*, was born. Offered in 1958 were many interesting items. A 1652 Massachusetts Pine Tree shilling, Small Planchet variety, in Fine condition could be ordered for $45, while a Fine 1776 Continental dollar in pewter cost $95, and an 1842 Second Restrike Proof half cent ("lacking in the Anderson-Dupont sale as well as a number of recent offerings") tempted purchasers at $150.

An 1857 Proof half cent with Reverse of '56 ("a similar specimen realized $101 on a $100 estimate in our Penn-New York auction last August") was listed at $85, while a Very Fine original 1804 large cent cost $195, and a glittering Proof 1855 cent was posted at $145. An array of nickel three-cent pieces included Proofs of many issues: 1878 $47.50, 1879 $9.50, 1880 $9.50, 1881 $9, 1882 $9, 1883 $8, 1885 $9.50, 1887/6 $57.50, and 1888 $9.

Perhaps a bargain, considering the description, was an 1858 brilliant Proof silver three-cent piece which was described as: "Extremely rare; not in the Anderson-Dupont sale or a number of other offerings since that time. We note in one of S.J. Kabealo's recent auction catalogues that a bid of $750 was received for a similar specimen; this is a fantastic 25 times the *Guide Book* listing. The specimen we offer is a brilliant Proof. Our price is $250."

These were the days when an Uncirculated coin was described as Uncirculated, and a Proof coin as Proof. Such distinctions as MS-60, MS-63, MS-65, MS-67, and MS-70 were unknown and, if presented in a catalogue, would have been laughed at! Large cent specialists, however, did know about the Sheldon Scale of condition, but that scale had basic steps and not the intermediate numbers we know now.

For those finding the 1858 Proof silver three-cent piece too expensive at $250, an 1864 in the same series could be purchased for $69.50, or an 1871 for $22.50. Brilliant Uncirculated examples of dimes in the 1830s, several different dates, were available from $8 to $10 each, while Uncirculated specimens of the 1880 and 1881 dimes cost $9 and $11. These were probably purchased from the Tatham Stamp & Coin Company, Springfield, Massachusetts, one of our regular suppliers in those days. Harold MacIntosh used to send shipments regularly. It seems that perhaps 100 or so of each date were acquired, a quantity which today (1984) would seem fantastic.

The word *investment* did not rear its head often back in 1958, but it was not unknown either. A roll of 50 1916-D dimes—yes, you are reading correctly, 50 pieces—was described by us as follows:

> 1916-D a most unusual, and perhaps unprecedented offer. One roll (50 coins) each in Good to Very Good condition. Every mintmark is full. The 1916-D dime is to the Mercury dime series what the 1909-S V.D.B. cent is to the Lincoln cent series. This date continues to climb in price steadily every year. We remember when 1916-D dimes were selling for $5 each; then they were hard to find for $10; a little later, for $15; then $20; then $25. A wonderful investment opportunity for $950.

An 1875 Proof 20-cent piece was offered for $47.50, which would prove to be about one-100th of the price it would sell for 25 years later! And then there was an 1828 Gem Brilliant Uncirculated quarter at $67.50 and an 1831 Uncirculated example of the same denomination at $18, followed by an 1857 Proof quarter ("this coin is from the Menjou Sale held by Schulman & Kreisberg") for $90.

A whole bunch of Proof trade dollars were available, including 1877 $57.50, 1878 $57.50, 1879 $47.50, and 1880 $47.50. A rare 1867 Proof quarter eagle was available for $160, and a 1907 Uncirculated piece of the same denomination for $17, and a Brilliant Uncirculated 1920 double eagle was featured for $47.50.

In the field of foreign coins, a 1935 New Zealand "Waitangi" Proof set, including the popular crown, in the original box of issue could be ordered for $125.

We had in stock a large number of Hard Times tokens, large cent pieces issued by political and private interests circa 1833-1834. Many different varieties were available from 75 cents each up to a few dollars.

Our Research Department proclaimed the discovery of an important piece: "NEW MASSACHUSETTS CENT DIE VARIETY DISCOVERED. In March 1983, while attributing a group of Massachusetts coins, Dave Bowers discovered a new variety. The new variety, a cent of 1787, is the first new reverse die of the 1787-1788 Massachusetts coinage discovered since the publication of the Miller-Ryder reference nearly 40 years ago." Then followed a detailed description of the distinguishing features of the newly discovered issue.

In those days the coin business, years away from being called the coin *industry*, was a close-knit fraternity. All dealers conducted business on a personal basis, computers were unknown, bid and ask prices were a thing of the future, and no one in our firm dreamed that if a customer had spent $10,000 to $20,000 with us in 1958, by 1984 he would be a millionaire!

Nearly Extinct: The Pristine American Eagle

By Bruce Lorich *1977*

My title refers not to nature and that symbol of majesty, the American eagle, but to numismatics and that rare denomination, the $10 coin, the eagle emblazoned in gold. The early species (those pieces minted until about 1880) are today seldom encountered in pristine Mint State.

I've been accused before of concentrating on coins about which little is known, and on coins which are relatively unpopular, and the $10 gold series is no exception. Unknowns appeal to me, as does the unpopular, and I believe that people whose curiosities are both open and untainted by the "join the bandwagon" syndrome belong in numismatics—because there remains so much to be explored, discussed, and revealed by collectors and other observers. This is the artistic side of "the science of numismatics"—the area where sound guesses following patient observation lead to insight, knowledge, and enjoyment.

In this sense, numismatics is merely a vehicle for revealment, a path down that often foggy road called human history. Observation of particulars (such as the rarity or availability of this or that year's or mint's coins) can roll back some of that fog—it can sometimes fill in what may be pretty safely taken as the facts surrounding a relatively unknown area of history. This, of course, is the classic use for numismatics: long before there was a fraternity of collectors (let alone investors) students of mankind looked at coins as a way of filling in some of the historical voids. In some cases we know of kings or queens only because a coin remains bearing a ruler's name, and less frequently a realistic portrait.

This vehicle into the past, numismatics, is an enduring one, for few other purchasable items have so widespread a background or offer such palpable clues to previous human activity as do coins.

Now that the motivation behind my observations on United States $10 gold coins has been set forth, we might reflect that the earliest eagles were the "stuff" of early American commerce: the coins of the period 1795 to 1804 (when mintage ceased, although the coins continued to be used) were the most convenient means of transacting business for fairly sizable sums. These capped bust coins are all, without exception, rare today in Mint State.

But the gold pieces of the late 1830s and the succeeding 40 years are what I would mainly like to comment upon here. Unlike the earliest type, these Coronet, or Liberty Head, coins were minted in huge quantities when the annual mintages are totaled. Yet most are of extraordinary rarity in pristine Mint State. Almost an extinct species, considered as a whole, with numerous specific issues nonexistent in the condition in which they were made.

In fact, specimens of these early years which grade between Extremely Fine and About Uncirculated if their surfaces are unmarred by excessive abuse, are prizes of pretty nearly the first order. Their scarcity tells us a lot about their times.

Turning the original use of numismatics around, to serve itself rather than the interests of history at large, we can readily see that the rough-and-tumble years when America was expanding into its present borders account for the paucity of Mint State examples of one of the most used of all gold coins—the $10 piece. We occasionally come across a Mint State Philadelphia Mint issue, for Philadelphia was a home of culture, breeding, learning and all that during the middle and later parts of the 19th century. But there were few collectors of coins, fewer still who could afford to lay aside a coin worth a week's, or a month's, wages. New Orleans was the commercial center of the Old South, a barbarous place for many years, a place where gold paid for debauchery, adventurous business schemes, and of course import-export debts. These as well as an even wilder countryside awaited the golden beauties issuing from the San Francisco and Carson City Mints—and it takes no imagination whatsoever to figure out why abuses of all kinds left their marks on the faces of our middle-years eagles.

Other events of the 19th century may not be so well remembered by all collectors. There was a horrible drought, causing bad financial times, in the 1830s. A war with Mexico for Texas and some pretty daring incursions into the wilderness in the 1840s. A bullion and paper money crisis in the 1850s and early 1860s which resulted in the final disappearance (into the melting pots) of all sorts of silver and gold coins. Tons of coins were exported for circulation or melting. Then came the Civil War and Reconstruction—years of hard money and, for most of the country's populace, a real struggle for survival itself; the aftermath of this emotionally horrendous war witnessed families in all parts of the North, South, East, and Midwest trying to put life in order again. Who could indulge in the luxury of putting aside large gold coins for an aesthetic purpose.

The nation awaited the fruition of the Industrial Revolution and a couple of decades of peace and fairly widespread prosperity—the 1880s—before even the well-to-do could afford to consider the very object of their energies for its artistic merits. And it is indeed the 1880s which began to leave for posterity a quantity of Mint State gold pieces, especially of the rarer $10 denomination.

In singling out the $10 gold piece as a rarity, I am not discounting the rarity of isolated years or mints of other gold denominations: anyone with a rudimentary knowledge of American numismatics can point out that certain quarter eagles, double eagles, and so forth are truly rare in Mint State. These other denominations, though, cannot be called rare as a whole for such an extended period of time, and the reasons are plain: the smaller denominations (the odd $3 coins excepted) were saved from use in small quantities—they were forgotten in drawers, buried in jars in the backyard—and the double eagle, being the unit of exchange for financial institutions, was kept in bags by banks and the government alike. While numbers of rarities exist among the other gold denominations, it is difficult to pick out any $10 gold piece (any date or mint) up until the very late 1870s which is not rare in Mint State.

Eagles have never been a popular size of coin among collectors. These reasons are several: they were expensive to save and expensive to collect in the days when face value was an important consideration; the numbers of issues (all mints considered) seemed to make collecting them prohibitive 50 years ago when collectors started to place considerable emphasis on date and mint sets; and they were just plain hard to find, so most collectors turned to other series.

These seem to me to be excellent reasons for pursuing the nearly extinct American gold eagle! You don't have to have them all—you don't even have to have one from each mint. Your own personal association with our country's turbulent but exciting past can be captured for you in an elegant manner in a single coin, a coin which will forever remain as testimony to one of the world's noblest struggles—the emergence of a powerful, democratic state. What more could any vehicle into the past provide?

The Legendary 1913 Liberty Head Nickel

By Q. David Bowers 1975

We are indebted to Clyde Mervis, Courtney Coffing, and the Amos Press, Inc. for much of the information in the article to follow. The interpretation is ours, drawing from several previously printed sources, including the excellent article "Liberty 1913 Nickel Offers Mystic Aura" which appeared in the December 1971 issue of The Numismatic Scrapbook Magazine.

1913 Liberty Nickel Offered for Sale

It is with great pleasure that we offer for sale the most famous American coin rarity: the 1913 Liberty Head nickel.

Over the years we have had many wonderful rarities come our way. The fabulous 1804 silver dollar, the exceedingly rare 1894-S dime (we have handled four of these), several 1838-O half dollars, several 1876-CC 20-cent pieces, two 1907 MCMVII Extremely High Relief double eagles, and others are familiar to readers of our catalogues and price lists. And yet there has been one coin—the "rarest of the rare"—which has eluded us. . .until now. The 1913 Liberty nickel. There are but five known specimens of this famous coin, and the piece we now offer for sale is among the finest of these.

The 1913 Liberty nickel is the best known of all American coin rarities. Much of this fame is due to the late B. Max Mehl, the most colorful coin dealer on the American scene during the first part of the 20th century. In his description of the Olsen Collection 1913 nickel in 1944, Mehl noted:

> I plead guilty to being responsible for making this coin so famous, having used it in all of my national advertising for a period

of about a quarter of a century, during which time it appeared in advertising totaling an expenditure of well over a million dollars!. . . Certainly this great coin will prove a most gratifying source of possession to the fortunate owner and also a profitable investment as well.

The ownership of a 1913 Liberty Head nickel has been a sure way to register its possessor in the "numismatic hall of fame." In recent years owners of 1913 nickels, particularly J.V. McDermott, Aubrey Bebee, and World-Wide Coin Company, have received tremendous publicity.

The presently offered coin traces its ancestry through the following owners: Samuel Brown, August Wagner, Col. Edward H.R. Green, Burdette Johnson, James Kelly, Fred Olsen, B. Max Mehl, King Farouk of Egypt, Edwin Hydeman, Abe Kosoff, World-Wide Coin Co., and now, Bowers and Ruddy Galleries. We are presently co-owners of the coin with World-Wide, having acquired half interest in the piece recently. The coin is now available for sale.

History of the 1913 Liberty Nickel

Under what circumstances were the 1913 Liberty nickels struck? Who made them? How many persons were involved?

At least 20 people have owned from one to five of the 1913 Liberty nickels. In recent years great attention has been focused on two particular specimens—the one sold when Aubrey Bebee cried a final "$46,000" at the American Numismatic Association convention in 1967, and bought the coin formerly owned by James V. McDermott; and the presently offered coin, which has been featured in many nationwide news stories, television features and has "starred" in the television series *Hawaii Five-O*. The presence of a 1913 nickel at a convention—both the Bebee specimen and the one offered now by us have been made available from time to time for display—has drawn thousands of additional visitors!

Numismatists, writers, and editors have sparred for years as they attempted to sift fact from legend. Doubtless the relentless radio campaign of B. Max Mehl, Fort Worth, Texas, of the 1930s helped make the coin the best-known, most sought American coin—and gave boost to coin collecting in general. The publicity campaign, which earned a special commendation for Mr. Mehl from the American Numismatic Association, helped make thousands of Americans more conscious of their coins and coin collecting as a hobby.

Some past owners hid their coin under a bushel. Others have generously and eagerly offered theirs for display as a major drawing card at a show or convention. Two specimens of this famous coin were exhibited at the ANA convention in Dallas, Texas, in 1953 when the Louis Eliasberg and J.V. McDermott specimens were viewed by the public.

Current owners of the 1913 Liberty nickel are: (1) Louis Eliasberg, Baltimore, Maryland; (2) Hon. R. Henry Norweb, Cleveland, Ohio; (3) Aubrey Bebee, Omaha, Nebraska; (4) World-Wide Coin Co. and Bowers and Ruddy Galleries, and (5) the R.J. Reynolds family in North Carolina.

The history of the 1913 nickel has long been shrouded in mystery. The actual facts probably remain buried with those persons who might have been able to account for them during their lifetime. Perhaps the true account would increase or decrease the value of the coins; as long as the mystery does continue, they will probably continue to be the cherished coins of our age.

The Liberty Head nickel was first struck for circulation in 1883. It was to survive 29 years. In the summer of 1912, James Earle Fraser was completing his designs for a Buffalo-Indian Head type nickel.

At this time we must set our personality stage, to position those who will be prominent as we attempt to unravel the threads of a still-complicated event.

The Secretary of the Treasury was Franklin MacVeagh; George E. Roberts was director of the Mint; John H. Landis, the superintendent of the Philadelphia Mint. On December 18, 1903, a native of Pennsylvania, Samuel W. Brown, had joined the staff of the Philadelphia Mint.

Brown was proposed for membership in the ANA in the April 1906 issue of *The Numismatist*, and vouched for by Stephen K. Nagy and Dr. Heath. Nagy, a Philadelphia resident, had joined the ANA about six months before. In the June issue of *The Numismatist*, 1906, Brown was assigned membership number 808.

Brown was assigned duties at the Mint as assistant curator of the Mint collection and later as a storekeeper.

In mid-1912, nickel activity at the Mint centered around the designs for the Buffalo-Indian Head nickel under preparation by Fraser, scheduled for production in 1913. Secretary of the Treasury MacVeagh approved the new coin design in June.

Clyde D. Mervis, writing in the July 1968 *Numismatic Scrapbook Magazine*, said, "Fraser's new designs were slow in coming, and since the Mint had a schedule to maintain with the new year 1913 breathing down its neck, the diemaker presumably went about his business of preparing advance dies, making up sets for the now-famous 1913 Liberty Head nickel.

"Satisfied the dies were satisfactory, he later showed the nickels to his superior for approval. The superior acknowledged the trial pieces, but told the worker the dies would not be used—to destroy them since the new Buffalo design had been approved and should be made ready in time for the year 1913. The worker is then reputed to have carelessly tossed the five trial coins into a desk drawer where they lay for some time."

On December 13, 1912, Mint Director Roberts instructed his Philadelphia staff: "Do nothing about five-cent coinage for 1913 until the new designs are ready for use." On that same day, the last Liberty Head nickel dated 1912 was officially struck at the Philadelphia Mint.

In March 1958, Lee Hewitt, editor of *The Numismatic Scrapbook Magazine*, wrote:

Various stories have circulated concerning the issuance of the 1913 nickels, but actual proof of the circumstances surrounding their leaving the Mint has never been documented. As coinage of the Buffalo type did not commence until February 21, 1913, the Mint had almost two months to strike the Liberty Head type and to supply all the demand from collectors, had the Mint been so inclined. Collectors, at least until recent years, have felt the Mint was unethical in striking a few pieces instead of including both types in the 1913 Proof set, therefore the coin did not bring a price commensurate with its rarity.

In addition to the five Liberty Head pieces, there is a 1913 Buffalo in copper and the Farouk catalogue, Lot 2029, listed a 1913 Buffalo without artist's initials (the 1913 Buffalo nickel in copper was an electrotype impression and not a trial striking).

Stories, theories, rumors, or what have you concerning these coins boil down to these main versions:

(1) They were struck to exchange for coins needed for the Mint collection.

(2) The coiner and engraver were amusing themselves and struck the pieces which years later found their way onto the numismatic

market.

(3) They were struck exclusively for a wealthy collector.

Regardless of the "whys" of the issue, under standard Mint practices of the period all that was necessary for those who were responsible for their striking was to pay the proof and medal fund eight cents for each coin and walk out of the Mint building with them.

In the September 1963 *The Numismatic Scrapbook Magazine,* Lee Hewitt commented, "Unless the order for the Buffalo nickel design was received in mid-summer of 1912, the engraving department probably changed the 1912 hub to 1913 as a matter of routine and the five specimens of the 1913 Liberty Head nickel are die trials."

Don Taxay, writing in 1963, was the first to disclose that Samuel W. Brown, the first man to publish, set a price on, and display all five 1913 Liberty Head nickels, was an ex-curator of the Mint cabinet who, in 1913, was still employed at the Mint as storekeeper. Taxay went on to say that in his opinion the 1913 Liberty Head nickels were not trial pieces or set-up pieces to test the dies, but, rather, they were made by or for Brown as a caprice.

Eric P. Newman, a former 1913 Liberty Head nickel owner and a well-known numismatic scholar, also wrote about the 1913 nickel in 1963:

> I still have the special leather case made for these nickels and formerly had the opportunity to study all five coins at one time. The important fact which I think should be further emphasized is that Samuel W. Brown, original owner of all five nickels, was guilty of deceptive practices from which one could conclude that the coins were improperly or unlawfully acquired by him.
>
> He worked for the Philadelphia Mint in various capacities from December 18, 1903, until his resignation on November 14, 1913. Although a coin collector and a member of the ANA since 1906, he kept the nickels he obtained, secreted for seven years and told no one about them. (This is in reference to the fact that no hint of the existence of the 1913 Liberty nickel was known until 1919.) He obviously feared disclosure of them. He then advertised in *The Numismatist*, beginning in December 1919, to buy for $500 (later $600), 1913 Liberty nickels which were then unknown and which he knew no one else could have. Why should he want to buy such a coin when he already had five of them?. . . The reason was to build up the price of the pieces he possessed.
>
> In the summer of 1920 he showed the pieces, privately, in the special case at the Chicago ANA convention and said the disclosure

was off the record. . . When asked, he did not disclose how he had obtained them. . . .

Such is a summary of what is now known or theorized about the origin of the 1913 Liberty Head nickels. As official records are lacking and the persons involved are no longer living, the true story will probably never be known for sure.

There are many other American coin rarities whose histories are similarly unknown. Take for example the illustrious series of pattern 25-cent and 50-cent pieces of the year 1916. So far as we know, there is no official record of how many were struck or to whom the several different die varieties were distributed. The famous 1894-S dime, described in detail on pages 22 and 23 of our *Rare Coin Review* No. 21, likewise has an origin shrouded in mystery, and there are several theories of how and why the pieces were struck. There are many other examples as well.

The 1913 Liberty Head Nickel and Numismatics

Now that the production of the 1913 Liberty Head nickels has been explored and remains as clouded as ever, let us trace the coins through their various owners, describe some, and attempt to visualize the mark left on numismatics by these owners and the attendant publicity.

Samuel W. Brown is the starting point for the pedigree of all known specimens. The October 1920 issue of *The Numismatist*, reporting on the ANA convention in Chicago the past August, commented:

> Samuel W. Brown of North Tonawanda, New York, was present for a short time on Monday. He had with him a specimen of the latest great rarity in United States coinage—the nickel of 1913 of the Liberty Head type. It was among the exhibits at the convention with a label announcing it was valued at $600, which amount Mr. Brown announced he is ready to pay for all Proof specimens offered to him.
>
> An explanation of its rarity is that at the close of 1912, the Mint authorities, not having received orders to use the dies of the Buffalo type nickel at the beginning of 1913, prepared a master die of the Liberty Head type dated 1913, and from this master die a few pieces—believed to be five—were struck in Proof. None of these are believed to have been placed in circulation.

The August 1944 issue of *The Numismatist* carried Brown's obituary, as follows:

> Samuel W. Brown, 64, of North Tonawanda, N.Y., died on June 17, after a year's illness. A native of Pennsylvania, he had resided

> in North Tonawanda for many years, taking an active part in civic affairs, serving as mayor for several terms, and for 10 years was a member of the board of education. Before leaving his native state he was employed for a time as storekeeper in the Mint at Philadelphia, and after located in New York State. He at one time was appointed a member of the Assay Commission. His former membership in the ANA was acquired many years ago, his number being 808.

At this point we mention that Brown's record of public service in North Tonawanda was certainly outstanding. This, coupled with the fact he openly advertised for 1913 Liberty Head nickels, would lead one to think Brown was secure in his position regarding the coins and risked no scandal or unfavorable investigation. It is certainly possible he obtained the pieces legally, although perhaps not openly. In the same manner, the superintendent of the San Francisco Mint, J. Daggett, acquired two or three 1894-S dimes at the time of issue and gave one to his daughter, Hallie. Although the reasons may have been different, it is interesting to note the existence of the 1894-S dime was not known to or suspected by numismatists until the year 1900, six years later—which, coincidentally, was the same number of years the 1913 Liberty nickel remained a secret.

In 1924, we find August Wagner offering the five coins through his stamp shop in Philadelphia for $2,000 for the lot. We do not know the actual sale price, but Colonel Edward Howland Robinson Green purchased the set of five and kept them until his death 12 years later.

Green was born in London, England, August 22, 1868, the son of Edward Henry Green and Hetty Howland Robinson. The elder Green died March 19, 1902, at the age of 80.

Before Green was 20 years of age, his right leg was amputated seven inches above the knee. Even so, he stood six feet, four inches, and weighed 300 pounds.

Just after reaching his 22nd birthday in September 1890, Green and "some of the boys" visited Chicago's red light district one evening. There he was charmed by Mabel Harlow, tall, redheaded, and attracted to money. She was variously known as Mrs. M.E. Staunton, Mrs. Wilson, Mrs. Kitterage, Mrs. deVries, or Mrs. Campbell.

Arthur H. Lewis, in *The Day They Shook the Plum Tree,* has Mary Cammack, Dallas, Texas recall Mabel. "Mabel was beautiful and had long, wavy, red hair which she could let down to her hips. She used to allow my older sister to comb it out for her. She used lots of makeup, but on her it looked good."

Green was given the Texas Midland Railroad by his mother, to play with as other children play with electric and wind-up trains. Green was never happier than when he rode in the cab of a steam engine on the TMRR. His palatial Pullman car was variously called 999, Mabel, the Lone Star, and again, 999.

Lewis tells how Green acquired the title "colonel." Green had gone to Terrell, Texas, in his Pullman, then called the Lone Star, on November 8, 1910. Terrell was his home, and it was election day. After returning from casting his ballot, Governor O.B. Colquitt and a party of friends met with Green, and the governor proposed a toast: "To 'Colonel' E.H.R. Green, the newest and finest member of my staff." On November 10, formal written appointment as lieutenant colonel came to Green from the governor.

Hetty Green, his mother, died on July 1, 1916, and on July 10, 1916, Edward and Mabel were married, after a courtship of 26 years. Estates were established at Round Hill, near New Bedford, Massachusetts, and Star Island overlooking Biscayne Bay, Florida. At Round Hill, in 1925, he established a flying field and hired Bert and Priscilla Hill to operate a training school.

At Star Island, Lewis writes, "To the rear of the projector was a vault containing the colonel's library of pornographic films, which experts considered the world's choicest."

Green died on June 8, 1938, at Lake Placid, New York, with Mabel at his side. Willard Snyder, Philadelphia stamp dealer, helped appraise the Green estate. He wrote:

> What also bothered collectors was that he hung on to almost everything, even when he had a complete monopoly. Take the 1913 Liberty Head nickels. If you were a coin collector when you were a kid you must have seen ads in magazines which read: "Will pay up to $10,000 for a 1913 Liberty head nickel."
>
> Naturally, kids went nuts examining five-cent pieces wherever they saw them. The ad was probably placed by Col. Green as a practical joke. The truth is 1913 was the year the Buffalo nickel was minted, and there weren't supposed to be any more Liberty Heads. . . He was simply having fun, providing excitement, and creating lots of new collectors.

Actually, the above recollection undoubtedly refers to one of the countless advertisements featuring the 1913 Liberty nickel which were placed by dealer B. Max Mehl in Fort Worth, Texas.

F.C.C. Boyd appraised the coins in the Green hoard. Buyer of all five 1913 Liberty Head nickels and the bronze (electrotype) was Burdette G. Johnson, St. Louis, Missouri. Johnson and Dayton, Ohio, dealer James F. Kelly then cooperated to offer the 1913 nickels to numismatists. In later years when Kelly prepared the Paramount International Coin Co. auction catalogue for the 1967 Miami Beach ANA convention he wrote:

> There has always been, and always will be, considerable mystery surrounding the origin of the 1913 Liberty Head nickel. For what it may be worth, it is my opinion that these coins were struck at the Mint during the period when the dies for the Buffalo nickel were being prepared. I base this opinion on extensive conversations with the late James Macallister, B.G. Johnson, and Ira Reed during that period when I handled three of these nickels.
>
> The reason for the person, or persons, involved in striking these coins and obtaining them from the Mint, along with witholding knowledge of their existence can only be speculation and never a known fact. . . .

Fred Olsen paid James Kelly $900 for one of the 1913 Liberty Head nickels in the late 1930s. It was auctioned by B. Max Mehl on November 7, 1944, for $3,750 and the buyer was King Farouk of Egypt. In 1949, the F.C.C. Boyd specimen of the nickel was sold through Abe Kosoff to Farouk for $2,750, at which time the Olsen coin was again offered by Mehl (who handled the sale of certain of King Farouk's coins) and was again sold for $3,750, this time to Edwin Hydeman. This is the specimen we now offer for sale.

Farouk was born February 11, 1920, at Abdin Palace, near Cairo, Egypt. The name Farouk is an appellation of the caliph, Omar, meaning in Arabic, "one who knows right from wrong." According to Hugh McLeave, writing in *The Last Pharaoh, Farouk of Egypt*, Farouk was at different times Farouk the man of the people; Farouk the pious; Farouk the omniscient; Farouk the lion-hearted; Farouk the Arab leader; Farouk the virile; Farouk the Casanova; Farouk the great gambler; Farouk the playboy; and, Farouk the prophet.

In 1938, just after being crowned king of Egypt, Farouk took a vacation at St. Moritz, Switzerland. Instead of skiing, it was complained that "his afternoons he spent shopping for watches and gold coins, which he collected by the hundreds."

Lavish entertainment was found at his private house on a bend of the Nile River, some 12 miles south of Cairo, called "Coin Farouk." Farouk was deposed as king in 1952.

In 1953 the government decided to auction the royal treasures. It took Sotheby's experts more than three months to sift and arrange the hoard which Farouk had assembled. They had the largest stamp collection in the world, some 8,500 coins and medals in gold and 164 in platinum, and 1,261 works of art in gold and silver, which included exquisite boxes, clocks, and ornaments by the great Russian jeweler and goldsmith Karl Faberge.

One of the best-known specimens of the 1913 Liberty Head nickel was that sold by Kelly to James V. McDermott, one-time steeplejack who later became an outstanding collector and coin dealer. His nickel became the best known of the five, because instead of safely ensconcing it in some safe deposit vault or museum, he had it mounted in a plastic holder and would generously loan it to different coin clubs for display.

McDermott was a professional coin dealer, benefiting in publicity greatly from this generosity. Soon his nickel became synonymous with his name, "McDermott nickel." Reportedly offered up to $50,000 for the coin, he preferred to decline all offers, continuing to make the coin freely available for exhibition purposes.

In his advertisement in *The Numismatic Scrapbook Magazine*, September 1957, McDermott refers to the ANA convention in Philadelphia: "Wow, it really was the biggest convention yet. I sure was happy to see so many old friends, also to meet folks I never sold coins to. Ouch! That man, P.B. Trotter, was there and trying to steal that thar 1913 nickel from me but the best he'd do was $19,000, so I still have it."

The reference was to Powell B. Trotter, a Memphis banker, who confirmed the offer and recently reported that he still would like to own a 1913 nickel someday. The $19,000 offer in 1957 was generous. In that same year we (James F. Ruddy and Q. David Bowers) purchased an Uncirculated 1894-S dime for $4,750 (current value: $100,000), and an 1804 silver dollar was valued in the $10,000 to $15,000 range.

James V. McDermott passed away September 29, 1966, in Milwaukee at the age of 68. Thousands of numismatists will long remember him as the man who made it possible for them to see the rare 1913 Liberty Head nickel. His widow Elizabeth (Betts), a familiar figure in the hobby, now became owner of the famous nickel. The coin was subsequently consigned for sale to the 1967 ANA convention auction in Miami.

The McDermott nickel unquestionably "stole the show" at the 76th annual ANA convention as the auction room was jammed to capacity, with little standing room for newcomers, as the historic event approached. Auctioneer James Kelly, who years earlier had owned three of the original five 1913 Liberty nickels, announced Lot 2214 to the tense crowd as cameras clicked and tape recorders whirred. After introductory remarks, Kelly cried: "We're starting the bidding tonight on the 1913 nickel. . . I have $38,000!. . . Can I hear $40,000?"

Aubrey Bebee, prominent numismatist from Omaha, Nebraska, bid $40,000, and Kelly continued, "I have $40,000, can I get $42,000?" A few moments later Abe Kosoff, standing together with Sol Kaplan, bid $45,000. Then came the winning bid, $46,000 to Bebee, amid the applause and cheers of the audience, now on their feet and making a mad rush to the auction podium to congratulate the principals!

Bebee's check and his new coin later went on display for the benefit of all who were not fortunate enough to have witnessed the big sale. Hundreds of photographs were taken by collectors, and many had their auction catalogues autographed by the principals, Mr. and Mrs. Aubrey Bebee, James Kelly, and Betts McDermott.

Later, Bebee turned down successive offers of $56,000, $60,000, and $75,000 for the coin, and an offered trade for an 1804 silver dollar.

A 1913 Liberty Head nickel—the one we now offer for sale, in fact—made headlines in 1972. On October 3rd of that year John B. Hamrick, Jr. and Warren Tucker, officials of World-Wide Coin Co., traveled to California and paid dealer Abe Kosoff $100,000 for the coin once owned by Kelly, Olsen, Mehl, Farouk, Hydeman, and then the California dealer. At the same time, an 1804 dollar was purchased for $80,000. The resulting check for $180,000 for the two coins, dated October 2, 1972, was pictured in magazines and newspapers all over America. The 1913 nickel then went "on tour" and was exhibited at major conventions. Thousands of collectors came to see this famous coin. In 1974 the television series *Hawaii Five-O* featured the nickel as the theme of one of its programs. Late in 1974 Bowers and Ruddy Galleries, which had earlier purchased the 1804 dollar from World-Wide, acquired half-interest in the 1913 nickel. Once again the famous coin made headlines!

Roster of the 1913 Liberty Head Nickels

Clyde Mervis and Courtney Coffing have compiled this genealogy of the known 1913 Liberty nickels. As already noted, all five coins were kept together through the first four owners.

(1) Samuel Brown (who presumably obtained this and the other four directly from the Mint); August Wagner; Col. Edward H.R. Green; Burdette Johnson; James Kelly; Dr. C.A. Bold; George Walton; Reynolds family.

(2) Samuel Brown; August Wagner; Col. Edward H.R. Green; Burdette Johnson; James Kelly; Fred Olsen; B. Max Mehl; King Farouk of Egypt; Edwin Hydeman; Abe Kosoff; World-Wide Coin Co. and Bowers and Ruddy Galleries. This is the specimen we now offer for sale.

(3) Samuel Brown; August Wagner; Col. Edward H.R. Green; Burdette Johnson; James Kelly; J.V. McDermott; James Kelly; Aubrey Bebee.

(4) Samuel Brown; August Wagner; Col. Edward H.R. Green; Burdette Johnson; Eric P. Newman; Abe Kosoff; Louis Eliasberg.

(5) Samuel Brown; August Wagner; Col. Edward H.R. Green; Burdette Johnson; F.C.C. Boyd; Abe Kosoff; King Farouk; Sol Kaplan and Abe Kosoff; Hon. R. Henry Norweb.

It seems probable that once the specimen we offer has been sold, it will be a long, long time until another specimen of the 1913 Liberty Head nickel appears on the market.

1913 Liberty Head Nickel Now Available

It is now our pleasure to offer for sale our choice specimen of the 1913 Liberty Head nickel, the specimen enumerated as No. 2 in the preceding listing. Its past owners read like a "Who's Who of Numismatics," and it is certain similar fame will accrue to its next owner.

Pricing the 1913 Liberty Head nickel is difficult. As our half interest in the coin cost us in excess of $100,000 cash, this would place a theoretical cost value on the entire coin of over $200,000. Few would dispute that this figure is a bargain, for in 1974 a 1907 MCMVII Extremely High Relief $20, a coin of which over a dozen are known (and of which we have handled three in recent decades), sold at auction for $200,000, with the buyer, a dealer, stating he would have gone to $250,000, had this been necessary. The 1804 silver dollar, a coin of which 15 specimens are known, was sold by us from our *Rare Coin Review* No. 21 (where it was listed at $200,000), and it was reportedly sold by our client to another dealer for $225,000—and presumably the second dealer-owner has since sold it for a profit. In Switzerland in 1974 a rare ancient coin was sold to a dealer for $314,000. Also in 1974 our friends at Paramount International Coin Company announced they had turned down a $500,000 offer for a rare 1907 pattern gold coin, and stated the coin was worth $1 million.

By any measure, the 1913 Liberty Head nickel is the most famous of all American coin rarities. More has been written about the coin, more advertising has been expended on this coin (with B. Max Mehl having spent over $1 million alone!), more publicity and news coverage has been given this coin than any other. The presence of a 1913 Liberty Head nickel at a coin convention will in itself assure the show of good public attendance, as has been demonstrated several times! What coin other than a 1913 Liberty Head nickel could have "stolen the show" at an ANA convention (reference: the 1967 ANA show in Miami)—the year's most important numismatic get-together. Considering the rarity of the coin and its incredible fame, few would dispute that a half-million dollars would be too high a price. We offer this coin, a superb specimen, the most famous of all American coins, for what we consider to be a very reasonable price. The 1913 Liberty Head nickel is currently available from us for. . . . . $300,000.

The coin was subsequently sold to Superior Galleries, who sold it to the Dr. Buss Collection. In 1985 the coin crossed the auction block at a Superior sale and fetched $385,000 and was acquired by Texas numismatist Reed Hawn.

The Coinage of Vermont 1785-1788

By Codman Hislop *1984*

The following article, by Codman Hislop, treats one of the most fascinating areas of 18th-century American coinage—the copper issues of Vermont. The author has lived for about 40 years in Dorset, Vermont, about an hour's walking distance from a structure considered by some to be the original mint house. "So far as the natives are concerned 40 years isn't enough, I'm still a 'summer visitor,' " Hislop relates. He is a retired professor of American Civilization (Union College, Schenectady, New York), the author of numerous books and articles, and is currently at work on new material pertaining to General Benedict Arnold's treason at West Point.

For further reading on the subject of Vermont Coppers, Rare Coin Review *readers may enjoy* Studies on Money in Early America *published by the American Numismatic Society, 1976, which contains an article, "Vermont Copper Coinage," by Kenneth E. Bressett;* Centennial Publication of the American Numismatic Society, *1958, which contains an interesting article by Eric P. Newman pertaining to Machin's Mills; and the classic* Early Coins of America, *by Sylvester S. Crosby, 1875, available in reprint form.*

Q. David Bowers and the Research Department of Bowers and Merena Galleries is planning to publish an illustrated book on the subject of Vermont coinage. Work is now in progress.

Reuben Harmon, Jr., of Rupert, Vermont, mintmaster to the Republic of Vermont, certainly did not think of himself as a "Colonial" when, in 1785, he petitioned the Vermont House, then sitting in Norwich, "for leave to coin a quantity of copper."

Nor did his fellow Vermonters who, for good reason by 1785, were ardent supporters of the recently won American Revolution. One remembers the anguished years of the New Hampshire Grants when the Green Mountain Boys organized to battle the sheriffs' posses riding in from New York to claim Green Mountain lands under King George III's grant to the Duke of York. "Colonials?" In the language of our time: No way!

By 1785 the expedient Republic of Vermont knew its future lay with the then painfully emerging United States of America. It was to take six more years of grinding political wheels before statehood was realized. In the meantime the Republic of Vermont and its neighboring states of the American Confederacy had overwhelming problems: a soaring inflation, mounting debt, British markets closed to American traders, and a currency of ragtag copper and silver coins, British and Spanish, a host of private tokens, counterfeits, and a paper money not worth putting in your pocket.

By 1785, when Reuben Harmon built his Mint House just east of the Mettowee, in Rupert, prices had advanced 20 times over what they had been 10 years earlier. In 1772 unskilled labor was paid 22 cents per day; by 1780 a farmhand was receiving 79 cents, and struggling on that to make ends meet. General Washington was bemoaning the blatant extravagance of those with money and their unrestrained importation of luxury goods, payment for which had to be made in a rapidly depleting hard currency the American states could ill afford to lose. The general, however, could cheer himself up by noting his land company in western New York was booming, selling off farms at one dollar per acre.

So Reuben Harmon, Jr., of Rupert (then spelled "Reupert"), in this time of economic crisis, elected himself and two Dorset neighbors, Abraham Underhill and Benjamin Baldwin, to produce a copper coinage with which Vermonters could carry on the small trade of households, of the baker, the candlestick maker, and the blacksmith. The Republic's legislature had been quite specific about the nature of the coins which would be struck at the mint on the Mettowee: ". . .all coppers coined by him shall be in pieces of one-third of an ounce, Troy weight each, with such devices and mottos as shall be agreed upon by the Committee appointed for the purpose by this assembly." One can be sure Harmon's Dorset neighbors, Abraham Underhill and Benjamin Baldwin, would watch the business with a sharp eye, for they were his sureties in the amount of $5,000.

Harmon seemed to be a solid citizen. With his father he came into Vermont from Suffield, Connecticut about 1768, part of that wave of Connecticut families whose numbers almost resulted in the name "New Connecticut" taking the place of "Vermont."

Reuben Harmon, Jr. was a member of that famous meeting in Dorset, in 1776, which initiated the moves resulting in the establishment of the Republic of Vermont, that "Vermon Res Publica," the Vermont house told Harmon, was to be the motto on those first coppers struck in 1785.

Reuben Harmon's labors as a mintmaster were innocent enough for the first two years. We have a picture of the strenuous business of sinking the quickly worn dies and striking the copper pennies from a letter written in 1855 by Reuben's grandson, Julian:

> ". . .my father gives me answers to your questions as follows. . .thinks Wm. Buel, of New Haven, cut the dies. The Mint House stood on Pillet [Pawlett] River, three rods from his father's house—storey and a half house, not painted—a furnace on one end for melting copper & rolling the bars, etc.; in the other [west] end, machinery for stamping,—in the center that for cutting, etc. The stamping was done by means of an iron screw attached to heavy timbers above and moved by hand with aid of ropes. 60 per minute could be stamped, although 30 per minute was the usual number. Wm. Buel assisted in striking the coins. 3 persons were required for the purpose, one to place the copper, and two to swing the stamp. At first the coins passed 2 for a penny, then 4, then 8, when it ceased to pay expenses. . . My father, Dr. John Harmon, also thinks there was a plough on one side of the coins. . . .

Copper pennies poured out of Rupert Harmon's Mint House, enough of them he hoped to drive out of the Vermont market the coppers struck by English speculators and confusion of debased coinage which was an affront to orderly business.

Those first pennies, struck in 1785 and the first half of 1786, proclaimed "Vermont" loud and clear. The device on the obverse, in the language of the numismatist, showed "the sun rising from behind a range of wooded mountains, a plough in the field beneath; the legend: "Vermons Res Publica 1785."

On the reverse, "an eye within a small circle, from which issue 26 rays, 13 long, their points intersecting a circle of 13 stars, and 13 short (rays), between the stars and the center." One suspects that "eye within a small circle" may well have had Masonic antecedents. But those 13 rays and 13 stars, in 1785 show clearly enough the Republic of Vermont's interest in the surrounding 13 United States. The legend on this reverse clinched the matter: "Stella Quarta Decima". . .the 14th Star.

In October 1786, Reuben again petitioned the Legislature; this time he urged it to extend his coin making monopoly ". . .for a further term of 10 years. . ." arguing that ". . .the present scarcity of a circulating medium for the coining of coppers within the state may be very advantageous to the public." For reasons which will soon become clear, Reuben Harmon's Dorset bondsmen, Abraham Underhill and Benjamin Baldwin, now disappear from the record.

The Legislature thought eight years would be enough, a suitable reward for "his great expense in erecting works and procuring a quantity of copper." The Committee on Coinage also seems to have been persuaded, perhaps by Reuben himself whose sights had recently been raised to visions of profit well beyond the borders of Vermont, that it should replace its "sun-rising-over-mountains, plough-in-the-field" coin with something more familiar, more like the English halfpennies which were not bound by state boundaries. So Reuben Harmon got his new coin, ". . .on the one side of which a head, with the motto 'auctoritate Vermontensium, abridged. . .' on the reverse, a woman, with the letters, Inde: Et: Lib:. . .for independence and liberty."

For smart operators these years of inflation and depression were also a time for great profit. Just when Captain Thomas Machin of Machin's Mills, near Newburgh, New York, and Reuben Harmon, of the Mint House on the Mettowee, joined forces is not certain; probably Machin's intriguing schemes influenced Reuben's second petition to the Vermont Legislature for a coin design which would forward those schemes.

Captain Machin, ex-British Army officer, ex-American Army engineer, is remembered best by historians as the ingenious ironmonger who stretched a huge chain across the Hudson River at West Point, a successful barrier to the British fleet. To Reuben Harmon, however, he was the proprietor of what, for devious reasons, was known as a "hardware manufactory" at Machin's Mills. What, in fact, went on at Machin's Mills was what Harmon seems to have decided to carry on in Rupert; a mint house whose coppers would find markets well beyond the limits imposed by his grants from the Vermont Legislature.

Captain Machin and Reuben Harmon were now set up for the long gamble. Machin's "hardware manufactory" had been supplying copper halfpennies bearing the devices of Connecticut; if not quite unlawfully, certainly they were unauthorized. But what he really hoped for were two potentially vastly profitable developments: first, contracts with state governments to issue their official coins, if and when they could be persuaded to authorize them. Second, and this would have been a memorable coup, to capture "a grant for coinage of money from the United States of America in Congress assembled."

By April 1787, this ambitious scheme was first formalized in a painfully detailed contract between Captain Machin and five partners. By June of that year the euphoria of this golden, or copper, opportunity had embraced our Reuben Harmon, Jr., and three additional partners in an even more formidable contract.

Both men had their working stamping presses. Harmon had the services of diemaker William Buel, of New Haven, Connecticut, and Captain Machin employed a James F. Atlee, an equally capable diemaker, and a metallurgist who could extract copper from the old brass cannon and the mortars of the Revolution which Machin melted down in his furnaces at Newburgh. When diemakers VanVoorhis and Coley of New York City joined this "hardware" combine that year, the members were ready to become, not regional mintmasters, but the coin makers of the new nation. The Machin-Harmon "hardware manufactory" might, just might, emerge as the national mint.

Between the dream and the reality, however, were unexpected miscalculations, economic and political, inevitable in a decade which saw the end of the American Revolution and the signing of the new Constitution of the United States.

From the numismatic evidence it seems likely that part of the partnership's "hardware-cum-coinage" operations was made of ". . .lightweight imitations of the British halfpenny, with a bust obverse and Britannia seated reverse." And there is little doubt most of these coins were minted within the sound of the Mettowee, for, according to Simms, in his *History of Schoharie County, N.Y.,* ". . .at Mr. Machin's mills perhaps a thousand pounds of copper was manufactured. . .in the year 1789; previous to which little seems to have been done."

All was activity, however, at Reuben Harmon's Mint House, until coinage ceased there when the partnership's operations shifted to Newburgh. I'm not going to describe the minute variants found among the identified "strikes" of Vermont pennies Reuben faithfully continued to issue in 1785 and later; they offer a happy hunting ground for the coin specialists, and proof of the primitive technology of metallurgy, for the dies quickly wore out, or cracked, and had to be replaced, each of them an "original," for the diecutter could never exactly duplicate the die he was replacing.

It was the wider market, however, which called for the labors of the four diesinkers employed by the Machin-Harmon "hardware manufactory." Their "Britannia" halfpenny imitation had an inter-state currency; in appearance it was close enough to the Vermont penny which replaced the first "sunrise-and-plough" coin of 1785. There were coppers turned out with a Connecticut legend, and probably coins for New Jersey, none of them official.

One suspects Captain Machin and Reuben Harmon were men in a hurry. Strange things took place in the mint house. Too many dies for too many different strikes, some dies childishly crude, and sometimes an inadvertent mixing of dies which produced those errors so dear to the collectors of a later generation.

The Vermont Legislature for instance, never authorized a coin bearing the bust of George III, Rex., dated 1788, with a reverse of a seated female, bearing the legend, ironically enough, "Inde: Et: Lib." We see Vermont coins with overstrikes on Connecticut pieces, on Nova Constellatio tokens, on English and Irish counterfeit halfpennies—all of these now commanding prices running into the thousands of dollars as numismatic rarities.

The Machin-Harmon "hardware manufactory" failed, probably, for two major reasons; the first, their reckless flooding of their markets with carelessly produced, counterfeit and underweight British halfpennies. The great dream of minting the coins of the new United States government died as the plans for a national mint matured in Congress in 1792. With the opening of the United States Mint at Philadelphia in that year, all such private mints as Captain Machin's and Reuben Harmon's were outlawed, though their rough coppers continued to circulate for decades afterward.

Our Reuben Harmon, Jr. must have seen the handwriting on the wall well before the establishment of the National Mint, for he left Vermont in 1790; the year after Captain Machin had used up his 1,000 pounds of copper. The partnership was dissolved. It's easy to believe Harmon found his new home in Ohio and his new business of making salt more rewarding than making money in Vermont.

Two brief footnotes: The original mint house which stood near the Mettowee, on the north side of what is now called Hagar's Brook, was moved several times. The first time, apparently, ". . .to a spot north of the house of John Harwood, Esq., in the town of Rupert." The same source, a letter written in 1856, goes on to say ". . .it was again removed from its third location to a site nearly opposite, where it remained until its final journey. . . This placed it on the farm of William Phelps, about a mile north of John Harwood's residence. . . Here it stood until last winter when it was blown down." It could have been that the old building was resurrected, for a structure now standing, a neat, red farm building among others, near the house of Bob Graf, on the west side of Route 30 in Rupert, has an attractive sign in front of it labeling it as "The Harmon Mint House."

1785-1985: A Numismatic Bicentennial

By Q. David Bowers *1985*

1985 marks an important bicentennial in American coinage: the 200th anniversary of state copper coinage. It was back in 1785 that Vermont and Connecticut, pioneers in the state copper coinage field, produced their first varieties, under contract with private citizens.

Your editor (Q. David Bowers) has always felt that state copper coins of the 1785-1788 year were among the most fascinating items associated with the American series. In recognition of this, we invited several well-known collectors and enthusiasts in the field to submit brief sketches or comments concerning the observance. These are presented for your enjoyment:

ERIC P. NEWMAN: One of America's foremost numismatic writers and scholars, has earned several Heath Literary Award honors given by the American Numismatic Association, has studied American coins extensively, has penned the authoritative works on Fugio Coppers, Continental dollars, and Virginia copper coinage, and has participated in many seminars and educational gatherings. His words follow:

The year 1785 was numismatically very significant in a distinctive manner and thus deserves the tribute of a bicentennial recognition.

The year 1785 saw Vermont, though not accepted as a state, authorize copper coinage to continue to assert its sovereignty by using legends on its coins to gain recognition as a separate republic (VERMONTENSIUM RES PUBLICA) and to be the 14th star in the flag (STELLA QUARTA DECIMA).

The year 1785 is the actual year of mintage in England and circulation in America of the Nova Constellatio coppers, even though some varieties are antedated 1783 to conform to the date of the 1783 silver and copper patterns from which the coinage was copied.

The year 1785 is the first public admission that counterfeit British-style halfpence were being minted in America as the petition for the 1785 Connecticut coinage franchise specifically stated.

The year 1785 is the year in which Continental Congress adopted the dollars and cents money of account system for the United States and approved coinage denominations for our future mint on a decimal basis.

The year 1785 is the date on three varieties (two obverse dies and two reverse dies) of counterfeit British-style halfpence the origin of which coppers is undetermined and which may be American because they are not listed in the 1868 publication of the immense collection of English coppers assembled by D.T. Batty of Manchester, England.

The year 1785 began the short cycle of state and federal officially franchised coppers which were the only privately minted coins circulated in the United States after independence.

My attraction to the state and federal franchise coppers and to those secretly made by Americans who coined without a franchise is based upon the great opportunity to do research about them. They are a product of natural economic necessity; they have diverse backgrounds and associated personnel; they suffered from the complications of inexperience; they showed the initiative of private enterprise; they have artistic charm and quaint mottoes; they were coined in a period of transition; and they circulated for over half a century.

How could anyone not be intrigued by studying and collecting what was started in 1785?

—Eric P. Newman

RICHARD AUGUST: Dick August, one of the foremost collectors in the field of state and related copper coinages, has gathered a cabinet comprising numerous rarities which many know only from reference book listings. Along the way he has taken time to study what he has acquired, with the result that his knowledge on different varieties and their rarities is of the first order. His tribute follows:

When I was five years old, my grandfather started to give me a few old coins as gifts. That was 1945, and the coins were Indian cents, Liberty nickels, and Barber coins. I can still remember the fascination and beauty that these coins, made before I was born, held for me. Time, history, and people were somehow locked up in these tiny little objects.

For many years I went on to collect United States coinage, when finally a gift of my own prompted me to collect early American colonial coins. It was a few days before Father's Day, and I decided to take the short trip from our Brookline home via the MTA to a coin show in downtown Boston. I was in high school then, I figured that I had $10 to spend on a present, perhaps a coin, which my father would remember forever. I scouted all the tables at the coin show and found nothing really interesting or unusual until I spotted this odd-looking large copper dated 1787 with a large eagle on it and the word "Massachusetts." I didn't know a thing about such coins, but I opened my *Guide Book* and discovered some 50 pages of coins, American colonial issues, I did not even expect had existed. How often I had opened this book without noticing these 50 pages. The coin was in Fine condition and the price then, some 25 years ago, was $10, which happened to equal the sum I had to spend. I took the "eagle" home, examining it all the way during my MTA ride. On the other side of the coin was a tall Indian, the emblem of the state of Massachusetts. The workmanship on this early coin was excellent. Later I would find out that Massachusetts coppers of 1787 and 1788 were generally the finest made colonial state coppers from a technical coinage viewpoint. On the eve of that first purchase I pored through all the pages of the *Guide Book* section on colonial coins. . .Pine Tree shillings, Oak tree shillings, Willow Tree shillings, Massachusetts coppers, Vermont coppers with ploughs on them, New Jersey coppers with horses on them, Connecticut coppers, Fugio with "Mind Your Business," Washington coinage and more.

That night I became an American colonial collector, and the coin that was to be a present ended up as my first colonial piece in my own collection! In fact, today Massachusettts copper is one of my favorite series, and I personally own the most extensive collection of these ever formed, lacking only one die variety. This took 25 years and I am still hunting for new die varieties, die states, and better grades.

Over the years I have found American colonial coins interesting to collect for many reasons. People I have met while collecting these coins have been as interesting as the coins themselves. Those who have owned these coins seem to have often left their own mark upon them. The coins themselves reflect "a time and history" interesting to Americans. Even though these coins do not have "United States" upon them, they are most worthy to belong in an American collection. The craftsmanship, beauty, devices and legends of these coins still speak of the colonist's sentiments, although sometimes in a folksy Latin: "Inde et Lib" for "Independence and Liberty," for example. I've always found, and still find, that the hunt for colonial coins is somewhat like the lure of prospecting and far more interesting than sending to the Mint for mint sets. Also, it never ceases to amaze me how truly rare these coins are in comparison with other United States issues and that still these coins are more affordable to me than some of those very early rare United States pieces.

And lastly, there is a great challenge in collecting coins. The first-hand records of this coinage are often incomplete or nonexistent, so it is often possible for a collector today to discover by studying the actual coins more about what really did exist. The coinage is so varied that it is not possible to ever get to the point of completion or boredom or perfection. Much like the realities of life, collecting this series involves an unending search. However, I've never seen this as any great frustration. I can't collect every colonial item, but I known I can form a unique collection in its own way. By selecting a certain section of colonial coins to stress in my collection, colonial state coppers and Fugio cents, I can add my own mark to these coins in the series. . .and so can everyone else. —Richard August

GARY A. TRUDGEN: Gary Trudgen has emerged on the collecting scene in recent times as a knowledgeable specialist in state coppers, particularly with regard to the coinage of Thomas Machin on the shores of Orange Pond, near present-day Newburgh, New York. A frequent contributor to *The Colonial Newsletter,* Gary writes in an interesting and authoritative manner:

The copper coinage of the early states, to me, is the most interesting area of American numismatics because it was the first domestic coinage of our new nation, following the Revolution. My interest in this coinage exists at several different levels.

First—The conditions under which the coins were made: This coinage occurred under relatively primitive conditions during the beginnings of our great nation. The United States had just won her independence from Great Britain and was loosely bound together by the Articles of Confederation. The federal government had not yet been established. To me, this period of American history, along with the American Revolution, is very interesting to study.

Second—The people involved with the coinage: The lives of the people who founded these early mints and sought coinage grants from the states and Continental Congress are fascinating to research and study. In many instances they were men of distinction. For example, Matthias Ogden and Thomas Machin were heroes of the Revolutionary War.

Third—Early American coinage technology: Understanding the methods and technology used by these early coiners demands detective-type investigation. Study of the coins themselves is required because there are no known extant coining implements and few contemporary coinage records from this era.

Fourth—Collecting the coins: I find that building a die variety collection of one of the state coinages is a real challenge because there are many rare varieties that were often created by early die failure. If collectors wish to increase this challenge, they can be very selective concerning the grade, strike, planchet condition and coloration of the coppers that they acquire for their collection.

For me, these state coppers open a window through time to the beginning of our nation. Imagine owning a piece of an instrument that was employed to bring about the birth of our nation! It so happens that with the state coinages there is just this opportunity. Some of the Machin's Mills imitation British halfpence were coined from brass cannons and mortars that were in all likelihood used during the Revolutionary War.

—Gary A. Trudgen

WILLIAM T. ANTON, JR.: Bill Anton has formed one of the finest collections of New Jersey coppers (1786-1788) ever gathered together, but at the same time he has an interest in many other contemporary copper series. A familiar figure at coin auctions and conventions, Bill is always eager to add specimens not already represented in his fine cabinet. He notes:

Since the tender age of four, I have been collecting coins. Some 46 years ago my dad, to whom I owe a great deal more than a pen could ever write, started me like many youngsters with Lincoln cents. To me at that time owning a Very Good Indian cent was a real treat. By the time I was six years old the bank on the corner where I lived knew my face very well, as I would every other day exchange a $10 bill for $10 in cents. Going through the rolls of "pennies" I would find all different dates, including over a period of time one 1909-S, about three of the 1909-S V.D.B.s, one 1914-D, and several of the other scarce dates. I learned that the hardest Lincoln cent to find in those days was the 1922 "Plain." I found one 1922 Plain compared to about seven 1922-D s for every two weeks of looking.

From Indian and Lincoln cents I quickly expanded to the entire United States series, going from there to federal paper money and to national bank notes. By the time I was 18 years of age I was a commissioned buyer at major auctions and private treaty for several collectors who had faith in my judgment as to what to buy and collect.

I must thank David Bullowa for introducing me to Americana. I made several visits to his dorm in Philadelphia and enjoyed listening to him giving me words of wisdom. This became rather routine for me as I went to Villanova University and lifted weights at the 52nd Street YMCA. After classes and on my lifting workout days, I would stop in at David Bullowa's coin shop off of Chestnut Street and talk coins before eating and returning back to my college campus on the Main Line.

I started dealing while still in college, but I maintained my collecting interest. To this date I am still a collector of coins in general and a specialist dealer in Americana in particular, mainly colonial coins, currency, and medals.

Americana colonial coins have become my major interest, with a special love and admiration for New Jersey copper cents. This was natural for me. I have lived in New Jersey all my life and grew up on a farm, playing and working a plow. I have loved horses since childhood and while attending Oakland Military Academy in my pre-teens I was member of the cavalry. I won every prize possible for horseback riding, racing, jumping, and show at the Academy for two active years of riding. Although my audience now looking at me may find it hard to believe, I was at one time lead exercise jockey at Saratoga raceway. New Jersey coppers, which show the motif of horse and plow, are part of me. I think they are the most beautiful coins in the world.

New Jersey coppers offer the perfect challenge. With 135 different horsehead die varieties presently known, any collector just startng out could put together an assembly of 90 different examples without too much difficulty and at very moderate prices. Colonial coins in general are greatly underpriced, in my opinion. A clean Fine piece is a very acceptable condition and can fit the budget of almost any age group. Other pieces are apt to be more expensive. I have to thank Dave Bowers for the genius that was applied in auctioning off the world-famous Garrett Coin Collection. Never before in modern numismatic history have so many colonial coins in top condition and rarity been offered for public auction. Even the great Chapman sales of decades ago didn't match up with the depth and magnitude of such an offering. The timing was right, the cataloguing was unparalleled, the numismatic world was mesmerized. I bought at the October 1, 1980 Garrett sale some New Jersey coppers that I never thought in my lifetime I would ever own. Many of the coins belonged to the granddaddy of New Jersey coppers, Dr. Edward Maris, and were so plated in this monumental 1881 book on same. I feel fortunate in my lifetime that this special event happened and I was there. More collectors should feel this way about coins they own. Too many people buy a coin and look for a profit the next day. I have found a very simple formula for making money in the coin business. First, be very discriminating when you buy. Now you can enjoy owning your coin while admiring and holding it for several years before selling. You will find at this time doubling your money is not at all out of the ordinary. Make the switch, readers, as I have, and buy your first American colonial coin. There are many books on all the different state coinages available in the marketplace. A good place to start is at the beginning of the *Guide Book* which includes nearly 50 pages on the subject.

—William T. Anton, Jr.

JAMES C. SPILMAN: "The year 1985, as well as being the 200th anniversary of the great copper splurge, will be the 25th anniversary of *The Colonial Newsletter*—how about that!," wrote Jim Spilman when he transmitted his comment. As editor of this scholarly newsletter, Jim has published information on many varieties and areas of colonial, state, and early American coinage and in the process has made many lasting contributions to our fraternity. For this issue of the *Rare Coin Review* he has the following to say:

"It is convenience only, that ought to be considered with respect to copper coinage, and not money or riches. It was going on this last idea, instead of the first one, that entangled the former Congress and the several states. They attempted to do what no other nation ever thought of doing, and which was impossible to do—that of exalting copper (coins) into national wealth."

So wrote Thomas Paine in *Thoughts on the Establishment of the Mint in the United States,* published in the *National Gazette* Philadelphia, November 17, 1791.

These thoughts of Thomas Paine pointed up a lesson learned with great difficulty by the individual states and by the newly formed federal government during the years 1785-1788. The concept that copper coins could be successfully produced by private contract was an attractive one—but it just did not work out. All those who played the game failed—and failure in those days, generally led to debtor's prison.

But they tried, and in the process was produced a unique series of events in the numismatic history of America and an even more unique series of state and federal coinage that remain today, 200 years later, a fertile field for fruitful research. In my mind, these four years in the first decade following the American Revolution are unequaled in the recorded numismatic history of any nation in the world. All the elements of mystery and intrigue, of invented genius, personal success and failure, of private enterprise and public service are intertwined—many just now being discovered, and even more awaiting discovery—all of these elements, and more, are present. There is something for everyone, from the "investor" to the collector to the research scientist, the beauty of it all is that the surface has been but lightly scratched.

The copper coinages of this period are truly "early American" in every sense. The largest group is, of course, the Connecticut coppers produced principally in New Haven by the famous "Company for Coining Coppers." Here we have more than 400 coinage dies used to produce almost 350 die variety combinations over the entire four-year period. The effort required to produce this quantity of coinage dies must have been awesome!

Then we have the copper coinage of Vermont produced by Reuben Harmon, Jr. of Rupert, Vermont during the same four years. During 1786 New Jersey granted a contract to coin copper to Walter Mould, Thomas Goadsby, and Albion Cox. Next was Massachusetts with both half cents. Then Thomas Machin of New York formed his infamous "Machin's Mills" organization and produced almost everything for everyone. If that were not enough excitement, the federal government requested proposals to produce a federal cent and eventually awarded a contract under questionable circumstances to James Jarvis and his associates who coined some 400,000 Fugio cents—our first American cent—before his operations fell prey to the impossible dream of creating wealth from copper coins.

With such a background, how could these early American coins fail to evoke interest? Even further back in time are many issues of earlier years including even those of the native American Indian tribes in their unique medium of exchange commonly known as wampum, or wampum-peage. If we were to follow the written colonial records that have come down to us we would speak of it as "peage" or even "peg." There appears to be no limit to the varied opportunities in "early Americana numismatics;"—yet, this segment of American numismatics is little known to the average collector. I hope this brief discussion will catch the interest of someone who wants to learn more of this fascinating era and that it will serve to lead them into this field that contains more opportunities and challenges than any other in numismatics.

—James C. Spilman

Ed. Note: It's appropriate at this point to suggest that interested Rare Coin Review *readers request a sample copy of* The Colonial Newsletter *from Jim Spilman, whose address is Box 4411, Huntsville, Alabama, 35802.*

ROY E. BONJOUR: The following tribute to the bicentennial of state coinage is by Roy Bonjour, the New York collector who has published several articles on the top subject of Vermont coppers in recent times and who has compiled a listing of known varieties of Ryder-15 and Ryder-30:

Why would anyone want to collect Vermonts? Certainly in this day and age when hymns are daily and routinely sung to the God "MS-65," these ugly ducklings have little place. I doubt if anyone has fallen in love with them at first sight. I believe that most of us who share love and fascination for these coins have gravitated toward them over a period of years. At least this is what happened to me.

As a history teacher I have always felt excitement when studying our colonial and post-Revolutionary period. It was only natural that when I returned to coin collecting I should choose this area of specialization. It was easy for me to start collecting colonials in the early 1970s because I was not jaded by the gods that now rule the collecting fraternity. In fact, I was so "stupid" that I refused to buy Brilliant Uncirculated Virginia halfpennies that were selling for $25 each. I preferred the worn version. This might indeed seem strange to most of you but I was naive in those days. I thought that one collected coins for the intellectual richness that they can bring; not necessarily for the financial reward. Put a circulated Vermont in your hand and close your eyes. Do you feel the presence of the Vermont farmer on your palm? Can you experience his loves and hates, share his problems? I can! Try holding an MS-65 silver dollar in your hand and all you feel is the cold of the vault where it spent most of its barren existence.

I approached the collection of colonial coins in a helter-skelter manner; no plan, just the *Guide Book* in hand. I decided to try a new approach and sent Dave Bowers a sum of money and told him to pick out some colonial issues which he thought I might enjoy. In a group of seven coins that arrived there were three Vermonts. I guess Dave's own love of Vermont colored his choices. At any length I was now in possession of my first Vermont issues!

I then started to research what I had. I was very fortunate to meet a Vermont collector, Harold Hauser, who proceeded to fill my files with articles on Vermont. I bought Crosby and read all the material I could find. Before I knew it, I was a Vermont specialist!

Much of what is being collected today is like ladies of the night. After you see through the glitter there is little substance. The Vermont, however, is like Eliza Doolittle. Once you remove the grime you discover her hidden beauty. I believe that knowledge holds the key to appreciating the coins of Vermont and unlocking the secrets of their charm. The landscape type is truly the most beautiful of all the state coppers. This design features a mountain range with a stand of pine trees on it. Just behind the mountain is a magnificent rising sun full of hope and promise. The American spirit radiates forth in this early primitive design. As an analysis of the coin continues, more and more of the Vermont hopes and aspirations are revealed. The coin becomes alive with American history!

After I studied the coins, I then turned to the people who made them. Here, history has assembled a cast of characters that could titillate the fancies of a movie producer. Unfortunately, much is unknown about what really happened during those years. In fact, I've recently published a paper which challenges some of the currently held beliefs. This is what makes Vermont so interesting!

Obviously there is more to collecting Vermont coins than their history. I like them because it was a short series containing only 39 types or varieties, with enough variation to make the pieces interesting. There are extreme rarities which I will never own, but hope springs eternal. Few dealers know enough about the series to identify the rarities, so each coin show is always filled with anticipation that an elusive coin is waiting to be discovered. Because there are relatively few Vermont collectors (compared to other series), great rarities can be bought for relatively reasonable prices. This was another reason that encouraged me to collect them.

In summary, I collected Vermont coins because they met all of my needs. They were collectible, that is, available at respectable prices. I found that they had significant historical interest and this provided an intellectual challenge. They even provided an outlet for the romantic in me to come out. They are, indeed, the perfect series!

—Roy E. Bonjour

ANTHONY TERRANOVA: "Tony" Terranova, a colonial dealer and specialist, has an intense personal interest in the things he buys and

sells. In recent years he has handled many important items among early American issues. Here he tells of his initial interest and his feelings concerning the field:

My interest in copper state coinage began about 12 years ago. I guess I was drawn at first to their reasonably affordable price structure. But, the more one looks at and handles them, the more one finds that each piece has a uniqueness all its own. From the crudeness of manufacture and wonderful range of colors to the challenge of locating them, each coin is "special." Sometimes even a piece that is not expensive may take a good period of time to locate.

To me, collecting something should not be a matter of simply spending money to instantly buy anything you want. Rather, there should be a hunt, a challenge. Colonial coins offer such a challenge.

The next time you handle a coin of this period, stop a minute and think about what it represents. This country's beginnings and attempts at a monetary structure are just two considerations. These little round copper discs are part of our American heritage.

—Anthony Terranova

Q. David Bowers: 30 Years in Numismatics

By Paul M. Green *1984*

It is a special anniversary for David Bowers, and as all collectors know, David Bowers is a special person. Few can point to a similar record of success in numismatics. The numerous books and articles, the important coins he has handled, now American Numismatic Association president, it is a combination that reads a little like a guide to all the things one person might do in numismatics. That David Bowers has done them all in 30 years makes it all the more interesting.

Perhaps the best news of all is that Bowers is hardly on the verge of retiring from the scene. His move in 1983 with Ray Merena to acquire the Bowers and Ruddy Galleries business from General Mills (which had purchased it from Q. David Bowers and James F. Ruddy in 1974) are hardly the actions of someone who has grown tired of the rare coin business. Ditto for his unopposed campaign last summer for president of the American Numismatic Association. As the following interview will show, Bowers is hardly stopping with his business or his likely role as chief spokesman of the hobby. He has always been active, and in 1983, his year number 30 in numismatics, the ideas, plans, and projects are many, matched only by the energy of Q. David Bowers to see them come to life.

Coins Magazine: Following the purchase from General Mills, how long did it take Bowers and Merena Galleries to get settled?

Bowers: There was a transitional period because nearly 100,000 customers in varying degrees of activity were involved. A number of these people had pending business with Bowers and Ruddy Galleries prior to the changeover, which was January 8, 1983, so on a customer by customer basis we had to take care of all clients who had open accounts, accounts receivable, coins that were waiting to be shipped, or other situations.

Coins Magazine: A lot of that was to be expected.

Bowers: Right, the first two months were taken up with the transition. At the same time, January 1983 saw us conduct the Roy Harte Collection sale, which was estimated to bring $800,000 but which soared to over $1.1 million, followed by record-breaking auctions of the Connecticut Historical Society Collection at $2.4 million in April, the George M. Hatie Collection sale, which grossed nearly $3 million in August, and other events.

Coins Magazine: Have your auctions further emphasized the general talk of new strength in the market?

Bowers: I read what a lot of people say about renewed strength or whatever. My feeling is that our customer base has been largely numismatists, or if they are investors they are numismatists first and investors second, so these people have been more immune to the cyclical effects than have people who are pure investors.

For example, the fourth session of the Garrett Sale was held in 1981 during the so-called soft market, but it still realized record prices. Then we had the Louis Eliasberg Collection of United States gold coins in October 1982, which broke all records and realized $12.4 million in a period of which the edge had been off of large purchases. In 1981 and 1982 there were many interesting alternative investment forms.

The rates on CDs were at an all-time high, the money market fund came into popularity. Coins had ridden a normal cycle peaking out in 1980, and some adjustment was to be expected just as I have seen three other times in the past. There were a number of things coming together to create the correction.

Now, in 1983, we have the situation that interest rates have dropped so money on deposit yields less than 10% which after taxes might be only 4% or so, we have international problems, record peacetime budget deficits and so on. A lot of people are turning to hard assets again and this has been manifested in interest in gold and silver. Many people believe that gold and silver prices will rise sharply, with numerous predictions appearing in print.

Historically coins have done better than putting your money in the bank, collecting interest and paying taxes on it. Charted over a long period of years, which tends to smooth out the cycle, coins have risen, depending on whose charting you read, 15%, 20% or more per year. Our own business has been really superb as evidenced by recent auction response plus the tremendous numbers of inquiries we are getting from collectors.

Our position now is that we are buyers of coins. I won't say we have more business than we can handle because we can handle what we have and handle it well, but our main advertising thrust in *Numismatic News* and elsewhere is *buying* coins because we have a strong need for top-grade material.

Coins Magazine: So that subtle change reflects the state of your business if not the market.

Bowers: Yes, I feel that just as economists take note of the help wanted index, someone studying the coin market could take note of the coin wanted to buy ads as related to selling ads. You go back a couple years and there were very few buying ads, now I notice that we're not the only ones wanting to buy. This obviously means that dealers and others have a faith in the future of the market, otherwise they would keep their money in the bank.

Coins Magazine: What areas were strong in the Harte sale?

Bowers: We found the collection of large cents brought record prices and far over estimate. Type coins seemed to be enjoying a renewed popularity, and there was good interest in almost anything you could consider desirable. If I were to pick a weak area, it would be military orders and decorations.

Coins Magazine: So you consider it a pretty successful sale.

Bowers: Yes, there were thousands of people interested in the sale and there were 710 successful bidders. When you figure there were only 3,000 lots, I think that shows that the market is broad and that the success was not due to three buyers competing against each other.

Coins Magazine: Is that experience backed up by your regular customers?

Bowers: We've always been broad based. It is my feeling that while I enjoyed selling the 1787 Brasher doubloon at $725,000, and an 1804 silver dollar at $400,000, as well as many other rarities, by far the majority of the business over the years has been to the average person who doesn't desire an 1804 dollar as it probably represents more than he or she has invested in a house. Rather the typical client is a methodical collector of half cents, type coins, tokens, large-size paper money, or whatever. A typical profile would be a person who is seriously interested in numismatics, who enjoys reading reference books and studying about coins and paper money and who gets involved.

I feel that education is not only part of success, it's everything that has to do with success. Because of this we stress heavily that people buy reference books and join the American Numismatic Association

(ANA). I've been in business 30 years now and we've always attracted customers who've stayed with us for a long period, and I feel this is due to being interested in more than just the customer's pocketbook.

Coins Magazine: Isn't the education aspect so important in areas such as grading and investment?

Bowers: I think it's significant to mention that as president of the ANA, and as past president of the Professional Numismatists Guild (PNG), and as author of many books, I have been called in as an arbitrator on countless disputes between people. Nearly all of the problems involving grading have been with newer collectors or investors, or collectors who haven't taken much time to learn about the subject themselves. I would rather sell the person a half dozen books and not sell them a single coin until they have done some reading before buying. I feel education is essential, and with education a customer can be successful. I don't think we've ever lost a customer because the customer knew too much.

Coins Magazine: Do you sense any division between collectors and others who are primarily investors?

Bowers: Well I think that almost all collectors are partial investors. Virtually everyone except perhaps museums who spends $10,000 of his hard earned money on coins has the hope, if not the expectation, that when the coins are sold in some future year that a profit will be made. They hope for some return and that's natural.

There are pure investors who don't want to learn anything about collecting. Well, this person might be successful, but I have yet to meet one who is *consistently* successful. It is just as if you went to a real estate office and said, "Sell me whatever you have," they would probably get all the property that has been listed for 10 years and no one wanted. The objective which the investor is trying to achieve becomes difficult to attain if the investor is not willing to take the time to learn what he is doing. It never ceases to amaze me how someone can be very successful in a career such as medicine, law, or business, and can save up his money only to spend it carelessly in the rare coin market. To me, education is the foundation of success in any venture, and coins do not represent an exception.

Coins Magazine: Is there still a role for the small collector or have the finances and so on passed him by?

Bowers: Part of my effort in coins has been to reach the small collector. Typically the person taking my "All About Coins" course that I have given at the American Numismatic Association headquarters each summer is not someone who wants to spend $100,000 on coins, but just wants to learn about the history of coins. In 1982 I gave a talk to the Worcester County Numismatic Club in Massachusetts, and the hall was just packed. Close to 200 people came there to see a variety of things. They weren't there to invest, they were there to learn about coins, to meet other collectors and dealers, and to simply *enjoy* the hobby. Of course, a number of them made purchases.

However, grass roots interest is not spectacular in terms of press or television coverage. When a reporter calls and says, "Well, you sold that 1787 Brasher doubloon for $725,000, tell me about it," I will do what I can to explain the issue, why it merited that price, its relation to other pieces, the setting of a world record, and so on. However, I would not expect a call from a similar reporter inquiring about the sale of a commemorative half dollar for $35. Coins that sell for large amounts of money in our auctions make news headlines. But, the fact is that at Bowers and Merena Galleries most of our time is spent with $35, $75, $200, and other pieces which we sell to the so-called "average collector." The Roy Harte Sale, the George Hatie Sale, and other spectacular auctions we have conducted are certainly exciting to read about, but when we return from the auction site in New York City and come back to our office, typically we find several hundred orders on hand for coins ranging from $5 to $50. However, reporters don't find these lesser transactions to be commanding importance.

One thing nice about numismatics is that it is cosmopolitan; there is room for everyone. There is room for the person who can afford the Brasher doubloon as well as the person who buys a Whitman folder and is trying to get every Lincoln cent with the Memorial reverse. I myself collect tokens. When I was conducting the Roy Harte Sale, I had a collector named Alan Weinberg come up with a token from Grass Valley, California and he wanted $20 for it. Here, amidst a sale that was to bring $1.1 million dollars, we spent 10 minutes talking about tokens and I bought a $20 token. You do not have to be wealthy to derive real enjoyment from numismatics or to buy important coins.

Coins Magazine: Would you share the concern over lack of design change discouraging young collectors in particular?

Bowers: I share this concern; I feel this is unfortunate. When I started in 1953 you could look in circulation, and the possibility of finding a 1909-S V.D.B. cent was there. I never knew of anyone among my friends who found one at the time, but at least there was a chance. I found 1921 and 1921-D dimes and 1909 V.D.B. cents by the dozens, in fact, I started saving them and found too many so I started spending them. In one afternoon I went to the Forty Fort (Pennsylvania) State Bank, where I used to do business, and just kept exchanging half dollar rolls until I got a complete set of Liberty Walking halves from 1916 to 1947 including extra 1938-Ds. It was possible and it was thrilling to do that.

Today, the collector would do well to find a Lincoln cent prior to 1959, although a friend of mine in New Hampshire found a 1905 Indian cent the other day. You would do well to find a Jefferson nickel from before 1960, or any pre-1965 dime, quarter or half dollar. There are really very few rarities among those items.

I feel the United States government is missing a large opportunity by not having a broadly based commemorative program. I will be the first to compliment Donna Pope, the Bureau of the Mint, and others for what they have done in recent times. In 1982 we had the Washington commemorative, which was well received and is an attractive design. Now we have the Olympic coinage, which is admittedly controversial as far as designs go. I personally feel that certain designs could have been improved, but at the same time the Olympics coinage program is definitely a step in the right direction. It is important to remember that we haven't had a commmemorative since 1954, and certain of the earlier commemoratives we had wouldn't win any prizes. So, collectors should be heartened by the fact that new commemorative programs are under way.

I would like to see the United states have a program similar to what Canada has in which they put out a new dollar each year. What would be wrong with a new dollar coin each year? Have a design competition each year. Over a period of 25 years have 25 different designs. It's certainly not going to confuse the monetary system, they don't circulate anyway. They will make collectors happy; if they are available at face value or near it the average collector can collect them. Even at twice face they would probably be a sellout, the Treasury would make money, the collectors would be happy and it would be an equation without a negative in it.

Coins Magazine: I've thought along the same lines many times.

Bowers: There is ample precedent in the field of stamps. There are over a dozen different commemorative stamps released each year, and this has been responsible to a large extent for the widespread interest in stamps. Wouldn't it be nice if a person could invest a small amount of money and get many different commemorative halves or dollars?

Coins Magazine: I had the feeling some were disappointed the Washington half did not spark more interest in commemorative collecting.

Bowers: It's like a piece of string, you can't push the market. The local bank here asked me about the new commemorative half dollars last year. Should they buy some? They wanted to know if anyone would buy them. I said, "Well if no one buys them I'll buy them." To make a long story short, they sent off an order for 100. When they came in they put up a notice in the bank, and by the end of the afternoon they were all gone. Remember, this is a small town bank. They obviously did not sell to numismatists, because numismatists had known about them for many months and could have ordered them in any number of other ways. They were sold to people, the members of the general public, who looked at one and took one.

I don't know how many people will be new collectors but I would guess that maybe 10 of those people are thinking about their Washington half and might turn into collectors. You have to look at the Washington commemoratives as a seed that might germinate a collector, rather than a vehicle for market speculation.

Coins Magazine: You recently have been elected president of the American Numismatic Association. After 30 years of great activity, what is ahead for David Bowers?

Bowers: I pledge a great deal of energy to the ANA. I feel the ANA is facing a number of major and very serious problems. Number one is the budget. While the budget deficit anticipated for last year was corrected during the months leading to the summer, still steps must be taken to increase income, or reduce outflow, or a combination of both.

The ANA should exist for the benefit of its constituency, for the benefit of collectors, and it would be desirable to review every aspect of the ANA and see how we could further education, how we can better serve the collector and so on, while still doing so in a financially responsible manner.

The ANA has a number of advantages including a beautifully equipped headquarters which is paid for. Under the direction of Ken Bressett, director of the American Numismatic Association Certification Service, the grading controversy has abated. The ANACS authentication and grading group seems to be performing a service that is desired by many people. The outreach through seminars has been good. We have excellent headquarters people who are dedicated and enjoy their work.

Coins Magazine: What about for Bowers and Merena Galleries?

Bowers: On the commercial side, I would like our firm to rededicate itself to service, quality, and value as we say in our ads and to deliver an increasing number of interesting and significant auction catalogues and price lists.

Coins Magazine: And for David Bowers the author and writer?

Bowers: I would like to do research in several areas. It's always been of interest to me to do a history of coin collecting in the United States. I have devoted chapters in some of my books to this, but still I think there is a lot to be said. In particular, our own time has not been covered in detail in any of the books I have written. In 1982, *Numismatic News* had vignettes of the 30 years since 1952. There were literally thousands of little events, many big events, and other occurrences that would be interesting to research. I would like to talk to the people who have been there. I myself participated in many of these events, but still others have much to add. I think writing a history of collecting in America from the earliest days in the 19th century right up to the present time would be quite interesting.

I consider it important to record what some of the people were and are like. I had the privilege of knowing B. Max Mehl. Now he is a legend. Jim Ruddy, who was my partner until he left the business in 1977, has become a legend in his own right. He attended one of our recent auctions as a guest, and several people, particularly young numismatists, came up to him and requested his autograph. It was certainly flattering to Jim.

I think some of these happenings and stories would be interesting to put in book form and to discuss in detail. It would be a tragedy to have all of this disappear. B. Max Mehl, when he died in 1957, took with him thousands of stories and anecdotes which were never recorded.

Coins Magazine: I can appreciate what you are saying. Once such people are gone, so are the stories and when they played an important role, it is as you said, a tragedy to have the information disappear.

Bowers: Early in 1983 I revised my book, *High Profits from Rare Coin Investment,* nearly doubling it in size. I put a lot of material in it which is probably irrelevant, a lot of material that has to do with history—but I think it all points to the fact that coins are interesting. It could have been filled with numbers and charts and computer printouts, but it went from 180 pages to over 300, and it was done by adding additional *numismatic* material.

This is an investment book but I feel that the tail of investment has been wagging the numismatic dog. Investment is a fine thing, but perhaps there should be more emphasis on numismatics and that's why I changed the emphasis there.

Coins Magazine: So you are looking more at the historical or perhaps even numismatic nostalgia?

Bowers: I feel maybe some more writing will come in an additional book not yet planned about coins, their stories, and how interesting they are to collect. Coins really are the footprints of history.

Coins Magazine: Well there seems to be a lot of movement away from the investment oriented, how-to-get-rich article and back to the coins are fun area. Almost a return to the basics that we all followed in the 1950s.

Bowers: I think the term "investment" has become diluted. There are a number of people who have discovered that the way to sell coins today and to make money is to take a coin worth perhaps $100 and say "I predict that this coin will be worth $1,000 in 1993." Whether it will be is a matter of question, but there are many buyers who will jump at the chance to spend $100 believing the "expert" knows something the buyer doesn't. I think the investment aspect was overdone a few years ago. Such aspects as true rarity, art, history, romance, and so on are deserving of more attention than they have been getting.

Coins Magazine: Well, in the marketplace there seems to be a great emphasis on buyers making profits *this week* as opposed to the long term, and coins rarely work that way, or at least that's my experience.

Bowers: People will say, "Oh my gosh, a Proof nickel three-cent piece was worth $3,000 in 1980, and today the same piece brings $1,500. What a terrible thing! It's really crashed; it's in the pits, I don't want to touch one." Well, that's all well and fine, but you have to remember that 10 years or so ago the coin was probably worth $150. So, if you look at it in that way, you can say if you had bought one in 1973 for $150 and sold it today for $1,500 you would have multiplied your investment by 10 times, and that's pretty good! You have to remove the passion of the boom marketplace and look at it with a more measured, distant view. In some 30 years of collecting and dealing I have seen a few people make short-term profits, but without exception, to my knowledge, anyone who has put together a high-quality collection of coins with care and discrimination, and who has held them for five years or more, has shown a very attractive overall profit upon their sale! This is a very remarkable statement, and it is one which can be matched in few if any other investment field known to me.

Coins Magazine: Well there are a lot of people who just get fun from collecting, and perhaps they have been ignored somewhat in the rush for big profits.

Bowers: I think if I were on the staff of *Numismatic News* it would be fun to do an article on the sale of the John Doe Collection and say things like, "A group of Very Fine average circulated Lincoln cents brought $3 and they sold to Bill Smith in the 10th grade at Peoria High School."

Coins Magazine: Well perhaps now that we've been reminded that coins go up and down we can get back to education and information and away from speculation.

Bowers: I didn't recommend that anyone rush out and send me a check to buy coins. I do feel, however, that they should rush out and send *you* a check and get a subscription to *Coins Magazine,* and *Numismatic News* first, not to overlook several other excellent publications currently available. I would also be happy to act as a sponsor to anyone who wants to join the ANA. If any of your readers want to do that, just have them contact me and I will send an application blank.

Coins Magazine: Are you still pretty optimistic about the hobby?

Bowers: Oh yes, I think it is good to count one's blessings. Every hobby has its problems. However, in coins and in the American Numismatic Association we have many favorable situations. We have a vital and active organization, lots of fine publications, good communications, and so many different things which benefit collectors and dealers alike. Perhaps someone should construct a philosphical balance sheet once in a while. Everyone is quick to throw a dart when they don't like something that happens, but it is important to remember that there are many plusses too.

Coins Magazine: Do you see a fairly bright future?

Bowers: I have spent my life in coins and have no plans to change. I enjoy it a lot and I have received many benefits. I have endeavored to give some of these benefits back to writing books (which often do not represent a profitable situation), giving talks, serving as an upaid instructor to many seminars, writing columns, and the like. I cannot envision a nicer profession to have been a part of, and I don't mean just from the business point of view, I mean the people and the experiences. It has been really marvelous!

Coins Magazine: If the first 30 years of Q. David Bowers are any indication, we will hear a great deal more from him. For his clients, his readers, and the hobby in general, that is some of the best news of the year!

Some Aspects of Coin Investment

By Q. David Bowers *1972*

The following article is adapted from an article which I wrote for The Forecaster, *an investment newsletter. The article covers a range of often-asked questions and, hopefully, will be of interest to our* Rare Coin Review *readers. (Later, some of this information was incorporated into the writer's book,* High Profits from Rare Coin Investment.

Introduction

It has been quite some time since I have written an article for *The Forecaster.* This has not been due to lack of intention, but, rather, has been due to lack of available time. 1971 was the busiest year I have ever experienced in the nearly two decades (since 1953) I have been in the rare coin business. To say that such strength occurred at a time when the international situation was uncertain at best and in which the domestic monetary situation was in more trouble than it had been for many years, is quite interesting—and shows the basic strength of the coin market.

Rather than concentrate this article upon a few coins, I will answer some questions that James F. Ruddy and I are often asked by investors and potential investors. It is my hope that you will find some of these answers valuable as guidelines for your own investment interests and requirements.

Over the years Jim Ruddy and I have advised many collectors. I use the term *collector* rather than *investor* for I have found that nearly every successful coin investor has had at least a modicum of collecting interest. The romantic and historical appeals of numismatics combined with a pride of ownership are hard to overlook—and this factor separates coin investment from holding, say, a printed stock certificate or a savings account deposit receipt.

I might further say that our customers have been quite successful in the past. In the course of buying countless collections over the years Jim Ruddy and I have never had a seller who has informed us of experiencing a loss when United States coins were held as a long-term investment—say for five to 10 years or more. On the other hand, experiences of remarkable profits are quite common. We have purchased many coins back from clients at five to 10 times or more the prices they paid us when they acquired the coins in the 1950s or early 1960s. Indeed, the rare coin market has done fantastically well for those who have approached coin collecting and investment from a serious and well-reasoned viewpoint.

Quantity as a Factor

What factor does quantity play in coin investment? Is it better to have a $5,000 coin, or 10 $500 coins, or a large number of 50-cent coins?

There is no definite answer to this. A charting of values over the years reveals that great rarities which cost thousands of dollars each in the late 1950s have soared in value since then—as have pieces which cost just a few dollars back then. My answer to these questions is that it depends upon the amount of money you want to invest. If you want to invest $100 per month in your coin collection-investment then it would be foolish to save up for two years and own just one coin—a coin costing $2,400. Rather, you would undoubtedly experience more satisfaction of ownership if you were to have a nice portfolio of coins in the $10 to $100 range per item. Even the inclusion of a few items priced at several hundred dollars would not be out of line.

Coin Price and Marketability

Does the price of a coin affect its marketability?

The price of a coin is usually based upon the rarity of a coin and the demand for it. As the coin market is an active one, prices have equated themselves with supply and demand. Thus an 1838-O half dollar, an Uncirculated specimen of which is now listed at $14,000 in the *Guide Book of United States Coins,* is an extremely salable item for there are only a few specimens known to exist (fewer than 20 coins in all) of this rarity. Of course, the number of people desiring 1838-O half dollars are few in number also—but the number of collectors desiring one of these, even taking the price into consideration, has always been more than the available supply—so despite the ups and downs of certain segments of the coin market, the 1838-O has always been a "blue chip." An 1838-O was worth more in 1960 than it was in 1950, was worth more in 1970 than in 1960, and will undoubtedly be worth still more in 1980. I would be absolutely delighted to write out a check for $14,000 for a Brilliant Uncirculated example today—knowing full well that a nice profit could be made on it. My problem wouldn't be selling it; it would be trying to find one to sell!

Prime American rarities—the 1838-O half dollar, 1876-CC 20-cent piece, and 1894-S dime are examples—can be likened perhaps to Rembrandt paintings in the art field. They are expensive to be sure, but when a choice one comes on the market it creates a lot of excitement—and invariably a new price record is set.

Rare Coins vs. Common Coins

The average investor, however, will not have an opportunity to own an 1838-O half dollar. If one cannot own great rarities, then should he concentrate on owning just common coins—coins of low value?

In answer to the preceding question I repeat the old aphorism: A common coin that is common today will always be common. A common coin by definition is common—and is not rare. To buy common coins in the hope that they will magically become rare is a futile effort.

The best path then, obviously, is to purchase coins that have a present scarcity—either realized or unrealized in the marketplace. A year or two ago I wrote an article for *The Forecaster* in which I recommended the purchase of common date Barber half dollars; coins which were in good demand yet which were not plentiful. Values have risen sharply since that time, and anyone who purchased common date Barber half dollars in Uncirculated or Proof condition would have a nice profit to show for it today. The other day Bowers and Ruddy Galleries, Inc. adververtised some common date (the term "common" is relative here: we refer to Barber halves dated 1892-1912 and excluding the more expensive 1913-1915 issues) Proof Barber half dollars at $179 each—and we sold out instantly. These same coins catalogue as low as $140 today. So, our firm now finds itself in the position of paying over catalogue value to buy more pieces for stock.

Are these Barber half dollars a good investment now at $179?

Before I answer that question I will mention (in case someone wonders) that we have but a solitary common date Proof in stock at the moment (when this article was originally written for *The Forecaster*). Proof Barber half dollars (I mention Proof Barber half dollars merely as an example of one of many similar situations) are of proven rarity. Look at the Proof mintages of the so-called "common dates" from 1892 through 1912 inclusive. Only one date, 1892, has a mintage of more than 1,000 pieces; it has a mintage of 1,245 specimens. More likely the average piece has a mintage of somewhere in the 700 to 900 range. Here is a coin of *proven rarity*. By buying such a coin you are buying a blue chip.

Let's consider what this means: Proof Barber half dollars are of known rarity. Taking the year 1902 as an example, we see that 777 were minted. Probably 400 to 500 survive today, some of which are impaired by scratches and other defects. To say that 300 to 400 really nice Proofs exist is probably on target.

What about the price history of the coin?

If you purchased one of these any time within my memory (since 1953) you would have shown a profit by holding it for a few years and then selling it. Such pieces are immune to speculative effects. I have never heard of anyone hoarding 1902 Proof half dollars and doubt if many, if any, people have more than just one or two specimens. So there is no risk in investing, say, $180 or so in a nice Proof example and then suddenly finding that a hoard of several thousand pieces has been dumped on the market. Indeed, not that many ever existed in the first place. So, such an investment is immune from hoarding considerations.

What about the buying and selling profit margin?

Being a choice early United States coin in limited supply, the 1902 Proof Barber half dollar is in strong demand by dealers. I would happily pay $150 for a choice specimen—and possibly others would pay even more. I don't know. However, this does illustrate that the margin between the buying and selling price of such a choice piece is relatively modest.

Price Appreciation

Will the 1902 Proof half dollar, a coin which might cost $180 today, be a good investment for the future? After all, quite a bit of profit has already been made by others on the coin, by people who might have bought them when they were cheaper 10 years ago.

This is a logical question and one which is reasonable to ask. Perhaps the quickest answer would be to say that 10 years ago isn't now, and we must concern ourselves with the present—not the past. Valuable objects in any field—Rembrandt paintings, IBM stock certificates, etc.—have a history of price appreciation over the years. Waiting to buy them for the prices of 10 or 20 years ago is not realistic. So long as the trend of our economy is inflationary, prices seem to be headed for an ever-upward spiral. Coins have shared in this spiral and will continue to do so. Today the number of available 1902 Proof half dollars, combined with the number of people desiring them, have set the price at approximately $180, or possibly a few dollars more. Again we remind our readers that we have picked the 1902 Proof half dollar merely as an example. The reasoning applies to many coins in the United States series.

What will make the price go up further?

Of course this is basic economics, but we might mention that if the number of collectors increases then the demand will also increase.

Will the number of collectors increase?

This seems quite likely. The average citizen is working an ever-shorter week. More and more time is being directed toward leisure activities. Coin collecting is an ideal leisure activity. It can be conducted in private, does not require a large amount of space (a fine collection can be assembled by an apartment dweller, for instance), can be easily stored, and so on. As leisure time activities increase, coin collecting will surely increase also. More collectors will bring a greater demand.

Then there is the consideration of monetary inflation. If the dollar continues to depreciate then the thought of paying $180 for a coin will not seem as important. It wasn't that long ago that $180 would have been a "big price" for an Uncirculated 1796 quarter (a coin which now catalogues $5,750). In fact, I remember Aubrey Bebee, the Omaha dealer, showing me a 1796 BU quarter with a prooflike surface at the American Numismatic Association convention in 1955, and stating he had paid $200 for it. This was a "staggering price" at the time. Today it seems absurdly cheap! I don't mean to suggest or imply that a 1902 Proof half dollar will be worth $5,750 in as many years, for I don't think it will. On the other hand, it would not be out of the question for it to be worth a nice profit over today's price in the foreseeable future.

Summing up all of the above in concise terms, my advice to you is: "Buy coins of proven scarcity and value." These coins have done well in the past and should do well in the future.

Coin Grading

What about coin grading? Is it better to buy, for instance, 10 coins in "Good" condition or one coin in "Uncirculated" condition?

From an investment viewpoint all grades of coins have done well. Scarce coins in lower grades such as Good and Very Good have been excellent investments over the years, as have been Uncirculated and Proof pieces. However, Uncirculated and Proof pieces and other higher-grade issues have been in stronger demand and are scarcer than lower-grade pieces, so the dealer's margin of profit is less.

Taking a miscellaneous example, let us consider an Uncirculated coin which sells for $50. A dealer might well pay $40 to buy the coin for stock, giving him a profit of 20%. It is the higher-grade pieces that turn over the fastest in a dealer's stock, so he is willing to take a smaller margin of profit for them. On some closely traded high-grade items the margin between buying and selling may only be 5% to 10%.

On the other hand, if the dealer were to have 10 coins in stock, all the same variety, that were priced at $5 each, he may only want to pay $2 to $3 per coin (for a total of $20 to $30 for the lot) to buy such pieces for stock, as more handling is involved. I am assuming that the latter coins are in circulated grades. From an investment viewpoint I would rather have on Uncirculated $50 coin than 10 well-worn $5 coins. There is no strict "right" or "wrong" to this—it is more a matter of personal preference. It has been said by others that collectors and investors should "buy the best grade they can afford." Generally I agree with this advice.

"Processed" Coins

In recent years an insidious evil has entered the coin market: the deliberate "processing" of lower-grade coins and selling them falsely as "Uncirculated" and "Proof." When you purchase coins for investment you are faced with the uncertainty of what they will do in the future. Will they go up in value or won't they? Of course, we both hope they will. Why add to this the uncertainty of whether your coins are in the right condition? Instead, be very sure you are getting the condition you expect. In a recent issue of *Numismatic News* (April 18, 1972) Virgil Hancock related the story of an "investment advisor" who made a fantastic mark-up by selling wrongly graded coins to unknowing buyers. One of many examples cited was, in Mr. Hancock's words: "a 1799/8 13-Stars silver dollar 'Choice Uncirculated,' which is only a nice Extremely Fine worth $340, but sold to the victim for $1,200."

There is a lot of money to be made by selling processed and treated coins. Such operations prey on the bargain seeker. An Extremely Fine large cent of 1853, a coin worth in the $15 to $20 range, "processed" and sold as a "Uncirculated" for $40 (much less than the going price for true Uncirculated) is no bargain at $40. In fact, you are overpaying by a factor of two to three times! And yet it is continually amazing how many collectors, particularly beginning ones, will fall into such a trap. While dealers are sometimes reluctant to discuss "processed" coins, if you want a discussion on the subject talk to the representatives of any numismatic publication the next time you are at a convention. This is a big problem, and the publications realize it. I might mention that ethical dealers do not "process" coins. Your best protection is to *buy from an ethical dealer.* Bear in mind also that a large advertising budget has little to do with a dealer's experience. Indeed, some of the most successful dealers enjoy a fantastically large business by modestly circulating price lists and auction catalogues to a selected number of proven clients who have been with them over the years. They do not need a continuing stream of new faces.

Do not overlook the grading problem. This is a big problem, as we have noted. It costs no more, in fact it is infinitely cheaper in the long run (when the time comes to sell your coins), to buy properly graded coins. Otherwise you are just kidding yourself and impairing the chances for the success of your investment. I don't mean to sound negative in an article which perhaps should be 100% positive, but I do want to clarify this danger and make you aware of it. In many years of buying collections I have seen large sums of money lost by collectors who were hoodwinked in this regard. "There is no Santa Claus in numismatics," Lee Hewitt (former owner of *The Numismatic Scrapbook Magazine*) has written. This is one of my favorite quotations—so I mention it here again.

Aspects of Timing

How long should coins be held?

This depends, of course, on your investment objectives. Generally speaking Jim Ruddy and I usually recommend a period of five to 10 years. At least this has worked out well in the past. If you purchase a rare coin this month and sell it six months from now all you are doing is making a profit for the dealer. You may not be able to realize the total amount paid. For instance, if you buy a $50 coin for which a dealer has paid $40, hold it for six months and it becomes worth, say, $53, then a dealer may want to pay $43 for it. This still represents a $7 loss for you. On the other hand, if the coin is worth, say, $300 10 years from now, selling it for $225 to $260 will make an attractive profit for you.

In my opinion, rare coins should be considered as a long-term investment, not as a short-term one. I have seen many fabulous profits made by collectors who have assembled fine groupings of coins over a period of years and then sold them upon their retirement. It is not at all unusual for us to pay $10,000 to $25,000 for a collection which originally cost the owner one-fifth or one-10th of that sum. I might add that this is a very gratifying aspect of our business. Whenever I look through old catalogues that Jim Ruddy and I prepared in the 1950s, I know the people who ordered from these catalogues can be nothing less than delighted if they still have the coins today. The coin market has done fabulously well for those who have bought choice coins and held on to them.

Some Guidelines

In a few sentences can you give me some guidelines for successfully investing for the future?

While the future is never certain, I would recommend the following—based upon what has done well for others: Buy choice condition coins of proven scarcity or rarity. Thus you are assured of purchasing coins that are in demand now and will be in demand in the future. Be very careful about grading and make your purchases from an established reputable firm. Be prepared to hold your coins as a long-term investment—say for five to 10 years or more.

Anyone who followed the above advice and ordered the selected coins across the board from one of Jim Ruddy's and my catalogues of 10 years ago would have seen his investment multiply in value several times in the interim. I don't mean increasing in value just if certain selected pieces were purchased—I am speaking of choice and rare United States coins in general as offered at that time. I have every reason to believe that with the current inflationary trends and the growth of coin collecting that choice and rare coins, purchased today, will likewise prove to be an attractive investment 10 years from now in 1982.

Our Poet Laureate

By Harvey Roehl *1983*

Harvey Roehl, the Vestal, New York reader who enjoys both our catalogues and interesting variations of the English language, submitted the other day some limericks which he wrote after reading a copy of our book, *U.S. Gold Coins: An Illustrated History* as well as other printed items we've issued.

Harvey was evidently intrigued by the story of B. Max Mehl, the late Fort Worth, Texas dealer who in his day sold some of the finest properties to ever cross the auction block:

A Texas promoter, B. Max,
Of coins had enormous big stax.
He worked through the mails
To produce some big sales
And hauled home his profits in sax!

We didn't tell Harvey that our *U.S. Gold Coins: An Illustrated History* book has sold so well that we are down to just a couple hundred remaining copies. In fact, we will have to produce a new edition soon, probably preceded by a few months when the book will be out of print. So, Harvey wished us luck with its sales:

Dave thought it time people were told
About our geat coinage in gold.
Since much moola it took
To produce this thick book
He hopes that more copies are sold.

Actually, once the new edition is printed, we certainly can use additional sales, for the book costs nearly as much to print as we are selling it for!

The ''affair'' between President Theodore Roosevelt and noted sculptor Saint-Gaudens, whereby Roosevelt, despite great opposition at the Mint, enlisted the artist (an outsider) to design a coin, inspired the two following verses:

Said Teddy, "Because I've got clout
The design of this coin I farmed out.
Those chaps at the Mint
Should get the hint
Of the worth of their work, I have doubt."

We think it a process quite quaint
To add to one's name the word 'Saint'.
We suspect it's done wholly
To impart an air, holy,
To those who do sculpture, or paint.

The Pleasures of Forming a Type Set

By Q. David Bowers *1977*

What to Collect

"What should I collect?" This is a question asked by many collectors. And, it is a question which is imponderable; a question for which there is no precise answer.

Many considerations enter into the final decision of what to collect. How much money is needed? Are the coins easily available? Will the collection be stimulating and interesting to me? What about its investment potential or lack of it? These are but a few considerations.

When I first began my numismatic interest in the early 1950s the question wasn't that much of a question. What to collect? The answer for most collectors was Everything!

Everything? Yes, in those days costs were low and a collector with modest means could reasonably hope to build complete or nearly complete sets of Indian cents, Lincoln cents, Shield, Liberty, and Buffalo nickels, Barber and Mercury dimes, Barber, Liberty Standing, and Washington quarters, and so on down the line. Date and mintmark collecting was extremely popular. Because of this, great pressure was put on scarce or *key* dates, with the result items such as the 1909-S V.D.B. Lincoln cent, 1885 Liberty nickel, 1916-D Mercury dime, and 1916 Liberty Standing quarter became among the most prized items in modern American numismatics. In fact, at one time it was our company's policy not to advertise 1909-S V.D.B. cents—for we would get too many telephone calls and orders for them, and prospective buyers would overlook the rest of our listings!

Also contributing to the date and mintmark collecting syndrome was the fact many series could be started from circulation and pocket change. When I first began collecting it was theoretically possible to find nearly all 20th-century coins in circulation, including scarce and rare dates. I remember spending one afternoon at the Forty Fort (Pennsylvania) State Bank, where I was befriended by one of the tellers, sorting through bank rolls of circulated half dollars. In the space of two or three hours I formed a complete set of Liberty Walking half dollars from 1916 through 1947, with some duplicates of what today are regarded as scarce dates—the issues of 1921 and the 1938-D. The idea of finding "a treasure in your pocket" was irresistible, and no doubt this brought many people into the coin collecting field.

Today, in 1977, the situation is far different. Recently I went on a weekend holiday trip through California's Mother Lode country on Route 49, which meanders through such quaint and picturesque Gold Rush towns as Mokelumne Hill, Jackson, Coloma, Grass Valley, Angels' Camp, Sutter Creek, Placerville, and Nevada City. Then I visited Virginia City, Nevada, years ago the headquarters town of the fabled Comstock Lode. Following a day among the old Victorian buildings and silver mines, I continued to Harrah's Hotel at Lake Tahoe. Not being what you would call a heavy gambler, I spent an hour or two playing with nickel slot machines in this well-known Nevada casino-resort. When I returned to my room I had a couple hundred nickels. Out of idle curiosity I looked through them to see how many 1942 to 1945 "wartime" pieces I might find or whether there would be any scarcities such as 1939-D or 1950-D. Not only did I not find any scarce dates, there wasn't a single nickel in the group dated before 1960! My, how times have changed.

Likewise, prices have changed. In my early days as a coin dealer I used to sell Brilliant Uncirculated 1909-S V.D.B. cents for $20 each. And, this "high" price was for a *rare* date. Such issues as 1909-S, 1910-S, 1911-D, 1911-S, and so on were just a few dollars each. I remember having a whole cigar box full of Brilliant Uncirculated 1931-S cents and selling them for $2 each! Indian cents weren't expensive either. Proofs from 1879 to 1909 were $2 to $3 each and the rare 1877 was $75 to $90. A collector could literally afford to buy one of just about everything—and in Uncirculated or Proof condition—and this is precisely what many did.

Now we are in 1977, and not in 1953. Things are different. We have to live with today. While yesterday is fun to think about, the fact remains it doesn't make too much difference to you right now that I used to sell Brilliant Uncirculated 1909-S V.D.B. cents for $20 each—if they now cost several hundred dollars each. The facts of life are if you want to buy one now you should be prepared to pay about $350.

The Type Set of United States Coins

A practical alternative is the *type set*. Actually, rather than being an alternative, I consider a type set in many ways to be superior to a collection of dates and mintmarks. I will go into the reasons why. . . .

First of all, what is a type set? A type set is a collection containing one specimen each of various *major designs*. Take, for example, half dollars. The date and mintmark collector seeking to assemble a group of 20th-century half dollars would want one each of the Barber halves from the Philadelphia, Denver, New Orleans, and San Francisco mints, one each of all of the Liberty Walking pieces minted from 1916 to 1947 from each of the mints, one each of the Franklin half dollars from 1948 through 1963, and one each of the Kennedy halves minted from 1964 to date. The total cost for an Uncirculated set would run into tens of thousands of dollars. A select 1901-S half dollar would cost well over $1,000, and such Liberty Walking halves as 1919, 1919-D, 1919-S, 1920-D, 1920-S, 1921, and 1921-D would be the best part of $1,000 or more each, with the 1921-S costing in the $5,000 range. If one were to start the Barber half dollar series with the first year in the 20th century, 1901 (as a matter of possible interest, 1900 is not the first year of the 20th century but is the last year of the 19th century), there would be over 200 half dollars in the collection!

Let me contrast that with a type set. A type set of half dollars, one of each design, would contain not hundreds of coins but, rather, just *six* individual pieces of the following designs: (1) Barber type minted in the 20th century from 1901 to 1915, (2) Liberty Walking type 1916 to 1947, (3) Franklin type 1948 to 1963, (4) Kennedy type in silver 1964, (5) Kennedy type in clad composition 1965 to 1974, (6) 1776 to 1976 bicentennial design.

The total cost for a type set of 20th-century halves? Well, one of the advantages of a type set is that one does not have to include rare dates. A Choice Uncirculated Barber half dollar will be the major item in the set. A common date in really select condition will cost about $625. If you are not persnickety about condition and want an "average" Uncirculated piece, then you can find one in the $300 range. A Liberty Walking half dollar in Choice Uncirculated grade will set you back nearly $20. A Choice Brilliant Uncirculated Franklin half dollar will cost you all of $3. A silver Kennedy piece will run about $1.75, and if you're lucky you should be able to find a clad Kennedy half dollar and a bicentennial half dollar either in your pocket change or at your bank for face value. The total expenditure for a Choice Brilliant Uncirculated type set of 20th-century half dollars is about $650. In worn grades such as Good or Very Good (for the early issues), a type set would cost less than $10. Your own collecting interests and budget may dictate some happy medium between the two extremes. One thing is for certain: a complete 20th-century date and mintmark set is expensive, even for the most affluent buyer!

In addition to financial reason, there also seems to be a logical reason to form a type set. Take as an example the Barber half dollar series. This design commences in 1892 and runs through 1915. A complete collection contains 1892, 1892-O, 1892-S, 1893, 1893-O, 1893-S, 1894, 1894-O, 1895-S. . .the list could go on and on, but you get the idea. What is the difference between each of these coins? Well, it is the presence of a tiny mintmark on the reverse or a different digit in the date. The only mark of distinction, for example, between an 1892 Barber half dollar and an 1899 Barber half dollar is a single date numeral. If you have the budget and inclination you can, of course, spend tens of thousands of dollars and assemble a complete Uncirculated set from 1892 to 1915. But, you still will have just one basic design. Once you have looked at one coin, so to speak, you have looked at all of them!

A type set, it would seem to me, offers a much richer experience. Buy one Choice Uncirculated Barber half dollar and then take the rest of the money you would have spent on a string of dates and mintmarks and buy one each of the other half dollar design types—a Liberty Seated half dollar Without Motto, a Liberty Seated half with IN GOD WE TRUST, one With Arrows, an 1807 to 1836 Bust type half dollar, and so on. For the same amount of money the entire panorama of United States half dollar coinage designs, as well as designs of other denominations, will be at your fingertips.

Forming Your Type Set

A good way to start is to aspire to collect one of each copper, nickel, and silver coin design. Gold coins are a separate subject, and they also can be collected by types, but my discussion here will center on the denominations from half cent through trade dollar.

A nice thing about a type set is you can begin with a collection of 20th-century design types and then work backward into history from there. Your first collection, a 20th-century type set, will serve as a building block.

What does a 20th-century type set contain? Here are the major designs: (1) Indian cent, (2) 1909 V.D.B. Lincoln cent, (3) 1909 to 1958 type Lincoln cent, (4) 1943 steel cent, (5) 1944 to 1945 shell-case alloy cent, (6) 1959 to date Lincoln Memorial cent, (7) Liberty nickel, (8) 1913 Type I Buffalo nickel, (9) 1913 to 1938 Type II Buffalo nickel, (10) 1938 to date Jefferson nickel, (11) 1942 to 1945 "wartime" composition nickel, (12) Barber dime, (13) 1916 to 1945 Mercury dime, (14) 1946 to 1964 silver Roosevelt dime, (15) 1965 to date clad Roosevelt dime, (16) Barber quarter, (17) 1916 to 1917 Type I Liberty Standing quarter, (18) Type II Liberty Standing quarter, (19) 1932 to 1964 silver Washington quarter, (20) 1965 to 1974 clad Washington quarter, (21) 1776 to 1976 bicentennial quarter, (22) Barber half dollar, (23) Liberty Walking half dollar, (24) Franklin half dollar, (25) 1964 Kennedy silver half dollar, (26) 1965 to 1974 Kennedy clad half dollar, (27) 1776 to 1976 bicentennial half dollar, (28) Morgan silver dollar, (29) Peace silver dollar, (30) Eisenhower dollar in silver, (31) Eisenhower dollar in clad metal, (32) 1776 to 1976 Eisenhower dollar in silver, and (33) 1776 to 1976 Eisenhower dollar in clad metal. Of course, you can revise such a type set to suit your own personal preferences. Perhaps there are too many Eisenhower dollars for your liking and you would be happy with just two of them—one to illustrate the 1971 to 1974 design and the other to show the 1776 to 1976 bicentennial motif. Or, you might want to expand the set to include some minor sub-types.

The costs involved are fairly moderate. A complete collection of 20th-century type coins as given above, all denominations from the cent through the dollar and all in Choice Brilliant Uncirculated grade, would cost about $1,900 to $2,000 on today's market. If you want "average" Uncirculated grade rather than Choice Uncirculated, the price drops many hundreds of dollars.

A complete type set in Choice Brilliant Uncirculated grade with several of the more expensive pieces being in Extremely Fine grade (such Extremely Fine pieces being the Liberty nickel, three Barber silver coins, and two Liberty Standing quarters) would cost about $400—and still would represent a magnificent display. Of course, if the entire set were completed in lower grades such as Fine to Very Fine, then the price would drop even more dramatically. So, the completion of a 20th-century type set is a goal which most collectors can reasonably hope to achieve.

Don Suter, who manages Bowers and Ruddy Galleries' popular Collection/Investment Program, spent a few hours recently with a pocket calculator and came up with some figures on earlier type sets. He considered a complete 18th-, 19th-, and 20th-century United States type set beginning with the half cent and cent of 1793 and containing one of each major design in the denominations from half cents through trade dollars. While the formation of a Choice Brilliant Uncirculated type set would be a virtual impossibility (such a set has never been offered on the market due to the unavailability of certain earlier pieces in this grade), the *theoretical* value of such a set was computed by Don Suter to be $329,410.

Well, even if the pieces were available in Choice Brilliant Uncirculated grade, few of us would have $329,410 to spend on them! So, what should you do? Here is where planning comes in. For $30,572 you can have a first-class type set which contains the following grades: issues from 1793 through 1799 are Fine, issues from 1800 through 1859 are Extremely Fine, and issues from 1860 to 1977 are Choice Brilliant Uncirculated. Such a collection would be a blue-ribbon show winner and the pride of any numismatist!

Still, $30,572 isn't exactly pocket change. What if you have a more modest budget? For $11,656 Don Suter came up with still another type set. This set contains issues from 1793 through 1900 in Good to Fine grade and 20th-century coins in Extremely Fine to Choice Brilliant Uncirculated condition.

Checking over Don's data sheet I found that $8,210 of the $11,656 was comprised of several coins which sold at $400 or more. These were: 1793 half cent at $525, 1793 Chain cent at $800, 1793 Wreath cent at $475, 1796 to 1797 type dime at $460, 1796 quarter at $1,250, 1796 to 1797 type half dollar at $4,200, and 1794 to 1795 type silver dollar at $400. If one were to subtract these seven coins, one would have a type set illustrating virtually the entire panorama of coinage from the 1790s to the present time—nearly 90 different designs in all—for just $3,446!

Should one be embarrassed for not having a *complete* type collection? I don't think so. Completeness is an obsolete legacy left over from the days of date and mintmark collecting. Completeness does not have a counterpart in many other collecting fields. For example, what is a "complete art collection?" There is no such thing. Well, then, what about a "complete car collection?" No one has such a thing, and no one ever will. Even Bill Harrah, who has over 1,500 different cars, does not nor ever will have a complete collection or even come close to it. Does this mean all car collectors feel inadequate? Of course not! If you were a car collector you might have, for example, a 1931 Model A Ford coupe, a 1956 Lincoln Continental, a 1955 Thunderbird, and a 1927 Cadillac.

These cars would furnish you with lots of pleasure and enjoyment. You wouldn't feel inadequate because you didn't have a 1932 Model SJ dual-cowl Duesenberg phaeton (a classic automobile valued in the $200,000 range). Or, in a more modern vein, few collectors of Jim Beam whisky bottles have or even desire a complete collection. Rather, they collect the designs which interest them the most.

I am a collector of obsolete currency—broken bank notes and scrip of the 1790 to 1865 era—from the six New England states. There were probably more than 20,000 different varieties originally made. Right now I have about 800 to 900 different varieties. If my interest continues to be strong, and I hope it will, I would consider myself to have a truly *superb* collection if 10 years from now I have 3,000 to 4,000 different. I know I will never have a complete collection, and I don't lose any sleep at night worrying about it. Nor do I feel unfulfilled or inadequate. On the contrary, I *enjoy* my collection immensely—and have spent many happy noon hours here at Bowers and Ruddy Galleries poking through old notes of the Vermont Glass Factory, the Cochituate Bank of Boston, and other long-ago issuers.

The other day a dealer sent me a $2 note on the What Cheer Bank in Rhode Island. The name of the bank apparently intrigued him, or perhaps there was something about the note, I don't know, but in any event he asked over $200 for this one piece of currency. Well, I don't have a note from the What Cheer Bank, and if I am not able to find one later for $10 to $20 or so (which is what most other obsolete notes sell for, and many sell for just $3 to $9) I will probably do without one. I certainly can afford $200 for the What Cheer Bank note, but feel it isn't worth $200 to me.

The same rationale can be extended to building a type set of United States coins. You may feel spending several thousand dollars for a minimum-grade 1796 through 1797 half dollar simply isn't your cup of tea. If you can't afford it, the problem doesn't present itself. If you can afford it, perhaps you don't want to buy one anyway. Well, then, don't! Do without it. At least that is what I would do.

Other Aspects of a Type Set

Now comes the *pleasure* part of building a type set. As your collection grows, become *involved* with the coins as you get them. Don't be a slave either to completeness or condition. Which brings up another point: buy whatever condition you are *comfortable* with. I am of a rather sentimental turn of mind and always like coins with stories. A worn coin always has more potential for this than does an Uncirculated one.

Take, for example, a Flying Eagle cent of the 1856 to 1858 design. A Choice Brilliant Uncirculated one will cost you in the $500 to $600 range. An average Uncirculated piece will cost a couple hundred dollars less. A worn piece in Good grade will cost less than $10. Close your eyes and try to think where a coin might have been. Chances are if the Choice Uncirculated coin could talk it wouldn't have very much to say. Perhaps it was in a bank vault from 1857 to 1912 and then has been in six different coin collections since that time.

But, what a story the worn one could tell! It spent dozens of years in circulation and experienced many, many things. Undoubtedly it was owned and touched by thousands of different people—a little girl buying a piece of candy with it shortly after it was minted in 1858, a miner buying a breakfast roll with it in Calaveras County, California, in 1866, a teenager using it as part of a streetcar fare in Boston in 1872, a sailor dropping it into a penny-operated scale in Coney Island in 1897, a bartender taking it across the counter in a Boulder, Colorado tavern in 1899, and so on—you get the idea. How fascinating it is!

From a more numismatic viewpoint, the formation of a type set enables you to become familiar on a first-hand basis with many, many different numismatic series. You'll own an 1883 Liberty nickel Without CENTS on the reverse—a coin which represented a design error and about which a several-page story could be written (it was involved in a number of minor frauds at the time of issue); you'll own a Morgan silver dollar to remind you of the huge 1878 Bland-Allison boondoggle and the wild and woolly days of silver mining in the West; you'll own an 1875 20-cent piece which is the size of a quarter and which was so unpopular with the public that the denomination was discontinued a few years later; you will own a two-cent piece from the 1860s; you'll own a trade dollar from the 1870s which undoubtedly has been to China and back; you'll own a silver dollar, perhaps dated 1799, and will think of what an immense amount of purchasing power it represented in its day—enough to pay a hotel bill for a week! You will become familiar with many, many different designs. If you look beyond the coin you will think of John Reich, Christian Gobrecht, Gilroy Roberts, J.B. Longacre, Laura Gardin Fraser, George T. Morgan, and the other engravers and designers who made them. You'll find certain designs to be very appealing (among my personal favorites are the 1795 through 1797 half cents, the 1837 No-Stars half dime and dime, the Indian cent, and the Liberty Standing quarters) and others to be downright ugly (I find it difficult to become excited about the artistic merits of an Eisenhower dollar). In your album you'll have the entire panorama of American coinage history from the opening of the Philadelphia Mint in the 1790s right down to the present day.

One nice thing about a type set is that you can customize it to suit your own likes and dislikes. You can collect the pieces you want and the grades you want. You might choose to spice up your type set—the cost really isn't that expensive—by salting and peppering it with a few out-of-the-way pieces. For example, in the Morgan dollar slot, rather than putting in a common Philadelphia Mint issue, you might want to include an 1877-CC so you will have a coin from that romantic mint in Nevada, near the famed Comstock Lode. The cost is modest. Or, in the Classic Head half cent series you may want to include that famous and unexplained die engraving error, the 12-Star 1828. Here, again, the price differential isn't great. Or, how about sprinkling some Denver, New Orleans, and San Francisco coins here and there—often at little or no extra cost. Don't be a slave to a formula or to *someone else's* ideas. Experiment! Innovate! Be different!

Read about each coin in your collection. How was it made? Why is the design what it is? What function did it play in commerce? Think about all of these things and you will become more *aware* of your collection—and the greater your awareness is, the greater your appreciation will be!

What about investment? When you spend a few hundred or several thousand dollars for a type set you are naturally concerned about the lasting value of your expenditure. If it's any comfort, I'll mention that type sets have been among the best investments in American numismatics. In my *High Profits from Rare Coin Investment* book I charted some of the dramatic increases of type coins. Specimens in Good, Very Good, and Fine grades have appreciated attractively, as have examples in Uncirculated and Proof preservation. It's a fact—check for yourself by looking through old issues of *A Guide Book of United States Coins*—that a type set in basic Good grade, a low condition, has appreciated extremely attractively over the years—and has multiplied in value many times over. The results have been far, far more attractive than those possible by buying a representative group of stocks, average real estate, and the like. In fact, a type set in Good grade has been nothing less than a super-spectacular investment! So, don't pooh-pooh a low-grade coin!

"What should I collect?" My answer to this: Form a type set! The formation of a type set will be interesting, challenging, and potentially financially rewarding. And, who knows, perhaps it will lead you into some specialty. Along the way you might discover that early large cents are indeed intriguing or that half dimes offer a special allure. Later, you might want to form a date collection of these—and when you do so, your appreciation of a specialized collection will be heightened by the general and broad overall view of American numismatics. What a wonderful collecting experience and education you have received by putting together your type set.

Attractive albums for holding your type set are available by mail from us or from your local dealer. And, you can get started at low cost right away—by gathering current coins at face value!

Before appearing in the Rare Coin Review, *this article was earlier part of the writer's "Numismatic in Depth Study" column in* Coin World.

Tom Becker Discusses Coin Collecting

By Tom Becker *1984*

Tom Becker, senior numismatist at Bowers and Merena Galleries, gives some views concerning the coin collecting scene.

How should I begin a coin collection? Which coins do you think would be best for me? How can I best enjoy the hobby side of coins and still hope to receive a good return on my investment? These are just a few examples of the kinds of questions I am asked nearly every day, and each is certainly deserving of an answer.

Rather than begin a complicated discussion covering every possible point of view, it would seem most productive if I simply related some of my personal preferences and experiences. Asking for advice is a lot like going to a doctor: it is always reassuring to know your prescription is for the same medicine the doctor has taken himself.

One of the primary reasons coin collecting has remained a popular and *alive* hobby is every collector and investor is free to pursue numismatics on his own terms and in his own way. What has worked very well for me and many others may not be right for you, but perhaps some of what I have to say could be modified to suit your own needs and interests.

Personally, I prefer concise and unusual coin collections. I like to select an interesting project which is within my means and can be completed within a reasonable amount of time. While I might dream of someday owning a complete set of MS-65 double eagles, I realize the possibility of completing such a set, even if I had the funds available, is a hopeless task. Furthermore, since I enjoy collecting *all* types of coins,

I have little interest in devoting all my time and extra income to one specialized collection.

Instead, I would rather build a complete collection of 1917 quarters, for example. This set contains only six coins; I can pick a grade range of coins that won't play havoc with my budget, and even as picky as I tend to be, I will be able to find just the right coins if I am patient. Should I then desire to acquire more Standing Liberty quarters, the set I already have can be easily expanded. If I choose to move on to another area of interest, then the collection I have built will remain intact as an important part of a larger assortment of coins. In the future, should I decide to part with my quarter set, I'll have something to sell that's both popular and interesting to a large number of potential buyers.

I have always been fond of Lincoln cents, yet the prospect of building a complete set holds little interest to me. There are simply too many coins to make it a comfortable project. Should I just forget Lincoln cents, even though I have a real interest in the coins? No, I would rather pick just my favorite issues, the San Francisco Mint coins, and build a complete set of these. My set will contain lots of low-mintage coins, including many of the key dates found in a complete set. Since I've trimmed the project down to a reasonable size, I can collect the coins I like the most in a higher grade and work towards building a nicely matched set. When I am finished I will have a beautiful little "penny" set containing most of the goodies and none of the fillers. Since I have built several of these sets in the past, I know that should I wish to sell my set, I will have no trouble at all finding an eager buyer.

Before starting to build another collection of coins, I try to remember the advice about writing I was once given by an English professor. His warning was should I be assigned a 500-word essay and I picked a topic that was too broad, then chances were very good whatever I had to say would be both incomplete and uninteresting. The same is very true in the field of numismatics. When viewed as a whole, the hobby can appear to offer a bewildering array of alternatives. It is far better to investigate and then dissect a series; pick out an interesting segment, and begin with a *workable* project. If I have done my homework, the new collection will be reasonably complete and interesting, both to me and to others.

Large cents have always been a favorite series of mine. But the coins are only appealing in the higher grade. My personal preference is for nice, glossy tan coins in Choice AU-55 or MS-60 condition. Because of this interest in choice coins, I began my large cent collection with the 1837 to 1857 years. This group of coins is available in the grades I like best. There are no "stopper" rarities in the series, and I realize the set would not take me a lifetime to complete. When I began building the set I found, with the exception of a few type collectors, I had little competition in the marketplace. Once I had the set completed I was presented with several pleasant options. I could expand the set backwards to include the earlier dates, or find many interesting varieties of the *Coronet* series listed in the *Guide Book*. As it turned out, I did both. My first "short" set of large cents was completed when I was 15 years old. While many years have passed since then, remembering all the fun I had building the set makes me want to begin another one tomorrow.

Building small, personalized collections has also allowed me the luxury of working on several projects at the same time. The purpose of being a collector is to collect. I enjoy the flexibility that building a tidy little collection affords.

Since I have been working directly with collectors for many years, I have seen firsthand just how ingenious and creative some numismatists can be when deciding on a collection. One need spend only a few minutes in the exhibit room at a major convention to see how clever a collector can be. One award-winning exhibit I remember well was titled "Women and Their Coins." This exhibit was assembled by the wife of the local coin club president and featured examples of United States coins designed by women. How many women coin designers can you name? To find the answer, one only needs to examine the commemorative half dollar series. Many of these beautiful coins were designed by Gertrude K. Lathrop, Laura Gardin Fraser, and others. And, of course, Elizabeth Jones, presently chief engraver of the United States Mint, is well known for her 1982 Washington commemorative half dollar. The deeper you dig and the more you investigate, the more fun numismatics can be. "Women and coins" is just one of many suggestions.

Customizing a coin collection to suit your special interests is desirable even if you have a large amount of money to spend on coins. If you are on a very limited budget, then it becomes necessary.

For many years I worked closely with a collector who, as far as I could determine, had unlimited funds to spend on his hobby. When we first met he had been collecting for about six months and had accumulated a hodge-podge of gold coins. Like the hungry shopper who goes to the grocery store without a list, he had randomly selected his purchases with little thought or direction. As a result, he had become frustrated and confused. His coins ranged in condition from damaged Fine to Uncirculated. Somehow he even managed to buy two obvious counterfeits! I proposed that before giving up on coins he should come up with a plan and start over. I suggested, given a weekend to prepare it, I could come up with a list giving a hundred different ways to collect gold! We made plans to meet again the first part of the week and then adjourned our meeting.

On Monday morning we began discussing some of the options I had been thinking about. I noticed the gleam returning to the collector's eyes as we talked. While reviewing his previous purchases, I pointed out he had already completed one set. "How on earth did I manage that?" he asked. "Well," I said, "you have a complete set of Type I $1 gold pieces struck at the San Francisco Mint." I then held up his 1854-S gold dollar and, pointing out that since this was the only coin of this type struck in San Francisco, it constituted a "complete" set! I then suggested we expand his one-coin set by obtaining *all* of the San Francisco Mint gold dollars. Since the set contains only seven coins, the collection progressed rapidly. When he finally added the rare 1870-S, both of us were very pleased with what he had accomplished.

For a number of years I worked with my friend in the building of special sets. Sometimes, after hours of burying his nose in the *Guide Book,* my friend would come up with a new idea. Responding to the challenge, I would often make my own suggestions. Later, I was commissioned to sell his collection. Modesty aside, I have to say it was one of the finest numismatic properties I have ever handled—all of this from an inauspicious hodge-podge of a beginning!

I could continue to illustrate the point of this article with many other examples of productive and enjoyable ways to collect coins. I know first-hand dozens of collections which have been great fun as well as financially rewarding endeavors.

Just as I did with my friend who loved gold coins, each day I work with collectors in all parts of the country who are doing the same sort of thing. Though I am surrounded by coins and spend many hours each week as a professional numismatist, the collector instinct in me has always remained enthusiastic. Over the years I have developed a high regard for good coins and an even greater respect and admiration for the people who collect them.

If you are at loose ends so far as collecting objectives are concerned, why not consider forming some "special" sets such as I have suggested? The possibilities are literally endless.

More Than Just a Coin

By Q. David Bowers *1981*

When you see a 1908 Barber dime do you see just an obverse and reverse, or in your mind's eye is there more to it? While a coin is a coin is a coin, so to speak, each coin is more than just a coin—it is a tangible link with history.

If you have a copy of my *Adventures With Rare Coins* book, then you may remember that the entire theme of the book is art, history, and romance—the nostalgic background that each coin offers.

1908, to go to our earlier example, was a wonderfully romantic era in American history. The airplane, following the first powered flight by the Wright brothers at Kitty Hawk (North Carolina) in 1903, was coming into its own, with many daredevils learning how to become pilots. President Theodore Roosevelt livened up newspaper columns with colorful comments, goings-on at the White House, and so on. His daughter Alice, who far from being sedate and "proper," publicly stated that she would "like to go out with as many men as possible." At one point the president said he could do a good job of being president or do a good job of being Alice's father, but it was hard to do both!

Speaking of Teddy Roosevelt, the teddy bear, named after him, was a popular plaything. It turned out to be a powerful political emblem as well. When William Howard Taft, his successor, was campaigning later, his managers thought it would be nice to have something like a teddy bear, so they came up with "Billy Possum." But, somehow, Billy Possum never caught on.

In 1908 the nickelodeon theatre was rapidly becoming a national craze. Thousands of storefronts were converted to movie houses which charged five cents admission and which often offered a continuous show. You would pay a nickel (a Liberty nickel, of course!), go through the door, and stay as long as you wanted to—watching the dangerous adventures of train robbers, perhaps a trip to the Arctic, or something more mundane such as scenery in Hawaii or, closer to home, in Yellowstone Park.

The automobile was likewise becoming a sensation, and although they were hardly inexpensive (many models sold for several thousand dollars each), business was good enough that dozens of different manufacturers entered the field. Of course, Henry Ford was one of these, and within a few years his Model T became an American trademark.

While my purpose here is not to give a history lesson, I have always found it interesting to associate a particular coin with the era from which it came. While satisfaction can be obtained by acquiring as many coins as possible, in today's times in which you want to make a coin-buying dollar go as far as possible, you can "stretch" your budget a bit by appreciating more and more the coins you buy. Perhaps you cannot afford to buy 25 or 50 coins that you desire to own someday. But, if you can afford to buy one, two, or several, you can enhance your enjoyment of these by doing some research once you get them home. Some of the most fascinating research has to do with their historical background. What was going on in America back in 1883 when that Indian cent was made? Or, that 1898-S silver dollar—what was San Francisco like just before the turn of the century when that piece was minted there? That 1834 large cent—who was president then, what did he do, and what would the large cent buy when it was new?

Yes, a coin can be more than a coin if you take time to study not only the obvious surface features of the coin itself but also go beyond the coin to learn of its history, art, romance, and background. It can be an exciting trip!

Louis Eliasberg's Collecting Experiences

By Louis Eliasberg 1978

The following article is excerpted from the address, "Why, When, and How I Assembled the Most Complete Collection of United States Coins," given by the late Louis Eliasberg at the Evergreen House, Baltimore, Maryland, November 9, 1975.

The Eliasberg Collection, which in 1976-1977 was on view at a loan exhibition at the Philadelphia Mint, is generally acknowledged to be the most complete grouping of United States coin dates and mintmarks ever assembled. Included are several unique coins, including the only known examples of the 1873-CC dime Without Arrows and the 1870-S $3 gold piece. Eliasberg's collection has been the subject of many news features, including a double spread color article in Life *magazine in 1953.*

Eliasberg, a prominent Baltimore banker, found his coin collection enriched his life in many ways. As an investment it was superb. By his own calculations it returned a profit of over 119% PER YEAR on a long-term basis! In addition, it furnished countless hours of collecting and fraternal activity. He was a generous man and was always willing to share his knowledge and experience with others. Our last visit to see him was in 1975. His death in 1976 marked the end of a lifetime of numismatic accomplishment. Eliasberg felt our friends and clients would like to learn about his collecting interests, so shortly before he passed away he gave us permission to use the following information.

The Investment Results of Collecting

The profitability of collecting coins can be measured in part by my own experience, which I am sure is unique. Based on the recent appraisal of my collection at approximately $15-$18 million, subtracting our cost from the minimum appraisal of $15 million, and dividing it by the 41 years I have been collecting, I find that I have averaged a minimum return of over 119% per year on the original cost, plus subsequent acquisitions. In fact, its value has doubled in the last 18 months.

A recent issue of the *Wall Street Journal* tells of a man, age 26, who buried 66 pounds of gold in his back yard six years ago. "That is my savings account," he says, noting its value had risen from about $37,000 to $145,000.

In a recent coin publication Bowers and Ruddy Galleries stated that at their latest auction sale the prices of the United States coins made the latest edition of the *Guide Book of United States Coins* obsolete.

How it Started

In 1934 I was intrigued by the clause in President Roosevelt's gold proclamation of March 4, 1933 which excluded from its provisions collectors of rare and unusual gold coins held for numismatic purposes. Feeling a strong desire to own gold, I started collecting coins. I realized the only way I could legally acquire gold was by becoming a numismatist. So, in 1934, to the extent of my means, I started buying gold coins as close as I could to the bullion value. I maintained a small book in which I recorded the cost of gold coins I had purchased; the various dates, denominations, and mintmarks. Later I started collecting minor coins.

The price of gold had been fixed at $35 per ounce. A $20 gold piece had 9,675/10,000ths of an ounce of pure 24-carat gold, or an intrinsic value in 1934 of just $33.86. As late as 1941 I bought $20 gold pieces from dealers in the price range of $32.85 to $34.75.

My purchases of coins, mainly gold, went on from 1934 to 1941. In 1942 a coin dealer, Stack's in New York City, advised me that the John H. Clapp Collection was for sale by the executors of his estate. I went to Washington and acquired it intact. Soon it was home in Baltimore and merged with the rest of my holdings

My secretary made a list of all known coins not in the collection. It was our job to find these missing coins either in auction catalogues or by direct contact with dealers. We pursued every catalogue and submitted what I considered to be fair prices. One of two things happened: either we were successful in our bids or unsuccessful. If we were unsuccessful, we noted the price at which the coin sold, and the next time a similar coin came on the market we raised our bid to a price we felt would enable us to acquire it.

In 1947 I sold a number of duplicates for about $100,000, and then concentrated on finding the remaining rarities I needed. Acquisition of the rarities presented quite a problem, as such pieces were very seldom offered. I flew to Los Angeles, Texas, and other places searching for the coins I needed.

In October 1942 Stack's called me from New York and offered me a rare 1838-O half dollar for $1,400, and I bought it. In 1975 two similar pieces sold at public auction, one for $50,000 and the other for $43,000.

In July 1945 Abe Kosoff of the Numismatic Gallery came to Baltimore and offered me a very rare 1822 $5 gold piece for $14,000—and I bought it. There are only three specimens known, and two of these are in the Smithsonian Institution. I have the only one not in the hands of the government.

In January 1946 I acquired the 1854-S $5 gold piece through Stack's and the Numismatic Gallery for $5,500. In the same month I acquired the unique 1870-S $3 gold piece through Stack's and the Celina Coin Co. for $11,500. The 1870-S came earlier from the collection of Virgil Brand.

When the William C. Atwater Collection catalogue came out in July 1946, with dealer B. Max Mehl's name on it, the Stickney specimen of the 1804 silver dollar, the 1884 and 1885 trade dollars, and a dozen other pieces I needed were offered. I took a plane to Mehl's headquarters in Fort Worth, Texas, and placed my bids. I was very happy when my bids captured all of the rarities and most of the other coins I had bid on.

Subsequently, the Numismatic Gallery in California telephoned and advised me they had a 1913 Liberty Head nickel for sale at the now unbelievable price of $2,350. Recently, a similar coin was offered for $300,000.

In February 1949 I acquired the 1841 $2½ gold piece in Proof condition from the Numismatic Gallery. The acquisition of this coin enabled me to complete the gold segment of my collection. Now, I needed only a few silver coins for a truly complete collection.

When the Adolphe Menjou Collection catalogue came out in 1950 I flew to California to buy the 1853-O half dollar Without Arrows and Rays and the 1873-CC dime Without Arrows. I attempted to purchase in advance the dime at twice the price the auctioneers estimated it to be worth, but they declined. I then made the trip to California and bid many times what I thought the dime was worth, but I failed to buy it. I was so provoked that I did not attend the second session to bid for the 1853-O Without-Arrows half dollar. The next night my friend, Joe

Stack, bought the half dollar for me. Six months later, Sol Kaplan, the new owner of the 1873-CC Without-Arrows dime I wanted, telephoned me to ask how much I would pay for it. I said $4,000, and the piece was mine. That completed my collection of American silver coins by date and mintmark varieties.

A Collecting Predicament

Of the rare coins I do not have in my collection, one is the very scarce 1861 Confederate States of America original half dollar—which is *not* a coin made by the United States. Only four of these were made in 1861. One was acquired many years ago by the American Numismatic Society, leaving only three potentially available for private ownership. In my 40 years of collecting I have never seen one of these offered, nor do I know the present owners of any of the other three.

This reminds me of a very interesting story—one of many told at the round table in the dining room of the Players' Guild, the famous New York club. Of all the Players' folklore—and there must be a hundred legends—the one I like best is Dr. Hoffman's story about the silver piece and the round table. "Judge not that ye be not judged," says the Bible. And this little yarn emphasizes that teaching.

One winter's evening a group of dear friends was sitting at the round table, when one of the members reached into his pocket and brought forth a small box covered with red velvet.

As he sprung open the lid, a shining silver piece was revealed, laying on a satin cushion. Said this man, "Some of you know that for years I have had a habit of collecting rare coins. Well, today I found this, a very rare treasure. It is a Confederate half dollar. Only three or four of these are known to have been struck; they are almost priceless. This is the only one left on the market, and although I paid through the nose for it, I consider it to be a bargain. Would you like to see it?"

Lifting the shimmering silver piece from its cushion, he laid it in the palm of the man sitting next to him. While the precious object was passed from hand to hand, the owner was being asked a barrage of questions. "How did you find it? Where?"

Pleased with their interest, the collector harangued on and on about his hobby until more than a half hour had gone by. . .and all felt enough had been said about coins and coin collectors. Then suddenly the collector said, "By the way, could I have my silver piece back now?"

Well, they couldn't find the thing. There was a moment of confusion, each man turning to the other until it became clear that no one seemed to have it. Each man admitted he had held it in his hand and looked at it, and then, each man swore, he had passed it to someone else.

No one knew where it was. A hasty search was made—chairs pulled away, tablecloth turned over, everyone standing up. But,no! After 20 minutes of frantic searching there was no place else to look. The precious coin was gone. "Someone here must have taken it then," said the disturbed owner, his face turning red. An officer of the club, who was one of the party, stood up and said, "Of course, we should all be searched. I offer myself first."

He called to a waiter and ordered a screen around the table. Every other man at the table promptly expressed his willingness to be searched also—every man except one, and he was not a member of the club but a guest of one of the group. He declared, "I will not be searched. I haven't stolen your coin. Why should I be subjected to such an indignity?"

There was s storm of protest. Why shouldn't he be willing if all the others were? The rebel shook his head. He didn't care about what others did; he simply defied anyone to put a hand into his pocket. "Then," said the secretary, "there is but one thing left to do. A valuable piece of property is missing. No one must leave this table until the police arrive. I will ask the waiter to call the station house."

All this time, patiently standing nearby was a waiter—very old, very deaf, and very deferential. He had been standing close to the table for several minutes, hoping to be noticed. He had something on his mind. There was no pepper pot on one of the other tables. Could he borrow the one from this table?

He lifted the old-fashioned pepper pot on the lazy Susan in the center of the table, and a gasp came from all of those distracted men. THERE lay the missing coin!

The strain was over. And now the secretary turned to the rebel. He said, "Will you please tell me why you were so stubborn about being searched? What was the big idea?"

The obstinate guest gave a great sigh of relief and then answered, "No one would ever have believed me, especially because I kept quiet in the beginning, not to dampen the enthusiasm of our collector friend here. The fact is I also am a collector of coins and, furthermore, that coin of his is *not* the only coin on the market. There is a duplicate of it which I purchased two weeks ago in Paris. I thought *mine* was the only one. I brought it here to show you tonight. It is in my pocket now. But, 10 minutes ago who would have believed me?"

Some Other Comments

There were many outstanding collectors after the turn of the century. The wealthy Chicago brewer, Virgil Brand, left behind him a collection valued at over $2 million. John Garrett of Baltimore assembled one of the finest collections of coins, now valued at many millions of dollars. Other outstanding collectors were Matthew Stickney, William F. Dunham, William C. Atwater, King Farouk, Fred Boyd, Josiah K. Lilly, and Waldo Newcomer.

Speaking of Waldo Newcomer, this reminds me that in the late 1930s I sat next to his attorney. For conversation, not realizing this man was Newcomer's lawyer, I remarked that I supposed he thought I was foolish for collecting coins. His reply, on the contrary, was that Newcomer—then one of the richest men in the city of Baltimore—owned a very valuable coin collection, along with stock in the Atlantic Coast Line, the Louisville & Nashville Railroad, Safe Deposit & Trust Co., and other fine companies. When the Depression came, the most readily marketable asset he had was his coin collection, which he sold at that time.

You may be curious as to where these collectors acquired their coins. They were obtained primarily through dealers. The first dealer in America was Edward Cogan. It appears that he started in 1856 when a friend brought into his curiosity shop a fake 1792 Washington cent and persuaded Cogan to buy it for 25 cents. Cogan showed it to a customer as a curiosity and was offered 50 cents for it, and the coin changed hands again. Then Cogan started a coin collection and commenced selling off his duplicates. In that way his entry into the coin trade began.

Subsequently, there were Henry and S.H. Chapman, who handled most of the important sales until B. Max Mehl, of Fort Worth, Texas was recognized as the outstanding dealer in the 1930s. Currently there are hundreds of dealers, many of whom are well informed and financially strong. Outstanding among this group are Stack's, Bowers and Ruddy Galleries, Don Kagin, Abe Kosoff, Abner Kreisberg, Paramount, and others.

Many years ago my collection was displayed all the way from New Haven, Connecticut to Texas, and as far west as Chicago. My exhibitions included a display at the Smithsonian Institution from May through August of 1960, which is the only time a private collection has ever been exhibited there. Dr. Stefanelli, [late] curator of the Smithsonian, advised me that the number of visitors during this period was 500,000.

In conclusion, if you are a coin collector, I hope you will derive the same degree of pleasure and happiness, even if not so much profit, as I have in assembling *my* collection.

On the other hand, if you do not collect coins and are desirous of selecting a few for pleasure or profit, it would be my suggestion first that you subscribe to *Coin World* and buy a copy of *A Guide Book of United States Coins.* Furthermore, in making your purchases you should buy them through reputable dealers. . . .

Little did your editor know at that time he would in 1982 catalogue for public auction sale the Eliasberg Collection of United States Gold Coins, which ultimately realized $12.4 million.

Observations Concerning Coin Collecting

By Q. David Bowers *1984*

Collectors

The coin hobby—indeed, some have called it an *industry*—is fascinating. Like a chameleon it is always changing. Collecting is different now from what it was 10 years ago in 1974, much different from what it was 20 years ago in 1964, and to a decade even further back in time, 1954, it bears only a slight resemblance! Undoubtedly a decade from now, 1994, will see changes which would amaze us if we could know of them in advance!

Having been involved in numismatics for three decades plus one year (my gosh, doesn't that sound impressive!)—since 1953—I have had a front-row seat during the changing panorama of persons, places, things, and events. And, I must say, it has been a lot of fun!

I am prompted to make some observations concerning coins and those who collect them!

Like snowflakes, no two collectors are precisely alike. One numismatist may aspire to own a type set of 20th-century American gold coins in Extremely Fine to Uncirculated grade, another may concentrate on looking through Lincoln cents in circulation in the hope of finding a prized 1972 Doubled Die, and still another may bury his nose in Dr. William H. Sheldon's *Penny Whimsy* opus to try to decipher the die variety of a worn 1798 copper cent.

One thing (among many things) I have learned is that it takes all kinds of people with different interests to make up our hobby as we know it.

There are, to be sure, lots of *numismatists*—the serious or advanced collectors about whom much has been written. I guess everyone aspires to be a numismatist, at least in theory. And, it is the numismatist who, again at least in theory, furnishes the true value for coins we all aspire to own. A glittering Proof 1895 Morgan dollar is worth $30,000—rather than the meltdown or metallic value of $7 or so—because it is numismatically desirable. Remove this feature, and what you have is a bullion item worth only about $7, as noted.

Then there are the dilettantes—casual collectors who care not a whit about the technical aspects of coins, but rather, simply enjoy owning a few Kennedy halves or perhaps a small set of worn Morgan dollars purchased through a newspaper advertisement. Still others find nothing better than the comfort of having a couple of dozen krugerrands or double eagles squirreled away in a bank safe deposit box.

For purposes of studying the coin market it is interesting to divide coin buyers into several observable categories. Of course, these categories represent my own observations and opinions. Observations of others may well differ.

The Casual Collector

The first category represents the person casually interested in coins, a citizen who perhaps has other hobbies. In any event he (or she) does not have time to really get involved in the coin hobby. And yet to this person coins are interesting. He may save every "wheat" Lincoln cent encountered in change (amounting to very few pieces these days), or he may order Proof sets each year from the Mint, or he may have purchased one of the new and quite attractive 1982 George Washington commemorative half dollars. Or, he may have done all these things.

Similarly, the casual collector is a candidate to respond to newspaper advertisements offering perhaps a starter collection of coins (an Indian cent, a worn Buffalo nickel), or a run of Morgan dollars ("special release from a government hoard"), or a group of Franklin half dollars ("minted in the days when American coins were made of silver").

There are specific dealers who concentrate on selling to those interested in coins only on a casual basis. Often the prices charged are substantially more than one would have to pay to an advertiser in *Numismatic News, Coin World* or some other numismatic publication. But, apart from whatever profit the dealer may desire, there is another reason for this. Advertising in the *Wall Street Journal, The New York Times,* and other widely circulated general interest publications is exceedingly expensive. Also, such advertising is a shotgun approach.

When one places an advertisement in *Numismatic News* or *Coin*

World, one can target one's message to people who are proven coin buyers—or at least if they are not buyers, they are interested enough to subscribe. On the other hand, readers of a popular newspaper are, for the most part, not interested in coins. Perhaps only one in 10 readers is a potential buyer. Thus, it costs much, much more to sell coins this way. While there are abuses, unquestionably many dealers who advertise in popular publications are doing valuable missionary work. By this route many are introduced to our hobby.

Some casual collectors stay "casual" forever. Others develop into investors, advanced collectors, scholarly numismatists, or perhaps a combination of these categories.

Investors and Speculators

The second category is comprised of those who are interested in coins as a medium for investment or speculation. While the serious numismatist with an academic inclination may look askance at those who are interested in investment only, I feel investors and speculators are a very imporant and very essential part of the market. Clearly, a good percentage of the money being spent in our hobby today is spent in this category.

The typical investor likes "numbers" and desires figures, just as the typical stock market investor or speculator likes numbers printed in the financial columns of the daily newspaper. For the investor and speculator, the numerical grading system is a godsend. Such terms as "Very Fine," "Choice Brilliant Uncirculated," and so on are not precise enough. Using such terms is almost like describing a coin as "nice" or "not nice."

There is security in numbers—a saying which is quite valid in the mind of the investor. Thus, VF-30 and MS-65 are numbers which can be added, subtracted, divided, multiplied, and otherwise studied. Similarly, the advent of bid and ask prices—something virtually unknown until the 1960s (although veteran Cincinnati dealer Sol Kaplan took a chalkboard with him to coin shows during the 1950s and listed bid and ask prices for Proof sets)—was a blessing. There is comfort in knowing a given variety of Morgan silver dollars has a $500 bid price and a $575 ask price in a specific category. The fact is a coin with a $500 bid may be offered legitimately for $450 but is simply written off as being "overgraded." On the other hand, an offering of a properly graded coin at $700 may be dismissed as "overpriced" (although the advanced collector will know well it may be a good buy). However, for the typical investor, nothing but nothing must happen to impair the "security of numbers."

While many investors go on to become serious numismatists, many others—perhaps the majority—are simply interested in coins for the sake of investment alone. They want action, or as they say in Las Vegas or Atlantic City, "play."

"Mr. Bowers?"

"Yes."

"It is nice to talk to you. I am John Doe, and I am calling from XYZ Coin Company in Boston. Did you know the price of type coins has advanced 58% during the past year? Right now I can put you into some type coins. Would you like to talk about it?"

The preceding is the introduction to a sales talk I received a few weeks ago (the name of the caller and the company have been changed) from someone who was sitting at a bank of telephones and had a list of numbers to call. Upon learning I was a rare coin dealer, he quickly excused himself to go on to the next number!

The investor is a fickle buyer. Four years ago, when the market for silver and gold was very strong, this type of buyer could not spend money fast enough! Savings accounts were cashed in, stocks were sold, loans were taken out—in order to jump on the bandwagon to buy MS-65 Morgan dollars, or Proof gold coins, or whatever. It didn't seem to matter, but it had to be in MS-65 or Proof-65 condition, for that is what various investment advisors recommended.

The investor has supported an entire group of coin sellers. The editors of newsletters catering to investors have become demigods, and their word is gospel. Beautifully prepared brochures, seminars held in convention centers, and even television presentations are part of the sales efforts. While attending a recent convention I had the TV set on in my hotel room. I was treated to a presentation by an investment-oriented "rare coin dealer" who was selling double eagles. Financial charts were in the background, a computer console was in the offing, and a distinguished-looking gentleman with a professonial demeanor solemnly stated his firm was one of America's largest and most prominent rare coin dealers and had expertise second to none. I paused to reflect that the person speaking was unknown to me, and, further, I could not recall having seen either him or his firm at any major conventions, auction sales, or other places where numismatists gather.

Although sales figures are not available, I would guess quite a few hundred of millions of dollars each year are spent by coin investors.

And yet such coin investors are quite frightened. They really don't know what to buy on their own. They follow as much advice as they can get—trying to move from one "hot" area to another. The typical investor cannot think for himself and, apart from studying bid and ask prices or recommendations, doesn't really know what to do. Auctions, a source of coins for advanced numismatists and collectors, are often frightening to the investor. If a coin goes too cheaply "something must be wrong with it." On the other hand, if it goes too high, "perhaps I paid too much."

The investor is an integral part of our hobby, and most large firms have at least a foot in the investment door. I have yet to meet any leading dealer—even the most numismatically inclined of them—who is not interested in and who does not respect the buying power of the investor. And, many investors go on to become advanced collectors and serious numismatists. What better way is there to learn all about forming a date and mintmark set of Morgan dollars than by buying an "investment roll" of 20 MS-60 pieces of mixed dates?

The overwhelming purchasing power of coin investors has resulted in sharp cyclical effects in the marketplace. Investors tend to swarm. They come all at once, then they go away just as quickly, leaving only a few behind. Hence, dealers in the coin investment market have difficulty planning requirements for personnel, office space, and overhead. One hundred people might be needed in one month, and then a staff of 20 people can take care of everything—with time left over—a year later.

With some missionary work on the part of a dealer, the typical investor can be made into a combination collector and investor, a person who appreciates the history and background of coins, who is able to think independently, and who enjoys the hobby for all it is worth. From a financial viewpoint, this type of investor historically has reaped wonderful benefits—moreso than the "come and go quickly" type. There are some things to do to insure success, however. One is to "shop around," for it is quickly learned that not everything one sees in print is to be trusted. Grading does differ from dealer to dealer as do prices and *true value received.* The second requirement for success is to get *involved,* to read, to subscribe to various publications, to join the American Numismatic Association and other groups, to attend local conventions, to spend some time with the coin hobby.

Advanced Collectors

The advanced collector can be classified in varying degrees. Typically, such a person begins strictly as an investor or as a casual collector but, as interest deepens, goes on to become more involved. Usually the advanced collector thinks for himself, although a trusted dealer can often furnish guidance.

One or more numismatic objectives—besides simply making a profit—characterize the advanced collector. He may be forming a type set of United States coin designs, he may aspire to own Connecticut or Vermont copper coins by die varieties, he may assemble a display of commemorative half dollars, or whatever. He does, however, collect with a purpose. Investment is important—all of us like to think when one's collection is sold, one can ultimately realize a profit—but for the advanced collector, investment is not the tail that wags the dog. Rather, investment is a fringe benefit, an "extra" that comes with serious coin collecting.

Whereas the pure *investor* gravitates toward series which offer a combination of large quantities available plus average high grades (preferably MS-65, as noted)—such usual items being Uncirculated coins from the 1930s onward in various series, as well as Morgan dollars—the *collector* will dip his toe in other waters, perhaps to form a set of Indian cents, or large cents, or patterns, or large-size $1 United States currency notes. If he does collect Morgan dollars or coins from the 1930s onward—and, unquestionably, these are delightful to own—then the usual objective is to acquire but a single specimen of each variety. The advanced collector would rather own 20 different varieties of Morgan dollars than a roll containing 20 pieces of the same issue.

The advanced collector realizes there is much useful information in print, so going beyond investment newsletters, he builds a library of reference books, and importantly, *reads* them. Soon it becomes evident that certain coins are rarer than one might normally think. All sorts of bargains make themselves known. It is realized—perhaps after studying the excellent series of books by David Akers—that there are many 19th-century United States gold coins which catalogue for nominal sums in *A Guide Book of United States Coins,* but which are available, when offered, for nominal amounts. It may be further realized that a certain Liberty Seated coin variety, which is 50 times rarer than a "common date," may be available for only slightly more than the "type" or "common date" price. Interest quickens! And, a significant collection is born!

The advanced collector usually purchases from many sources. He knows the characteristics and idiosyncrasies of the various retail dealers and coin auction houses. He subscribes to a dozen mailing lists and does business with as many different dealers, perhaps dropping one or two occasionally because of bad experiences and, conversely, trying out occasional new entries into the professional field.

It is the advanced collector who provides the price structure of the coin market. A pure investor paying $30,000 for an 1895 Morgan dollar is buying it on the hope that sometime, someday, someplace an advanced collector will desire that 1895 dollar for his collection of Morgan silver dollars by date and mint. Otherwise, as noted, one might as well melt it down for $7 worth of silver! While it can be argued that investors may buy coins simply to sell them to other investors, an analysis will show such thinking is not much different than a Ponzi coupon scheme. Or, perhaps it is like musical chairs—when the music ends, the last buyer will not be able to find a seat!

Indeed, the advanced collector is essential for the integrity of the coin market. Sometimes intense activity by pure investors has pushed the price of certain coins up to the point at which advanced collectors do not desire them. Someday such prices will come down, especially if investor interest turns elsewhere. How far will they come down? To the point at which they may become interesting to advanced collectors. Other coin areas are untouched by investors. Thus, whether investors buy or don't buy is not important and is not part of the market structure. Thus, the pricing structure of such pieces is rather "solid" and is unlikely to drop. On the other hand, it is not likely a great surge of investor interest will suddenly occur in such a series either. Rather, the price movement of this type of coin tends to be steadily upward over a long period of years, in response to growing collector demand.

What type of series am I referring to? One might as well use the 1794 large cent—an example proposed by Dr. William H. Sheldon many years ago (in 1949). In good economic times and bad, in hot coin markets and cold ones, 1794 cents have appealed mainly to advanced collectors and have inched upward in price year by year. They don't have much "play" or "action," but they certainly are interesting to collect. And, like the proverbial tortoise, 1794 cents have crossed "the investment finish line" with results far better than certain well-publicized "hares."

Scholarly Numismatists

Scholarly numismatists make up the fourth category in the present discussion. While many advanced collectors are scholarly numismatists as well, I use this term as a catch-all for collectors who are not responsive to price movements, but who, rather, collect for the pure *joy* of it. Undoubtedly, most people who save Civil War tokens (emergency money made in 1863) are of this leaning, for such pieces are inexpensive, are hardly a part of the investment mainstream, yet yield a generous amount of history and fascination when studied. Similarly, collectors of broken bank notes and other obsolete currency, Hard Times tokens (issued during the period 1833 to 1844), medals issued by the Mint decades ago, and so on, fit into this category, as do most members of the new generation of numismatic bibliophiles.

Concerning the latter category, several dealers now make it their exclusive trade to buy and sell out-of-print auction catalogues, reference books, and other numismatic literature. I doubt if "investment" is a consideration for nine out of 10 buyers in this category. Rather, the name of the game is enjoyment.

Scholarly numismatists usually don't spend much money. Scholarly numismatists are nice to correspond with, enjoyable to talk with at conventions, and make being a rare coin dealer worthwhile from an *aesthetic* viewpoint, but one advanced collector putting together a date and mintmark set of Morgan dollars is apt to spend more than 23 scholarly numismatists who are aspiring to collect "good for" tokens from New York, Nebraska, or New Mexico, or who are assembling sets of auction catalogues issued in the 19th century by W. Elliot Woodward.

I personally enjoy relating to and with scholarly numismatists. It imparts a degree of "fun" to the numismatic scene. When cataloguing the group of Hard Times tokens acquired with the Garrett Collection from The Johns Hopkins University, I found many of the pieces were jumbled together loosely in a small cardboard box. A previous appraiser had attached little significance to them, and apart from a few scarce varieties, had simply lumped them together as a single entry valued at $500 for the lot. I found the tokens to be interesting and decided to catalogue them individually, and to illustrate most of them. The results are now history. The "low value" pieces sold for *tens of thousands of dollars* when they crossed the auction block! Obviously, officials of The Johns Hopkins University were delighted. And, I had a good time cataloguing them! Still, such "scholarly" or semischolarly pursuits remain the icing on the cake in my business, for the everyday expenses of doing business around here must be met by selling more popular items, by more "commercial" activities. Still, it is enjoyable to spend time in the area of research, although, more often than not, there is no bottom-line profit when the year's financial statement is read.

Good, Better, Best?

In various fields of human endeavor it is popular to say that one thing is "better" than another. Thus, to some a Mercedes-Benz automobile is better than a Lincoln Continental, while to others Acapulco is a better place to visit than Waikiki. Similarly, those involved in one category of numismatics often consider themselves to be better than those involved in other categories. The scholarly numismatist may look down his nose at the pure investor, while the pure investor in turn may think the scholarly numismatist is missing the boat entirely! This trend is also evident among dealers.

Those professional numismatists who can from memory attribute large cents of the year 1794, or pattern nickels of the year 1882, may look askance at someone who rents a convention hall to lecture 300 eager investors on the virtues of Morgan dollars. In my opinion, there is no "best." It could just be the person giving a seminar about silver dollars is doing more for our hobby than someone sitting in a small room and explaining to three fascinated listeners the difference between a 1794 cent attributed as Sheldon variety 46 and one attributed as variety 47 or 48.

Numismatics is like America; it is a melting pot. Remove the equivalent of one ethnic group or nationality, and things would not be the same. Nor, upon serious study, would many people want things to be different.

As 1984 is now upon us, and as it is early in the year, I am prompted to make some comments concerning the state of the market. Let me say at the outset I feel today is one of the best times to buy coins in recent years! Why is this? Because the market is quieter than it was back in the late 1970s and early 1980s. While a certain percentage of readers only want to buy things when they are "hot," history has shown the greatest profits—and I am now orienting these comments toward investment—have gone to those who have swum against the current, to those who have developed contrary thinking.

If everyone is rushing to buy item X because it is "hot," then perhaps, just perhaps, you should stay away from it. Instead, buy item Y, which no one seems to want. If you are buying for the short term—if you are buying in January with the hope of making a profit in May—then you probably will lose no matter what you do. Buying and selling on a short-term basis is wonderful for dealers who sell to you, but from your viewpoint, it is apt to result in a negative situation. Rather, think of the long term.

I have yet to meet a serious coin collector who has built a nice set of United States coins over a period of years and who, after holding them for five years or more, has not made a really wonderful profit. As I have met thousands of collectors and bought thousands of coin collections over the years, this is truly a remarkable and dramatic statement! On the other hand I have met dozens of people who have bought investment groups and packages and who have wanted to sell them at a profit a year or two later, but who have sustained losses. Clearly, long-term thinking is "the way to go." If you will think on a long term basis, it won't make much difference if an item is "quiet" now. Sooner or later it will have its day in the sun. At that time you will own the piece and will stand to reap the greatest benefit.

Grades Overemphasized?

I personally feel that emphasis on certain condition grades is misplaced. Today entirely too many people are focused solely upon MS-65 or Proof-65 pieces. I must confess that I am responsible for some of this. Back in 1974, when the first edition of my *High Profits from Rare Coin Investment* book appeared, the market was much different than it is now. It was the case in many typical instances that a Choice Uncirculated (MS-65 by present day ANA standards) coin sold for, say, $250, while a worn Extremely Fine-40 coin fetched $100. As it didn't cost a great deal more to buy Choice Uncirculated examples, I recommended this grade in my book.

In the ensuing decade, things have changed dramatically. The EF-40 coin that was worth $100 back in 1974 has increased in value to say, $300—not bad! But, the Choice Uncirculated coin that was worth $250 back in 1974 is now worth $3,000! Needless to say, anyone who bought one of these back in 1974 is tickled pink. But, what about now in 1984? In my opinion, an EF-40 example might be a better buy at $300 than an MS-65 piece at $3,000. After all, an Extremely Fine piece has nearly all of the original design sharpness, has the same amount of artistry and historical background, and has just about everything the MS-65 coin does except some added sharpness and mint lustre. While an MS-65 coin is definitely worth more than an EF-40 coin, is it worth 10 times more? You may think it is. But, you may also feel, as I do, that by contrast an EF-40 piece may offer certain opportunities. I know that in the field of Morgan silver dollars, many collectors have gravitated toward MS-63 and MS-63/65 coins, simply because many issues are available at fractions of the MS-65 listings. Still, for the serious collector with an adequate budget, there is no doubt that a display of MS-65 Morgan dollars is a truly wonderful thing to own.

Then there is the matter of various collecting areas. While my own firm has been as active as any in the field of Morgan and Peace dollars—coins unquestionably right at the top of the popularity parade—many numismatists have overlooked other series and have concentrated on series such as Morgan dollars, which have furnished the focus of "investment interest." And yet there are many other areas equally deserving of attention in recent years, the prices of which in many instances are incredibly cheap!

Want a Challenge?

Take out your copy of *A Guide Book of United States Coins* and contemplate building a date set of large cents from 1816 (when the design changed to the *Coronet* type) through the end of the series in 1857. Aspire to assemble a set averaging EF-40 in condition and consisting of dates and major varieties. With due credit to that familiar red-covered reference book, the prices of the different dates (with a few major varieties included) look something like this:

1816 $75, 1817 13-Stars $75, 1817 15-Stars $100, 1818 $75, 1819/8 $90, 1819 $75, 1820/19 $80, 1820 $75, 1821 $250, 1822 $80, 1823/2 $425, 1823 $625, 1824/2 $200, 1824 $100, 1825 $80. . .on through to 1848 $60, 1849 $70, 1850 $60. . .on to the last year of the series, 1857 Large Date $70, and 1857 Small Date $80.

There are many sleepers to be found in such a group. For example, did you know that an 1857 large cent with Large Date, which catalogues $70, is at least 10 times rarer than an 1849 which catalogues for the same price? Isn't this interesting? I think so!

The great "rarity" in this series is the 1823, which will cost you all of $625. While this certainly is not "cheap," it is much less than some relatively common Morgan dollars in MS-65 grade might sell for! Indeed, an entire set of large cents by dates and major varieties from 1816 through 1857 would cost you less than $10,000—or, to put it another way, about the price of an "investment pair" of 1895-S Morgan dollars in MS-65 grade. And yet the collection of large cents can be a real challenge. While, offhand, you might think all you have to do is whip out your checkbook to acquire a set in one fell swoop, that is not the case. I imagine the formation of a nicely matched Extremely Fine set will take the best part of a year's time!

Each cent will have its own personality, its own characteristics, its own degree of difficulty. You will find price does not have a great deal to do with availability. For example, the 1817 15-Star large cent, a major numismatic mystery (why was it created?), is not at all easy to find in Extremely Fine grade, although it catalogues for only $100. My own firm, which handles quite a few rare United States coins, may not have more than one of these per year! Other firms rarely have them either.

I am not "pushing" large cents, and I have no significant vested interest in the large cent series, (apart from whatever pieces we may have in inventory from time to time—a small fraction of our stock), but I am just prompting you to think for yourself—to take advantage of some of the numismatic opportunities that are "out there." The next time someone tells you that "all coins are overpriced"—or some similar pat statement—think for yourself, and you will find there are literally "acres of diamonds" just waiting to be picked up. However, you have to look for them!

The field of colonial and early American coins is largely asleep. Today, many important pieces—even great rarities—can be obtained for tiny fractions of what they would have cost you a few years ago. View this as an opportunity. Take out your *Guide Book* and study carefully pages 13-57. If you have an intellectual curiosity you cannot fail but be attracted to some of the issues, each of which has its own characteristics and history.

Commemorative half dollars are fascinating! While these are not on the popularity parade in investment circles, still they have a high degree of numismatic interest. A set of 48 different design types from 1892 through 1954 is, in effect, 48 different stories—48 different numismatic events—48 chapters of history. And while you are at it, don't just buy commemoratives. Buy the Swiatek-Breen book, buy the Iacovo book, buy the Taxay book (if you can find one; it is out of print), read what other writers have had to say about the pieces. It is all part of the "Grand Program."

The present article is not meant to exclude numerous other areas of numismatic endeavor which are equally worthwhile. There are many sleepers to be found among British halfpennies by date, among the coins of Queen Victoria by design type, among American Liberty Seated and Barber coinage, among world crowns, among encased postage stamps, and among the pieces in many other areas.

Coin Cycles

I was there in 1980 when coin prices reached a peak. Perhaps you were there also. Coming together all at once were many factors. Gold had risen to an historic high, providing much glittering excitement. Silver touched $50 at one point, creating so much interest many dealers were faced with long lines of people selling the precious metal. In the process, numerous dealers made hundreds of thousands or millions of dollars' worth of profits. The logical place to spend these profits was to make a "splash" in the rare coin market—by buying rarities, thus driving prices upward.

The American dollar was called into question, especially when Arab oil interests demanded payment in gold. During the Jimmy Carter administration we had the spectre—make that the *reality*—of double digit inflation. OPEC caused additional concern. "Tangible assets" became a new and popular investment medium, and many banks, pension funds, financial advisors, and others in the world of finance became attracted to the field. Coin prices have always moved in cycles (in modesty I note that I was the first numismatic author to study coin price cycles, having written extensively on the subject, beginning in 1962 and 1963 in *Coin World),* and 1980 saw a peak.

Today in 1984 we are not likely to see a repeat of the events that came together four years ago. And, it may be possible that we will never see these events in concurrence again. It is important to realize this. Otherwise, thinking about 1980 prices can "spoil" your outlook! Look at 1980 as a phenomenon. If you want to chart coin prices you may wish—as one investment advisor has suggested—to leave out the peak of 1979 through 1980, for it is not representative. Similarly, in the field of rare books, there are certain prices were achieved in the height of the market in 1929—and this was over a half century ago—which have not been achieved since!

It is more comforting to observe that with the exclusion of the 1979 through 1980 years, coins have followed a more or less steady trend upward, with due respect to cycles. A survey of coin prices of 1976 or 1977 will show, for the most part, that a really nice profit could be made by selling coins now that were purchased back then. Spectacular profits could be shown by selling coins purchased just a decade ago, in 1974.

A Fine Position

Today, in 1984, the coin market is at the finest position I have ever observed. Consider the advantages:

In terms of buying opportunities, there are many excellent possibilities. Enough important collections have come on the market in recent times that even such rarities as the 1804 silver dollar and 1787 Brasher doubloon can be obtained by those who can afford them.

More appropriate to the average reader of the present article, such pieces as Indian and Lincoln cents, Buffalo nickels, half dimes, Liberty Seated silver dollars, $3 gold pieces, Barber coins, half cents, and the like are relatively inexpensive, with rare dates often being available for slightly more than common or "type" prices. Opportunities! Opportunities! Opportunities! And, as noted earlier, there are many advantages to considering pieces in grades other than MS-65 and Proof-65, with VF, EF, AU, MS-60, and MS-63 coins often being at the bargain level.

Although it is not particularly associated with the coin market, the American Numismatic Association offers many services to those interested in the hobby. If you question the authenticity of a piece, the American Numismatic Association Certification Service can render an opinion. Similarly, the American Numismatic Association can grade a coin for a fee. And, there are several private organizations which also offer expert authentication and grading, the International Numismatic Society among them. This is a nice protection and assurance.

Are you interested in camaraderie and companionship? In today's world of computers, the threat of atomic war, and other impersonal situations, it is nice to know that coin collectors are a close-knit fraternity. Join a coin club! What fun it is to spend an evening—or an afternoon—"talking shop" with other collectors, meeting dealers, watching slides, and, in general, immersing yourself in your hobby. Attend a convention! Visit a coin auction! There are many possibilities.

How to Study

There is more numismatic information available today than ever before. *Coin World, Numismatic News, The Numismatist, Coins Magazine, CoinAge,* and other publications have a wealth of data—ranging from investment articles, personal opinions and market reports, to numismatic current events, not to overlook seemingly endless offerings of coins and numismatic services. The field of reference books offers you in-depth information on just about any topic of interest, ranging from how many national bank notes were printed in White River Junction, Vermont during the last century, down to estimates of the investment potential of the 1903-O Morgan dollar.

In winter, when the daylight hours are short, why not spend a few hours each week curled up in your favorite armchair with a numismatic book? Spend a few hundred dollars on books and read them—and you will be right up there in the forefront of coin "experts." And, you will have a lot of fun.

Speaking of fun, why not make 1984 a year of numismatic enjoyment? Get involved as much as you can. I do not have to welcome you aboard what many have called the "world's greatest hobby"—for you already have an interest or you wouldn't be reading this. But, I can encourage you to expand that interest. When I entered the field of rare coins back in 1953, I was very lucky. Today, I am very thankful for all numismatics has meant to me over the years. In addition to being a business, it has been a way of life. The collectors and dealers I have known, the experiences I have had, the things I have done—they have been wonderful!

I will never forget that night back in 1979 in New York City, when the 1787 Brasher doubloon, which I had spent several days cataloguing, fetched $725,000 in furious auction competition, culminating in virtual pandemonium. Less dramatic, but still important, was the day—which I also will never forget—when I sat down at my typewriter and wrote my first "Numismatic Depth Study" column for *Coin World*, never dreaming that during the ensuing years nearly 1,000 additional articles would be sent by me to that publication!

The dealers and collectors I have known will always be fond memories—and those I didn't know, legendary figures such as the Chapman brothers, Virgil Brand, and others, will be nostalgic in a different way. Equally important, I have the anticipation that in coming years I will meet many other collectors. The schoolboy who does find one of those 1972 Doubled Die cents in circulation is just as interesting to talk to, in a way, as the collector of territorial gold $50 pieces!

Numismatics: Different! Diverse! Delightful! I would not want it to be any other way.

Hans Schulman Remembers Virgil Brand

By Hans M.F. Schulman *1984*

It was 1926. . . The place was Amsterdam, site of my family's rare coin business. . . I was 13 years old. . . .

My father always got home around 6:00 in the evening. He had his Dutch gin and then went to dinner. Dinners at our home started not later than 6:30. Father was generally very cheerful, enjoying his relaxation after a typically busy day in the Jacques Schulman numismatic house. This was located on one of Amsterdam's beautiful canals, and was the establishment founded by Jacques Schulman, run in 1926 by the two sons (Max and my father) and my uncle, Andre. The father of the present-day (1984) Jacques Schulman, my cousin, is still at the same address.

"What's the matter, Max?" my mother asked on that beautiful warm June day in 1926. The sun was shining into the dining room, and it was the month in which the days are longest. A cheerful aspect prevailed. Except for my father. "Aren't you feeling well, Max," my mother insisted.

"BRAND DIED!" That was all Father said. My mother turned to me and my younger sister, Elly (who, in 1984, lived in Michigan), and directed, "You children must keep quiet. Don't ask your father anything; don't bother him."

I didn't understand what "Brand died" meant, but I didn't dare to ask. We ate quickly; it is a rare situation to eat quickly in a Dutch household. We got up and went to our rooms.

After weeks of hearing the name Brand mentioned I dared to ask what this meant, this Brand situation.

"You'll understand who Brand is when we don't have the money to keep you in that luxurious school," Father said. When I continued to show my lack of understanding, Father got annoyed.

"You know I go all the time to America, we earn our living selling rare coins, and we have lost our best customer. We have to spend less money. We will go on shorter vacations."

But in my 13th year I did not fully comprehend what was going on. The school, the friends, the birthday parties continued as before. We went for six weeks on vacation to Switzerland. Father mentioned Brand's name less and less at home. I forgot it. Life didn't seem to have changed. In 1927 I heard the name Brand at the dinner table again.

My father was not a man to talk about the office, once he was home. But the Brand matter broke the habit of not talking "shop."

What happened in 1927? The estate of Virgil Brand found a good number of unopened packages. Many of the unopened items came from Amsterdam and carried the Schulman label. Virgil did not open all the packages as he received them. There were so many parcels coming in that Virgil didn't have the time to work on everything right away. It seems in 1926 he was at least a year or two behind in opening packages!

The estate advised that they were not going to pay for unopened packages and that they did not accept the statement sent by the firm of Jacques Schulman in Amsterdam. They were going to return all unopened packages. . . My father's firm started legal proceedings in Cook County, Illinois, quite a daring action from so far away in Holland.

A settlement was reached by which packages that arrived after June 20, 1926 could be returned, but all those which arrived before June 20, 1926 would have to be paid for by the estate. The amount of the purchase price in United States funds came to $300,000.

Later when I grew up and entered into the business—it was 1937 then—I came across certain pieces in the inventory which had been in the unopened Brand packages permitted to be returned. These coins had been returned in the very late 1920s and had come to rest in the inventory when the Great Depression started. We still had these in 1937. Finally most of them were sold at a loss. Coin prices had been going lower and lower, a discussion that was to become familiar once again years later around 1980.

It was not the only time our firm was caught in a $300,000 debt which was hard to collect. It happened again in 1952. My father had long since passed away, having died in 1943 in Sobibor, Poland, a camp not far from the infamous Auschwitz.

I had opened a numismatic business in New York in 1939, calling it Hans M.F. Schulman, so as not to confuse it with the Amsterdam firm. Father, in 1939, sent a short wire when war broke out: "DON'T RETURN.

OPEN BUSINESS IN YOUR NAME AND BECOME AN AMERICAN." Hollanders were always proud to become American citizens and generally were good Americans. I followed Father's instructions and am proud to be an American today.

The $300,000 owed to me in 1952 was an unpaid amount by His Majesty King Farouk, who abdicated in 1952, fled from Egypt, and left his coin collection in Cairo. He settled in Rome in a small flat, sad and lonely. The demand to "Please pay your bill!" was answered by a wire: "Coins are in Cairo, the Egyptian government must pay you." Wires certainly have played an important role in my life! That was easier said than done. I was thinking of Father and Brand. Will I get matters settled as he did in Cook County?

I went into the Egyptian Supreme Court. My argument was that the Egyptian government had confiscated American property. The invoices stated clearly, "Title does not pass until paid for."

Winning the trial was only the beginning. Getting part of the $300,000 in coins and part in American dollars took 18 months of discussions with the authorities and involved permission from customs, currency control, inland revenue, and so on. However, in the end I succeeded.

Twice a sum of $300,000 has been important in the same numismatic family. It is quite a strange coincidence. Another time and I'll tell more about Farouk and other unusual numismatic events. . . .

Garrett Collection Breaks Records

By Q. David Bowers *1980*

Over $7 Million Worth of Coins Sold in 622 Lots
1787 Brasher Doubloon Sells for Record $725,000

The book of coin price records will have to be rewritten following our spectacular sale of the Garrett Collection, sold to the order of The Johns Hopkins University on November 28 and 29, 1979. The sale, one of four scheduled events offering Garrett coins, realized a total of $7,069,650. The world record price for a rare coin was set when Lot 607, the finest known example of America's most famous coin, the 1787 Brasher doubloon, was knocked down after furious bidding for $725,000. The buyer, Mr. Martin Monas, stated that he was purchasing it for a client, one of America's most prominent numismatists.

Interest was lent to the sale when a surprise guest, Mr. Milton Brasher, the great-great-grandson of Ephraim Brasher, was introduced to the audience. No, Mr. Brasher did not personally own a copy of the famous doubloon, but he certainly was appreciative of the Brasher family history. Brasher, he related, is a Huguenot name and has always been pronounced as "Brazier."

The term "world's record price" lost its meaning after the first several lots, for virtually everything in the sale set a new record. Some of the highlights are listed on the second page following.

A total of $7,069,650 worth of coins found new buyers for the sale.

The next scheduled sale in the Garrett Collection will be held in Los Angeles, California on March 26-28, 1980. Information concerning participation in the upcoming Garrett Collection sales can be obtained by writing to our office.

Highlights of the Sale

HALF CENTS

1793 Extremely Fine	$10,000
1795 Uncirculated	$30,000
1796 EF pole to cap	$14,000
1797 About Uncirculated	$14,000
1836 original Proof	$9,000
1845 original Proof	$9,500
1849 Small Date restrike Proof	$6,800
1856 Proof	$9,500

LARGE CENTS

1793 chain AMERI AU-50	$29,000
1793 chain AMERICA Uncirculated	$115,000
1793 Liberty cap AU	$36,000
1794 S-24 Uncirculated	$17,000
1794 S-48 Very Fine	$14,000
1794 S-56 Uncirculated	$16,000
1795 Jefferson head Fine	$7,500
1797 S-138 Uncirculated	$15,000
1803 S-254 Uncirculated	$11,500
1803 S-258 AU	$12,000
1838 Proof	$11,000
1847 Uncirculated	$10,000

SMALL CENTS

1856 Flying Eagle Proof	$4,200
1857 Proof Flying Eagle	$5,800
1859 Indian Proof	$2,500
1860 Proof	$1,800
1877 Proof	$3,200

TWO-CENT PIECES

1864 Uncirculated Small Motto	$4,500
1866 Proof	$1,700
1873 Proof	$2,100

HALF DIMES

1794 About Uncirculated $7,500
1795 About Uncirculated $9,000
1796/5 Choice BU $60,000
1802 Extremely Fine $45,000
1805 Extremely Fine $10,000
1829 Uncirculated $4,000
1831 prooflike Uncirculated $5,500
1838-O About Uncirculated $7,000
1840 Uncirculated with drapery $5,000
1841 Choice Uncirculated $5,500
1847 Proof $6,500
1856/4 Proof $13,000
1859 regular issue Proof $8,000
1860 transitional Uncirculated $7000
1864-S Choice BU $6,000
1866 Proof $3,200

HALF DOLLARS

1794 Extremely Fine $5,800
1795 MS-60 Uncirculated $18,500
1795 MS-60 Uncirculated, finer $34,000
1796 15 obverse Stars VF $32,000
1796 16 Stars Fine $17,000
1797 Extremely Fine $30,000
1806 Uncirculated $28,000
1797 old style Uncirculated $35,000
1813 Uncirculated $9,000
1815 About Uncirculated $3,400
1822 Uncirculated $12,500
1836 Lettered Edge Proof $34,000
1836 Reeded Edge Proof $28,000
1853-O no arrows or rays VF $40,000
1854 Proof $21,000
1856 Proof $16,000
1861 Proof $6,000
1866-S no motto Choice BU $22,000
1873-CC no arrows Choice Uncirculated $30,000
1876 Proof $3,500
1877 Proof $6,000

1916 Walking Uncirculated $2,400

PATTERN HALF DOLLARS

1838 J-73 . . . . $6,000
1838 J-76A $9,000
1838 J-79 . . . . $11,500
1839 J-95 . . . . $17,500
1872 Amazonian, J-1200 . . . . $23,000
1877 J-1501 . . . . $25,000
1877 J-1503 . . . . $12,500
1877 J-383 . . . . $15,000
1877 J-1520 . . . . $25,000
1877 unlisted variety, similar to J-1534, struck in silver $32,500
1877 J-1535 . . . . $24,000
1879 J-1597 . . . . $17,000

ALUMINUM PROOF SET

1866 aluminum Proof set $40,000

GOLD DOLLARS

1850-O AU $4,600
1854-S AU $6,750
1854 Type II Brilliant Proof $90,000
1858-D Extremely Fine $2,700
1860 Proof $9,000
1861 Proof $12,500
1865 Proof $17,000
1866 Proof $10,000
1873 Proof $8,500
1874 Proof $15,000
1877 Proof $12,500
1880 Proof $8,750

$3 GOLD PIECES

1854 Proof $45,000
1860 Proof $21,000
1861 . . . . $25,000
1865 . . . . $40,000
1866 Proof $34,000
1873 Proof $44,000

1874 Proof $42,000
1876 . . . . $27,000
1877 . . . . $35,000

$4 GOLD PIECES

1879 with Coiled Hair $115,000
1880 with Flowing Hair $65,000

HALF EAGLES

1795 Small Eagle reverse AU $60,000
1798 Small Eagle reverse EF $110,000
1809/8 Uncirculated $25,000
1810 Uncirculated $14,000
1815 About Uncirculated $150,000
1818 Uncirculated $22,000
1819 Uncirculated $85,000
1824 Uncirculated $47,500
1828 About Uncirculated $70,000
1829 Large Planchet Uncirculated $165,000
1829 Small Planchet AU $65,000
1834 With Motto Uncirculated $34,000
1838-D Extremely Fine $2,800
1839-C AU $16,000
1839-D Extremely Fine $3,500
1860 Proof $18,000
1865 Proof $21,000
1866 Proof $23,000
1873 Proof $21,000
1874 Proof $26,000
1876-S Gem Uncirculated $34,000
1877 Proof $21,000
1879 Proof $16,000
1880 Proof $18,000
1891 Proof $11,500
1892 Proof $10,000
1908 Proof $24,000
1909 Proof $23,000
1910 Proof $19,000
1911 Proof $18,000
1912 Proof $26,000

1913 Proof $19,000
1914 Proof $24,000
1915 Proof $27,000

TERRITORIAL GOLD

Templeton Reid
Quarter eagle VF $47,500
Half eagle $200,000
Clark, Gruber & Co., 1860 issues
Quarter eagle Uncirculated $12,000
Half eagle Uncirculated $9,000
Eagle AU $6,400
Double eagle AU $40,000
John Parsons & Co.
Quarter eagle VF $85,000
Half eagle VF $100,000
Conway half eagle EF $100,000

COLONIALS

1785 Uncirculated Vermont copper Ryder-2 . . . . $6,800
1788 AU R-23 . . . . $10,000
1776 Massachusetts "Janus" copper $40,000
1788 Uncirculated half cent $4,500
1787 Uncirculated cent $5,000
1787 Uncirculated cent, finer $10,000
1786 New York Non Virtute Vici EF $12,000
1787 Nova Eborac nearly Uncirculated $8,750
1787 Excelsior with eagle on globe facing left AU $17,500
1787 Excelsior transposed arrows VF $26,000
1787 Indian with New York reverse EF $21,000
1787 Indian with the eagle on globe reverse AU $37,000
Clinton copper Very Fine $29,000
1787 New York Immunis Columbia copper struck over New Jersey issue
Uncirculated $21,000
1787 Indian copper with George III reverse $20,000
1783 Nova Constellatio patterns
Bit in silver $97,500
Quint in silver $165,000
Quint in silver $55,000
Mark in silver $190,000

The Austin Collection

By Q. David Bowers *1974*

A Record-Breaking Auction: Standing Room Only!

The Austin Collection sale held on May 31 and June 1, 1974 by American Auction Association (division of Bowers and Ruddy Galleries, Inc.) will be forever remembered as one of the outstanding numismatic events of our time. Up for bidding in the two-day event were 1,874 lots of choice United States and world coins. From the very start it was evident that countless price records would be shattered. When all was said and done new levels had been set in many different series. Outstanding was the $50,000 paid by a buyer from Connecticut for the rare 1877 pattern $50 gold piece in copper (Lot 1115), an all-time world's record price for *any* copper coin, to our knowledge!

Shortly before 7:00 p.m. on Friday, May 31st, the auction room began to fill up with eager bidders from all parts of the world. We had expected a record attendance, for only once in a great while does an event like the Austin Collection sale occur. Many of the coins in the sale had not been on the market for many years, we knew there were more than just a few once-in-a-lifetime opportunities.

As the clock approached the opening time the room filled to overflowing. In fact, we had to send out for extra chairs four times! One of our dealer friends came over to say "I didn't know there were this many auction bidders in all the world! I've never seen anything like it!" Virtually every major coin firm in the world was represented, either in person or by proxy.

The Austin Collection

The Austin Collection was assembled over a long period of years by one of America's most prominent numismatists. Quality and rarity were important precepts when the stellar grouping was formed. In addition, several other fine consignments with the same emphasis completed the offering. The result was a sale catalogue which had few equals in numismatics: a catalogue with rare, important, and significant offerings in many different fields—areas as diverse as silver dollars, American gold coins, tokens, British crowns, and Spanish issues. Indeed, if divided into major parts the Austin Collection would have made *several* definitive catalogues!

The sale catalogue itself was a large 8½ x 11″ two-column format and contained 128 pages. Hundreds of fine-quality illustrations reproduced on high-grade glossy paper made the catalogue a delight to the eye. Copies of the catalogue, destined to be a numismatic reference for many years to come, are available for $5 postpaid from Bowers and Ruddy Galleries. The $5 price includes a list of prices realized.

The following are some of the many sale records and highlights of this action-filled sale:

United States Silver Dollars

The Austin Collection catalogue contained one of the finest offerings of silver dollars to come on the market in many years. Issues ranged from the first year of this denomination, 1794, to the end of Peace dollars in 1935. Along the way many finest-known coins, Uncirculated and Proof examples, and other choice pieces were featured.

Lot 1, an Extremely Fine 1794 dollar with mint adjustment marks, opened at $16,000. Auctioneer George Bennett quickly called out one bid after another, and in a matter of seconds the 1794 had a new owner at $20,000; a new record price for this date in this grade. Lot 18, 1798 silver dollar described as "Brilliant Uncirculated, sharply struck. A gem coin," fetched $9,750, thus more than doubling in value since the same piece was sold earlier (in November 1972 as Lot 75 of the Robert Marks Collection sale) by the American Auction Association. Lot 41, an Uncirculated 1801 dollar with some surface friction, fetched a new high of $3,000.

Lot 56, a Proof Liberty Seated dollar of 1844, found a new home at $4,100, a figure which set a new record price at over three times catalogue value! A prooflike Uncirculated 1851 original dollar (Lot 68) touched the $11,000 mark, likewise a landmark price. Following was Lot 69, a Proof 1852, at $5,250, also a record figure. Lot 74, a Proof 1858 dollar, fetched $2,500; Lot 77, an Uncirculated 1859-S, $1,100; Lot 78, a prooflike Uncirculated 1860, $925; and Lot 100, a beautiful Uncirculated 1872-CC, which catalogues $1,500 but which sold in spirited competition for a record $6,000, or four times catalogue price! Among Morgan dollars two 1889-CC Uncirculated coins (Lots 125 and 126) at $2,600 and $2,400; an 1893-CC Uncirculated (Lot 136) at $16,000; and the rare 1895 Proof (Lot 139) at a record-smashing $8,500 are especially noteworthy. Rounding out the Morgan dollars was Lot 157, a Proof 1921, at $6,250, also a new record.

United States Copper and Nickel Coins

The Austin Collection catalogue featured three examples of the rare 1856 Flying Eagle cent: Lot 280, a Proof with minor spots, at $3,000; Lot 281, a Proof with some planchet marks, at $2,200; and Lot 313, a lightly toned Proof, at $2,350. Also significant were: Lot 285, a Proof 1864-L cent, at $9,500; Lot 292, an Uncirculated 1869/8 cent, at $550; and Lot 307, an Uncirculated 1888/7 cent, at $3,000.

In the two-cent piece series an Uncirculated 1865/4 (Lot 352) leaped to $675; an Uncirculated 1869/8 (Lot 356) touched $3,500; a Proof 1870 (Lot 358) brought $200; an Uncirculated 1871 (Lot 359) realized $230; a Proof 1872 (Lot 360) sold for $335; and the last date in the series, Lot 361, a Proof 1873 with Closed 3 in date, was awarded at $675.

A Proof 1877 nickel three-cent piece with some spots (Lot 363) brought $650; a Proof 1881 of the same denomination (Lot 364) brought a whopping $170; and a Proof 1884 three-cent (Lot 365) likewise set a new record, this one at $220.

The nickel five-cent pieces in the Austin Collection featured many choice issues. A Proof 1879/8 (Lot 380) brought $300; an Uncirculated 1918/7 (Lot 409) sold for $8,250; and Uncirculated 1919-D (Lot 414) left all old price records behind at $775; and a sharply struck Uncirculated 1926-D (Lot 427) shattered all precedent at $1,100.

United States Silver Coins

Half dimes sold at the Austin Collection sale included: 1792 half disme VF/Fine (Lot 443) at $2,000; 1794 AU (Lot 444) at $1,750; 1794 EF+ (Lot 445) at $1,250; 1795 Uncirculated (Lot 446) at $2,200; 1797 16-Star variety (Lot 449) at $1,950; 1831 Uncirculated (Lot 453) at $420; 1846 Proof (Lot 459) at $1,550; and a lovely Proof 1857 (Lot 464) at $900.

There were likewise many highlights among dimes. Examples: 1796 Uncirculated (Lot 475) at $2,800; 1797 Uncirculated (Lot 476) at $3,200;

1814 Uncirculated (Lot 483) at $1,450; 1820 Small 0 Uncirculated (Lot 484) at $1,200; 1830/29 Uncirculated (Lot 490) at $2,100; 1837 Liberty Seated, no stars. Toned Uncirculated (Lot 493) at $1,100; 1846 Proof (Lot 494) at $1,750; 1853 Arrows Uncirculated (Lot 495) $390; 1873 Arrows Uncirculated (Lot 499) at $575; and 1916-D Mercury Uncirculated (Lot 505) at $1,500.

Twenty-cent pieces included a Proof 1875 (Lot 535) at $800; a prooflike Uncirculated of the same date (Lot 537) at a record-breaking $1,150; and two 1878 Proofs (Lots 544 and 545) at $925 each.

Quarter dollars commenced with Lot 546, the prooflike Uncirculated 1796 quarter from our great Terrell Collection sale (May 1973). Many bidders' hands were in the air and an atmosphere of excitement prevailed as this coin, one of the finest known examples of the first American quarter dollar, came up for bidding. Finally just one hand was left, and auctioneer George Bennett announced the record-setting figure of $18,500! Other quarters included 1804 Uncirculated with rubbing (Lot 547) at $6,000; 1806/5 Uncirculated (Lot 549) at a record $7,750; 1819 (Lot 554) at $2,200; 1853 With Arrows and Rays (Lot 565) at a new record $1,250; 1896-S Uncirculated (Lot 595) at $2,900; 1913-S Uncirculated (Lot 624) at $1,850; 1918/7-S Uncirculated (Lot 638) at $4,500; and a complete set of Brilliant Uncirculated Washington quarters (Lot 673) at $1,475.

Half dollars in the Austin Collection auction were also memorable, and bidding was brisk as choice specimens came up on the sale block. An Uncirculated 1794 with rubbing (Lot 675) fetched $3,500; an Extremely Fine 1796 16-Star half dollar with some adjustment marks (Lot 678) sought a new level at $8,750; a lovely AU 1797 (Lot 679) fetched $13,500; an Uncirculated 1806 (Lot 681) reached $3,300; an Uncirculated 1837 (Lot 734) left its $425 catalogue value behind and sold for $2,700; an Uncirculated 1874-S (Lot 738) brought $1,150; a 1921 Uncirculated (Lot 757) made $1,500; and two 1921-D Uncirculated halves (Lots 758 and 759) sold for $1,750 apiece.

Rounding out the American silver coins in the sale were many choice commemorative half dollars. Examples are: 1893 Isabella quarter (Lots 901 and 902) $255 and $245 respectively; 1936 Albany half dollar (Lots 911 and 912) $180 and $175 in that order; and a complete set of silver commemoratives (Lot 979) at $13,500.

United States Gold Coins

All bets were off and all guesses as to what coins would sell for were not important as the section featuring United States gold coins came up for sale on Saturday morning, June 1st. Seated in the room next to your reporter was the main consignor. In his copy of the sale catalogue were personal notations as to the price he paid and the price he hoped each lot would sell for.

What happened there cannot be adequately described in print. It was an *experience* that can only be felt. Suffice it to say that those in attendance will never forget what happened, and they will never forget the prices that were realized.

Symbolic of the sale was Lot 1045, an Uncirculated 1834 $5 With Motto. This coin catalogues $3,000, however the consignor had paid double catalogue or $6,000 for it a year and a half earlier. It would be very nice if it brought close to $8,000 at our sale, he said. Well, there wasn't much worry about that, we assured him. We had several mail and telephone bids in the $8,000 to $9,000 range, including a high bid of $8,900. A nice profit was in the offing, our consignor mused.

But the roomful of bidders was to make the $8,900 bid seem *conservative*. No, the coin was not going to sell for $8,900—a figure which in itself would have been nearly three times catalogue!

"Do I hear $9,250?" the auctioneer cried.

"I have $9,250. How about $9,500? I have $9,500. Now $9,750."

"$15,000!" shouted a voice from the back of the room. Fantastic! A new record price. Our consignor was beaming from ear to ear!

"I have $15,000 now. How about $16,000? I have $16,000!" said the auctioneer as three or four other hands indicated that the bidding was far from over!

"$17,000! $18,000! $19,000! $20,000! $21,000! $22,000! $23,000! $24,000! $25,000!"

Now just two hands were remaining in the air. "$26,000!"

Now just one hand was raised. "$27,000! Going once! Going twice! Going three times! Sold for $27,000!"

Spontaneous applause filled the room as the sparkling little 1834 $5 gold piece, a coin which catalogues $3,000, sold for *nine times catalogue* to a bidder from Massachusetts.

The highlights from the gold section were many, as price record after price record was trampled in the dust. Here are just a few of the pieces and what they sold for: 1796 $2½ No Stars variety. AU (Lot 989) $14,500; 1798 EF $2½ (Lot 990) $4,750; 1806/4 $2½ AU (Lot 991) $3,750; 1824/1 $2½ AU (Lot 992) $4,250; 1827 $2½ Uncirculated (Lot 993) $7,750; 1831 $2½ Uncirculated, some marks (Lot 994) $4,950; 1845-D $2½ Uncirculated (Lot 999) $1,600; 1854-O $3 Uncirculated, some handling marks

(Lot 1006) $2,100; 1855 $3 Uncirculated (Lot 1007) $2,700; 1864 $3 Uncirculated (Lot 1015) $2,300; 1871 $3 Uncirculated (Lot 1021) $3,500; 1884 $3 Proof (Lot 1031) $7,500; 1795 Small Eagle $5 Uncirculated (Lot 1037) $13,500; 1806 $5 Uncirculated (Lot 1042) $3,200; 1838-D $5 Uncirculated (Lot 1049) $4,000; 1795 $10, Uncirculated with rubbing (Lot 1058) $12,500; 1804 $10 AU (Lot 1062) $4,250; 1838 $10 Uncirculated (Lot 1063) $3,500; 1861-S Paquet $20 EF-AU (Lot 1075) $5,000; and 1907 MCMVII $20 Uncirculated (Lot 1077) $5,200.

"I will write you the nicest letter you've ever received," said our consignor as the second auction session ended.

Starting the third session at 2:00 p.m. Saturday were additional gold coins. A Carolina Bechtler $5 in AU grade (Lot 1085) brought $1,850; an 1849 AU Norris, Grieg & Norris $5 (Lot 1086) broke all records at $3,100; and a high-grade 1854 Kellogg & Co. $20 (Lot 1090) fetched $2,100.

Other United States Issues

Early in the third session several outstanding United States pattern coins came up for sale. A rare 1916 pattern half dollar, Judd No. 1798, fetched $6,750. A unique 1866 pattern $5 in white metal, J-545, (Lot 1114) brought $2,400.

Lot 1115 then had its turn. The piece, a choice Proof copper striking of the 1877 $50, had ealier appeared in our Robert Marks Collection sale in November 1972. At the Marks sale our consignor had purchased the coin for a then record $15,000. Now it was the consignor's turn to sell, and the piece was again on the market. What would it bring now? We knew the consignor would make a profit, for we had a number of mail bidders in the $15,000 to $22,000 range. The coin opened up at just over $20,000. About two minutes later it turned out that $20,000 would have been one of the bargains of the century. Thunderous applause broke out as the piece sold for $50,000, a world's record for a copper coin! Again the sale proved that if there is a finer investment than rare coins, we've yet to learn what it is (in the meantime the Dow-Jones Industrial Average closed at a new low for the year).

United States paper money in the sale comprised a number of popular and interesting issues. Lot 1171, a $10 "bison note" in New condition fetched $260; a rare Uncirculated $10 refunding certificate, Lot 1173, fetched $2,100, and many National Bank notes attracted wide bidding interest.

Excitement prevailed when Lot 1201, a fractional currency shield bearing the autographed signature of Francis E. Spinner and decorated with extra notes (45 notes instead of the 39 usually found on shields) and official Treasury department ribbons and a wax seal, came up for bidding. The previous record for a fractional currency shield, not one with extra notes, was set at $2,600 in our sale of the Matt Rothert Collection in 1973. That record wasn't to stand for long. In furious bidding the shield soared to $5,750 and became the property of a Maryland buyer!

The large offering of tokens and medals in the sale attracted many specialists in these series. A new record for a Feuchtwanger three-cent piece (Lot 1218) was set at $2,100. A rare Philadelphia token, a variety which was worth $28.50 in 1884 according to the catalogue description for Lot 1243, went to $1,050. A Charleston, South Carolina token with the inscription "Good for One Glass of Soda Water" (Lot 1246) brought $575. An Erie Canal medal in silver (Lot 1252) found a new owner at $800. Interest in the upcoming bicentennial celebration might have furnished the reason for the record price of $2,600 realized for Lot 1257, a large silver medal from the 1876 Centennial Exhibition.

Coins of the World

Several hundred lots of ancient coins, minor and silver world coins, crowns, and gold coins of the world completed our Austin Collection event. A beautifully toned Proof 1911 Canadian half dollar (Lot 1388) sold for $1,500, indicating strong interest in the coinage of our northern neighbor. This was followed soon thereafter by a bid of $450 for an Extremely Fine 1948 Canadian silver dollar (Lot 1413), surely a record price for this date in this grade! The most expensive Canadian coin was a lovely Proof 1925 nickel (Lot 1366) which sold for a record $1,750. Also high on the list was an 1864 pattern Proof cent of Newfoundland (Lot 1431) which fetched $1,500.

Also setting a trend was the rare 1865 Newfoundland pattern five-cent (Lot 1433) in Proof condition which sold for $1,700. The low-mintage Newfoundland 1946-C five-cent in Extremely Fine grade (Lot 1435) brought $200. The many talers and other issues of Germany attracted wide interest. An 1811-C mining taler of Westphalia (Lot 1530) fetched $575; a 1927-F three-mark piece observing the 400th anniversary of Durer's death (Lot 1537) sold for $400 in Uncirculated grade. Then followed a large collection of German porcelain coins, mainly from the 1920s and 1930s. Bidding was active, and many price records were set.

Among coins of Great Britain an Uncirculated 1797 set of Soho Mint "cartwheel" coins from the farthing to the twopence (Lot 1584) brought

$550; an 1848 "Godless" florin in Proof grade (Lot 1590) sold for $450; a VF+ 1658 Cromwell crown (Lot 1595) realized $1,600; a lovely VF+ 1692 crown of William and Mary (Lot 1597) brought $850; and a 1736 AU crown of George II (Lot 1600) went to a new owner at $950.

One of the greatest rarities of the Spanish Empire, a 1620 50 real or "cincuentines" coin of Philip III was featured as Lot 1749. Worldwide interest was centered on this beautiful Extremely Fine example, and it sold for $5,300.

Toward the end of the sale another major rarity came up for sale: a lovely Uncirculated one-dollar undated (1916) presentation piece struck in gold for the coronation of Yuan Shih-Kai as leader of the Imperial Hung Hsien regime in China. Wide bidder interest pushed the price up to $3,000.

Additional Comments

The Austin Collection will never be forgotten by those who attended it. As has been the case with all of our previous auction sales, the strength of the coin market was vividly demonstrated, and many new price records were set.

The Lessons of History

By Q. David Bowers *1981*

For many years I have carefully studied the rare coin market. Indeed, as a dealer who invests large sums of money in inventory, it is only prudent to do so. I have found that like any other field of commercial activity, the price of rare coins tends to move in cyclical patterns.

Interestingly, the entire market does not move in concert. While one series is high in popularity, another will be low. Then when the low series becomes high, perhaps the series that was high earlier then becomes low.

The year 1979 and the first part of 1980 saw a time of frenzied market activity. Prices reached historic highs, only to fall in many instances later in 1980 and through the present year (1981). Like all previous coin peaks, the market activity was caused by specific reasons. Such factors as increased nationwide publicity concerning rare coin investments, publicity of the past track record of rare coin price appreciation, concern that money in savings accounts would not equal the inflation rate (historically, investment in coins has outpaced the inflation rate), general euphoria caused by the rise in price of silver and gold, and other considerations contributed to a run-up in value.

By the spring of 1980 the effort had run out of steam. Silver and gold bullion prices fell, interest paid in the money market rose in levels which approximated the return historically attainable with rare coin investments, few new articles on coin investments appeared in the popular press (for it was a "tired" subject; reporters went on to other things), and, equally important, many people who had bought earlier decided to take profits.

Now, in the autumn of 1981, some coins that cost $1,000 a year and a half ago now cost $500 or $750. I said some, not all. Certain series—Hard Times tokens, obsolete currency, numismatic books, and so on are higher priced today than they were a year and a half ago. As noted, not all things in numismatics move in the same price pattern at the same time.

As prices are lower today, more people should be buying coins, right? Wrong! Fewer people are buying coins today. Why? The answer is popular psychology. Everyone likes to jump on a bandwagon. When full-page advertisements in *Coin World* and *Numismatic News* trumpet the desirability of a certain issue, thousands of people rush headlong to that issue without thinking any further about it. When the market is quiet, the same buyers lose interest. Many people have trouble thinking for themselves.

And yet those who think for themselves historically have done the best. The famous financier Bernard Baruch claimed to have made his considerable fortune by buying against the trend. When people were rushing headlong to buy stocks at what Baruch considered to be unreasonable prices, he sold his holdings. Then when the stock market was quiet and few people were interested in buying, Baruch was on the front-line writing checks.

So it is with the coin market. Various series in the market have peaked from time to time over the years. In 1956-1957 Proof sets saw a peak; then in 1964-1965 rolls, Proof sets, Lincoln and Indian cents, and certain coins reached all-time highs; in 1973-1974 gold coins had a sharp run-up to a peak; and in 1978-1980 gold coins, "type" coins, and certain other series increased in value to historic highs.

After each and every one of these market peaks price levels subsided. History teaches us the lesson that it was far more profitable to have bought United States Proof sets in 1958 or 1959 than it was in 1956 or 1957. It was extremely profitable to have bought Proof sets, rolls, and Indian and Lincoln cents in 1976-1978 compared to a few years earlier. And, those who bought gold coins in 1976, when the market was for all purposes "dead," saw their investments multiply many times over in most instances when the market rose again.

The future is unknown, and there is no way of telling what 1985, 1990, or the year 2000 will bring. However, the basic appeal of coin collecting—the beauty of the designs—the tangible link with romantic history that the pieces offer, the thrill of working on and completing sets, and so on—will always be with us. It seems to me that in recent years hobbies have become more popular than ever. Whether the hobby be home photography, macrame, French cooking, planting a garden, or collecting coins, the trend has been for increasing numbers of people to participate. Coins are small, easily handled, easy to learn about (more excellent numismatic books are available now than at any time in our history), and can be collected in privacy—an ideal hobby for someone who lives in an apartment or condominium (the growing housing trend in 1981). The outlook seems to be bright.

Right now, the autumn of 1981, the market is quiet. If you were an active purchaser a year and a half ago, you may want to review the emotions which caused you to buy at that time. The coins, currency notes, and other pieces have not changed since then. A 1907 Proof Barber quarter that had certain features in March 1980 still has those same features today in 1981. The coins have not changed; psychology has.

While the decision of how and when to spend your money is ultimately your own, the lessons of history amply show that quiet periods in any market—whether the market be coins, stocks, real estate, or whatever—bring the greatest financial reward to those who swim against the tide. Are you one of them?

The King of American Coins

By Q. David Bowers *1974*

The United States Silver Dollar of 1804

It is with great pleasure that we offer for sale what is undoubtedly one of the most famous and finest-preserved specimens of "The King of American Coins," the United States silver dollar of 1804.

The coin here offered obtained by us from World-Wide Coin Company of Atlanta, Georgia, has achieved a fame accorded to few, if any, other United States coins. In recent years it has appeared on the cover of *Coin World, Numismatic News,* and numerous other numismatic publications. It has been on nationwide television, it has been featured in news stories, and has attracted the admiration of countless thousands of viewers when it has been exhibited at conventions. There is no alert numismatist anywhere in the world who has not heard of this famous coin!

Over the years we have had many wonderful coins pass our way. Included have been unique and extremely rare coins—virtually every issue listed in the *Guide Book,* as a matter of fact. No coin has given us a pride of ownership greater than the magnificent 1804 silver dollar offered here. In the past other dealers and prominent collectors have shared our feelings. The ownership of an 1804 silver dollar has in the past been a sure way to register its possessor in the "numismatic hall of fame." The inclusion of an 1804 dollar in the sale of a collection has invariably made that sale a landmark event to be remembered for all time.

The late Texas dealer, B. Max Mehl, who was without question the most prominent professional numismatist of the early 20th century, handled a large share of the prominent collections which came on the market during that time. His appreciation and admiration of the 1804 dollar was unstinted. Perhaps no more colorful and romantic reason for wanting to own an 1804 dollar can be found than the description written by B. Max Mehl when he sold the W.F. Dunham specimen in 1941:

> In all the history of numismatics of the entire world there is not today and there never has been a single coin which was and is the subject of so much romance, interest, comment, and upon which so much has been written and so much talked about and discussed as the United States silver dollar of 1804.
>
> While there may be coins of greater rarity (based upon the number of specimens known), no coin is so famous as the dollar of 1804! This is due to the fact that this great coin was the first coin of United States mintage to have been recognized as the rarest coin of the United States from the very beginning of American numismatics more than one hundred years ago. And it is today, as it always has been, the best-known and most sought-after coin, not only among collectors, but among the public in general as well.

Research by Eric P. Newman and Kenneth E. Bressett has revealed that 1804 silver dollars were struck at the Philadelphia Mint between about 1834 and 1859. Their book, *The Fantastic 1804 Dollar,* tells the story of these famous coins. No United States silver dollars were minted in the year 1804. In the 1830s it was deemed desirable to prepare specimen Proof sets of United States coins for presentation to foreign dignitaries, royalty, and others. As no regular-issue silver dollars had been made at the Mint since 1803 (coinage was suspended in 1803, and from that point onward the half dollar became the largest currently minted silver coin of the realm) the Mint had two choices when preparing these beautiful Proof sets, intended to display our nation's coinage to its best advantage. The first possibility would have been to include no silver dollar at all. As the silver dollar or "crown" silver coin has traditionally been the showpiece denomination of each nation's coinage, this possibility was rejected. To have the smaller-size half dollar as the centerpiece silver coin would not have been satisfactory. The second possibility was to mint silver dollars of the last-used (and thus most familiar) design, the style used from 1798 to 1803. These coins were given the distinctive 1804 date. Thus the sets contained a beautiful crown-size coin.

During the mid 19th century the U.S. Mint officials were building the National Collection of rare coins. At the same time the Mint actively traded coins with and sold coins to collectors—sometimes openly, other times secretly. The appeal of the 1804 dollar was recognized, and the Mint struck additional pieces for distribution to collectors.

The most famous and best-recorded sale to a collector involved the coin acquired by pioneer American collector Matthew A. Stickney (1805-1894) of Salem, Massachusetts, in 1843. In their *Fantastic 1804 Dollar* book Messrs. Newman and Bressett quote this letter. We reprint part of it here. The letter is dated July 2, 1867, and is from Stickney to Edward Cogan, a New York dealer:

> I was applied to by letter, July 4, 1866, by Mr. T.A. Andrews of Charlestown, Massachusetts, for the Dollar of 1804, which he understood I had in my possession and wished to obtain by purchase, for a friend in California, or information where he could get another. In reply I stated: "I have a genuine Proof dollar of the United States coinage of 1804. I do not dispose of my coins not duplicates, at any price. It is not likely that if I parted with this dollar, I could ever obtain another, as I have been told by a gentleman (W. Elliot Woodward, Esq.), largely engaged in selling coins at auction, that he thought it might bring one thousand dollars."
>
> On the 18th of November, 1866, Mr. Andrews wrote to me again, offering in the name of his friend "$1,000.00 in currency or the value in gold coin," saying: "I merely make the offer as requested to do, being aware that you stated that you did not dispose of coins except duplicates." I declined the offer on the 23rd of the same month.
>
> Of the genuineness of my United States dollar of 1804, I think there cannot be entertained a doubt, as it was handed me directly from the Cabinet of the U.S. Mint in Philadelphia, on the 9th of May, 1843, by one of its officers (Mr. W.E. DuBois), who still holds the same situation there, and can testify to it. . . .

The presently offered coin, known through the years as the Idler specimen of the 1804 dollar, was struck at the Philadelphia Mint circa 1858-1860. It was evidently acquired by Philadelphia dealer William Idler at or near the time it was minted. The knowledge of this specimen was first made public when John W. Haseltine, Idler's son-in-law, sold the Idler Collection in 1908. Mr. H.O. Granberg of Oshkosh, Wisconsin, became the new owner of the 1804 dollar.

On October 19, 1908, Haseltine wrote to Granberg and mentioned that Idler had the coin forty years earlier (in 1868—but this may have been an approximation, rather than a precise date), but that Idler forbid Haseltine to mention it. The coin was subsequently sold from the Granberg Collection into the celebrated collection of William C. Atwater, who died in 1940. On June 11, 1946, B. Max Mehl sold the Atwater Collection, including this 1804 dollar, for the Atwater family. At the sale it was purchased by Mr. Will W. Neil of Abilene, Kansas.

When the Neil Collection was sold by B. Max Mehl on July 17, 1947, he illustrated the 1804 and gave it a full-page description. The description, including Mr. Mehl's exclamation points, reads in part:

> The CELEBRATED "KING OF AMERICAN COINS"—The 1804 DOLLAR! Lot No. 31. 1804 United States Silver Dollar! The famous Idler specimen. The best-known specimen of this great rarity. . . .

Mr. Edwin Hydeman acquired the coin from the Neil sale. It remained in the Hydeman Collection until March, 1961, when it was auctioned by A. Kosoff. It was acquired for $29,000 by a buyer whose name was not disclosed. It remained in a private collection until 1972 when it was advertised by Mr. Kosoff, acting on behalf of the owner, for $100,000. The coin was acquired by the World-Wide Coin Company of Atlanta, Georgia. The new owner widely exhibited the coin, featured it in many displays, and made possible the viewing of this famous piece by thousands of collectors all over America. In October 1973, we acquired the coin by outright purchase from World-Wide. The purchase price was not disclosed, but it was in excess of $110,000, which was the previous high price paid for an American silver dollar (this price was paid by Ralph Andrews for an Uncirculated 1794 silver dollar which was sold by Superior Galleries in October; James F. Ruddy was the underbidder at $108,000).

The coin is attractively and evenly toned. It has the sharpness of Extremely Fine at the centers (due to striking, as is characteristic). Struck as a Proof coin, the 1804 retains Proof surface in the fields. In their book Messrs. Newman and Bressett note that the Idler specimen has "the clearest edge lettering of any 1804 dollar."

There are two considerations involving the pricing of this coin. First, as an 1804 dollar it is of immense value. Second, as one of the very finest known examples (Mr. B. Max Mehl, who handled more 1804 dollars than any other dealer before or since, said that this identical coin is "the best known specimen of this great rarity.") this coin is of even greater interest. In our *Rare Coin Review* No. 18 we noted how undervalued coin rarities are in relation to rarities in the art field, or even in the field of rare stamps for that matter. A rare painting has sold for over $5 million and many have broken the $1 million mark. A rare stamp has fetched over $300,000.

We believe that this 1804 silver dollar, one of the finest known specimens and certainly the most famous specimen of the "King of American Coins," will bring immense pleasure to its next owner. When one considers that $110,000 was recently paid for an Uncirculated 1794 dollar, a coin which is not nearly so well known as the 1804, then a price of $250,000 would sound inexpensive for this 1804. At the price we ask we belive the next owner will be making an outstanding purchase. The pleasure of owning the most famous specimen of "The King of American Coins" cannot be measured. The investment value can, however. Each of the past owners has made an attractive profit upon the sale of this coin, and with the strength of the coin market and the relatively low price for which this coin is available, we are sure the next owner will likewise do well with it.

The Idler specimen of the 1804 dollar, a magnificent coin which will bestow fame upon the collection of its next owner, is available from us for . . . . $165,000.

Index

A

Adams, John W., 31, 36
Adventures With Rare Coins, 45, 165
Akers, David, 180
Alpert, Don, 63
American Auction Association, 201, 202
American Express, 88
American Journal of Numismatics, 32, 34, 77, 82
American Numismatic Association, 47, 49, 51, 63, 74, 98, 99, 101-103, 105, 106, 109, 119, 131, 133, 134, 137, 140, 145, 179, 184, 188
American Numismatic Association Certification Service, 137, 188
American Numismatic Society, 111, 170
Americana Museum, 47
Amos Press, Inc., 97
Anderson-Dupont Sale, 89
Andrews, Ralph, 216
Andrews, T.A., 81, 215
Anka, Paul, 87
Anthon, Professor Charles, 33, 40
Antiquarian Bookman, 14
Anton, William T., Jr., 123, 125
Apache mine, 24
Appleton, William S., 33, 40, 82
Arizona and New Mexico Express Company, 24
Arizona Weekly Miner, 23, 24
Armington, J.R., 59, 60
Arnold, General Benedict, 111
Arthur, Chester Alan, 28
Assay Commission, 103
Atlantic Coast Line, 172
Atlas mine, 24
Atlee, James F., 115
Atwater, William C., 169, 172, 216
August, Richard, 120, 122
Auschwitz, 192
Austin Collection, 201-204, 207, 208

B

Balaban, Sydney, 64
Baldwin, Benjamin, 112, 114
Bangs & Co., 39, 41
Bank Note Reporter, 50
Bank of America, 88
Bank of Mutual Redemption, 55
Bank of New England, 56
Bank of Prescott, 24
BankAmericard, 88
Barber, Charles E., 16, 29
Barnum, P.T., 27
Baruch, Bernard, 210
Batty, D.T., 120
Beardsley, Marcus W., 57, 59, 60
Bebee, Adeline, 107
Bebee, Aubrey, 98, 99, 107, 108, 145
Beck Collection, 64
Becker, Tom, 161
Bennett, George, 202, 204
Betts, C. Wyllys, 33
Blake & Co. Express, F.W., 21, 23
Blake, Edward B., 23
Blake, Edward Meador, 23, 24
Blake, Francis Wheeler, 21-24
Bland-Allison Act, 158
Block & Co., 22
Bold, Dr. C.A., 107
Bolen, Mr., 77
Bonjour, Roy E., 127, 128
Bowers and Merena Galleries, Inc., 21, 131, 135, 137, 161
Bowers and Ruddy Galleries, Inc., 14, 49, 98, 99, 107, 108, 131, 143, 155, 157, 168, 172, 201, 202
Bowers, Lee, 47

Bowers, Q. David, 11, 27, 45, 63, 89, 97, 106, 111, 119, 124, 127, 131-141, 149, 151, 165, 175, 178, 195, 201, 209, 213
Bowers, Wynn, 47
Boyd, F.C.C., 105, 108
Boyd, Fred, 64, 172
Brand, Virgil, 169, 172, 189, 191-193
Brandywine Company, 50
Brasher doubloon, 40, 133, 135, 187, 189, 195
Brasher, Ephraim, 195
Brasher, Milton, 195
Breakfast at Tiffany's, 87
Breen, Walter, 75, 186
Breen's Encyclopedia of United States Half Cents, 1793-1857, Walter, 75
Brenner, Victor David, 15
Bressett, Kenneth E., 214-216
Brevoort Collection, 36
Bright's disease, 24
British Museum, 64
British Overseas Airways Corporation, 88
Broadway, 28, 40
broken bank notes, 14, 15, 48
Brooklyn Bridge, 28
Brousand Academy, 76
Brown, Samuel W., 98, 99, 101-103, 107, 108
Bruce, Alamanda Pope, 58
Buel, William, 113, 115
Bullowa, David, 124
Burton, O.A., 57
Bushnell, Charles I., 31, 35-42
Buss, Dr., 109

C

Cammack, Mary, 103
Campbell, Mrs., 103
Carter, Jimmy, 187
Celina Coin Co., 169
Century Collection, 71
Chapman, Henry, Jr., 31, 36, 37-41, 124, 189
Chapman, Samuel Hudson, 31, 36-41, 124, 172, 189
Chicago Daily News, 28
Chinese Exclusion Act, 28
Civil War, 36, 48, 55, 58, 76, 95, 181
Clapp, John H., 168
Clark, Ed, 48
Clark, Gruber & Co., 61
Clark, Jackson, 59
Clark, Murray, 47, 49, 50, 55
Clark's Trading Post, 47-49
Cliburn, Van, 87
Clogston Collection, 81
Cochituate Bank of Boston, 157
Coffing, Courtney, 97, 107
Cogan, Edward, Sr., 39, 40, 75, 172, 215
Cogan, George, 40
Cogan, Richard, 40
Cohen, Jerry, 73
Coin Collectors' Journal, 43
Coin World, 14, 45, 49, 68, 160, 173, 176, 187-189, 210, 213
CoinAge, 14, 188
Coins and Collectors, 18
Coins Magazine, 14, 131-140, 188
Colburn Collection, 42
Coley, Mr., 115
Collecting Rare Coins for Profit, 11
Collection Investment Program, 13
Collins, Thomas Bronson, 59
Colonial Newsletter, The, 122, 125, 127
Colquit, O.B., 104
Commercial Coin Co., 50
Comstock Lode, 152, 159
Coney Island, 158
Confederacy, 112
Confederate States of America, 57, 58
Connecticut Historical Society, 132
Connor, Mr., 77, 78
Constitution, 21
Continental Congress, 120, 122
Cook, Byron, 50
Copenhagen Restaurant, 56
Coulter, Mayre B., 52
Coursel, Justice, 60
Cox, Albion, 126
Crane, Ichabod, 83-85
Criswell, Grover S., 48, 50, 51, 55
Crosby, Sylvester S., 33, 37, 42, 82, 111, 128
Currency Times Past, 50

D

Daggett, J., 103
DeHavilland Comet, 88
deVries, Mrs., 103
Diana, goddess, 29
Diners Club, 88
Doolittle, Eliza, 128
Doty, James Alexander, 59
Doughty, F.W., 40
Drake's Plantation Bitters, 27
DuBois, Patterson, 32, 33
DuBois, W.E., 215
Duesenberg cars, 11
Dunham, William F., 172, 214

E

Early Coins of America, The, 37, 111
Edison Illuminating Company, 28
Edison, Thomas, 28
Edward, Dr., 77
Eisenhower, Dwight D., 88
Elder, Tom, 70, 72
Electric Boat Company, 73
Eliasberg, Louis, 65, 99, 108, 132, 167, 173
Ely, Herman, 76
Embvry, Don, 50
Empire Coin Company, 88
Empire Topics, 89
Ewing, Thomas, 22
Exodus, 87

F

Faberge, Karl, 106
Fairfield County Coin Club, 72
Fantastic 1804 Dollar, The, 214, 215
Farouk, King, 64, 65, 98, 100, 105-108, 172, 193
Ferreri, John, 50, 53
Fielding's Travel Guide to Europe, 88
Finn, Leonard, 53
Finotti, Rev. J.M., 76

First National Bank of Prescott, 24
Fitzgerald, F. Scott, 11
Forbes, 87
Ford, Henry, 166
Ford, John Jay, Jr., 35, 43, 56, 62
Ford, Robert, 27
Forecaster, The, 141, 143
Forty Fort State Bank, 136, 152
Franklin Bank, 57
Franklin Bank of Boston, 53
Franklin, Ben, 12
Franklin County Bank, 57, 59-61
Fraser, James Earle, 99, 100
Fraser, Laura Gardin, 158, 163
Frossard, Edouard, 31, 35-42, 75, 76, 78, 81, 82, 86

G

Gainsborough Collection, 64
Gallo, Ray, 69
Garrett, John, 172
Garrett, T. Harrison, 32, 124, 132, 182, 195
General Mills, 131
George III, King, 112, 116
Gimbel's, 63
Goadsby, Thomas, 126
Gobrecht, Christian, 158
Gold Rush, 11, 152
Graf, Bob, 117
Granberg, H.O., 215
Graphic Co., 55
Great Depression, 67, 172, 192
Great Gatsby, The, 11
Grecian Bend mine, 24
Green, Col. Edward Howland Robinson, 98, 103-105, 107, 108
Green, Edward Henry, 103
Green, Hetty, 104
Green, Mabel, 104
Green, Paul M., 131
Greenhound & Newbauer's Northern Express, 22
Gret, Samuel Simpson, 59
Guide Book of United States Coins, A, 16, 89, 121, 125, 127, 142, 159, 163, 164, 168, 173, 180, 185, 186, 213

H

Hall & August Bank, 14, 15
Hallowell, Maine, 15
Hallowell, Massachusetts, 15
Hamilton Bank" of Boston, "The, 54
Hamrick, John B., Jr., 18, 107
Hancock, Virgil, 146
Hard Times tokens, 32
Harlow, Mabel, 103
Harmon, Dr. John, 113
Harmon, Julian, 113
Harmon, Reuben, Jr., 111-117, 126
Harper, Terrence G., 57
Harrah, Bill, 156
Harrah's Hotel, 152
Harte, Roy, 132, 133, 135
Harwood, John, Esq., 116
Haseltine, John W., 36, 40, 77, 215
Hatie, George M., 132, 135
Hauser, Harold, 128
Hawaii Five-O, 98, 107
Hawn, Reed, 109
Heath, Dr., 99
Heath Literary Award, 119
Heaton, Augustus G., 30
Hewitt, Lee, 100, 101
High Profits from Rare Coin Investment, 11, 13, 45, 67, 138, 141, 159, 184
Hill, Bert, 104
Hill, Priscilla, 104
Hill, Roland, 49, 50
Hinmar, H.B., 71
Hislop, Codman, 111
Historical Account of Vermont Paper Currency and Banks, 56
History of Schoharie County, N.Y., 115
Hoffman, Dr., 170
Holiday Inn, 88
Holland, Henry, 76
Hollinbeck Coin Company, 71
Hoober, Richard, 50, 61
Howard, Thomas, 27
Humboldt Register, 22, 23
Humboldt Salt Mining Co., 22
Hutchinson, William H., 59, 60
Hydeman, Edwin, 98, 105, 107, 108, 216

I

IBM, 11, 144
Idler, William, 215, 217
International Numismatic Society, 188
investment (coin), 11-14, 90, 167, 178, 180, 182
Issues of the Mint of the United States, 82

J

James, Jesse, 27
Jarvis, James, 126
Jenison Collection, 82
Jenks, William, 77
Johns Hopkins University, 182, 195
Johnson, Burdette G., 98, 104, 107, 108
Jones, Elizabeth, 163
Judge, H.M., 23
Jumbo, 27

K

Kabealo, S.J., 89
Kagin, Don, 172
Kahn Collection, 64
Kaplan, Sol, 107, 108, 170, 177
Kelly, James F., 98, 105-108
Kirtland Safety Society, 62
Kitterage, Mrs., 103
Knickerbocker, Diedrich, 82
Kosoff, Abe, 21, 63, 64, 98, 105, 107, 108, 169, 172, 216
Kreisberg, Abner, 63-65, 73, 90, 172

L

Lackey, Samuel Eugene, 59
Lafayette Bank of Boston, 54
Landis, John H., 99
Last Pharaoh, Farouk of Egypt, The, 105
Lathrop, Gertrude K., 163
Laurel and Hardy movies, 11

Leidman, Julian, 50, 52
Leventhal, Ed, 55
Levick, J.N.T., 76, 82, 86
Lewis, Arthur H., 103, 104
Life on the Mississippi, 28
Lilly, Josiah K., 172
Lincoln cents, 15, 16, 18
London Zoo, 27
Longacre, J.B., 158
Lorich, Bruce, 93
Los Angeles Times, 63
Louisville & Nashville Railroad, 172
Low, Lyman H., 32, 40
Luchow's Restaurant, 28

M

Macallister, James, 105
Machin, Thomas, 114-116, 122, 126
Machin's Mills, 111, 114, 123, 126
MacIntosh, Harold, 89
MacVeagh, Franklin, 99
Madison Square Garden, 27
Manhattan Life Insurance Company, 23
Maris, Dr. Edward, 82, 125
Marks, Robert, 202, 206
Marvin, William, 76
McDermott, Elizabeth (Betts), 106, 107
McDermott, James V., 98, 99, 106, 108
McDonald, Douglas, 21
McDonald's, 88
McGroty, Joseph, 59
McLeave, Hugh, 105
Meador, John Frank, 24
Meador, Sarah E., 23
Medlar, Bob, 50
Mehl, B. Max, 73, 74, 97, 98, 104, 105, 107, 108, 138, 149, 169, 172, 213, 214, 216
Menjou, Adolphe, 64, 90, 169
Merena, Ray, 131
Mervis, Clyde D., 97, 100, 107
Merwin, Mr., 40
Metacomet Bank, 14
Mickley, Joseph J., 38, 41, 76
Miller, Henry C., 90
Monas, Martin, 195
Monograph of United States Cents and Half Cents, 82
Moore, Dudley, 59
Morgan dollar, 1895 Proof, 13
Morgan, George T., 16, 29, 158
Moskowitz Collection, 64
Mould, Walter, 126
Mount Washington Cog Railway, 48
Moxie, 27, 47
Muldaur, Maria, 53
Muscalus, Dr. John, 55

N

Nagy, Stephen K., 99
National Gazette, 125
Nautilus, 73
Neil, Will W., 216
New England Bank Note Co., 55
New York Numismatic Club, 72
New York Times, The, 40, 176
New York *Tribune,* 40
Newcomer, Waldo, 172
Newman, Eric P., 101, 108, 111, 119, 120, 214-216
Nichols, Major, 40, 43
North American Currency, 48, 50
Norweb, Hon. R. Henry, 99, 108
Numisma, 31, 37, 38, 41, 76-78, 86
Numismatic Gallery, 64, 169
Numismatic News, 14, 17, 133, 138-140, 146, 176, 188, 210, 213
Numismatic Scrapbook Magazine, The, 57, 97, 100, 101, 106, 147
Numismatist, The, 15, 51, 99, 101, 102, 188

O

1812 Overture, 28
OPEC, 28, 187
Oakland Military Academy, 124
Obsolete Bank Notes of New England, The, 50
obsolete currency, 48-51, 55, 62
Ogden, Matthias, 122
Olsen, Fred, 97, 99, 105, 107, 108
Only in America, 87
Ophir Mining Company, 23
Owyhee Avalanche, 23

P

Paine, Thomas, 125
Paramount Internation Coin Corporation, 71, 105, 108, 172
Parish, Daniel, Jr., 40
Parker, Edward W., 57
Parkinson's Law, 87
Parmelee, Lorin G., 32, 36, 39, 40
patterns, 32, 33
Peck Mining Company, 24
Penn-New York Auction, 89
Penny Whimsy, 175
People's Bank of Patterson, 48
Peters, Jess, 55
Phelps, William, 116
Piedmont Cattle Co., 24
Pittman Act of 1918, 13
Pizza Hut, 88
Players' Guild, 170
Poillon, W., 40
Pope, Donna, 136
Pope, J.O., 22
Prince and the Pauper, The, 28
Professional Numismatists Guild, 68, 134
Proskey, David, 40, 43

Q

Quarterman Publications, 50

R

Rand McNally's *Road Atlas,* 15
Rarcoa, 50
Rare Coin Galleries, 63
Rare Coin Review, 12, 45-47, 67, 102, 108, 111, 125, 127, 141, 160, 216
Raymond, Wayte, 43, 69, 72
Reed, Ira, 105

Reich, John, 158
Rembrandt, 46, 143, 144
Rettew, Joel, 63
Revolutionary War, 112, 115, 122, 123, 126, 127
Reynolds, R.J., 99, 107
Rhodes & Lusk Express, 21
Rives, Beverly, 47, 48
Rives, John, 47, 48
Roaring '20s, 11
Robbins, Charles P., 23
Roberts, George E., 99, 100
Roberts, Gilroy, 158
Robinson, Hetty Howland, 103
Rockefeller, John D., 28
Roehl, Harvey, 105
Roosevelt, Alice, 165
Roosevelt, Theodore, 150, 165, 168
Rothert, Matt, 207
Ruddy, James F., 16, 17, 67, 89, 106, 131, 138, 141, 142, 147, 148, 216
Ryder, Hillyer C., 90

S

Safe Deposit & Trust Co., 172
Saint-Gaudens, Augustus, 16, 65, 150
Sampson, H.G., 35, 39, 40
Sanford Bank, 14
Saratoga Raceway, 124
Saxe, James, 59
Schilke, Olga, 67, 69, 72-74
Schilke, Oscar G., 45, 46, 67-74
Schulman, Elly, 191
Schulman, Hans M.F., 63, 90, 191
Schulman, Jacques, 191-193
Schulman, Max, 191
Scott, George, 59
Scott, J.W., 40
Seavey Collection, 36
Sheldon, Dr. William H., 64, 175, 181, 183
Sheldon Scale, 89
Shield Earring design, 29
Shipkey Collection, 64
Shultz, Norm, 65
Simms, Mr., 115
Smith, H.P., 35, 40
Smith, Justice, 60
Smithsonian Institution, 169, 172
Snyder, William, 104
Social Club of Charles Town, 33
Society of Paper Money Collectors, 49, 52
Sotheby's, 106
South Royalton Bank, 55
Spangenberger, Hank, 69
Spilman, James C., 125, 127
Spinner, Francis E., 207
Spurr, Marcus, 59
St. Albans Raid, 57, 58, 60, 61
Stack, Joe, 170
Stack, Morton, 72
Stack's, 168, 169, 172
Standard Catalogue of United States Coins, 71
Standard Oil Trust, 28
State Bank, 55
Staunton, Mrs. M.E. 103
Stefanelli, Dr., 172
Steigerwalt, Charles, 40
Stickney, Matthew A., 169, 172, 215
Stonington Bank, 56
Stravinsky, Igor, 28
Strawberry Patch Restaurant, 69
Strobridge, William Harvey, 39, 40, 75
Studies on Money in Early America, 111
Suffolk Bank, 55
Sun, 40
Superior Galleries, 109, 216
Suter, Don, 13, 155, 156
Swager, Charles Moore, 59
Swiatek, Mr., 186
Symmes' Theory of Concentric Spheres, 85

T

TWA, 88
Taft, William Howard, 165
Tatham Stamp & Coin Company, 89
Taxay, Don, 33, 101, 186
Tchaikovsky, 28, 87
Teaparty Co., J.J., 55
Terranova, Anthony, 128, 129
Terrell Collection, 204
Texas Midland Railroad, 104
Thoughts on the Establishment of the Mint in the United States, 125
Time, 68
Treasury Department, 29, 51
Treavis, Squire Turner, 58
Triple Cities Coin Exchange, 17
Trotter, Powell B., 106
Trudgen, Gary A., 122, 123
Tucker, Warren, 18, 107
Twain, Mark, 28
Twilight Tunneling Co., 22

U

U.S. Gold Coins: An Illustrated History, 149
Ugly American, The, 87
Underhill, Abraham, 112, 114
Union Army, 76
Union College, 111
Unitas, Johnny, 88
United States Coin Co., 12

V

Van Winkle, Rip, 82, 83
Vanderbilt, William H., 28
VanVoorhis, Mr., 115
Varieties of the Copper Issues of the United States Mint in the Year 1794, 82
Vermont Glass Factory, 157
Vermont Obsolete Notes and Scrip, 52
Villanova University, 124

W

Wagner, August, 98, 103, 107, 108
Wait, George, 56
Wall Street Journal, 176
Wallace, Caleb McDowell, 59
Walnut Grove Water Storage Co., 24
Walt, George W., 51
Walton, George, 107
Washington, George, 56, 112
Weinberg, Alan, 135
Wells Fargo & Co., 21, 22, 24
Wesley, John, 33

West Point, 111, 114
West River Bank, 56
What Cheer Bank, 157
Whitefield, George, 33
Whitman folders, 135
Wilson, Cal, 75
Wilson, Mrs., 103
Wismer, David C., 50-53
Woodward, William Elliot, 31, 33, 35, 41-43, 75-78, 81, 82, 86, 182, 215
Worcester County Numismatic Club, 135
World, 40
World-Wide Coin Co., 18, 98, 99, 107, 108, 213, 216
Wright brothers, 165

Y

YMCA, 124
Yellowstone Park, 166
Young, Bennett H., 58
Young, Brigham, 62
You're Just a Three-Dollar Bill, 53